Catholicism in the American West

Number Thirty-nine:
The Walter Prescott Webb Memorial Lectures

Catholicism in the American West
A Rosary of Hidden Voices

Edited by
Roberto R. Treviño *and* **Richard V. Francaviglia**

Introduction by
Steven M. Avella

Contributions by
Anne M. Butler
Michael E. Engh, S.J.
Matthew Pehl
William Issel
Gina Marie Pitti
and **Roberto R. Treviño**

Published for **the University of Texas at Arlington**
by **Texas A&M University Press**
College Station

Copyright © 2007 by the University of Texas at Arlington
Manufactured in the United States of America
All rights reserved
First edition

The paper used in this book meets the minimum requirements
of the American National Standard for Permanence
of Paper for Printed Library Materials, z39.48-1984.
Binding materials have been chosen for durability.
∞ ♺

Chapter 6 "Faith and Justice" previously appeared in *The Church
in the Barrio: Mexican American Ethno-Catholicism in Houston,*
by Roberto R. Treviño, pp. 176–205. Copyright © 2006 by the
University of North Carolina Press. Used by permission of the
publisher, www.uncpress.unc.edu.

Library of Congress Cataloging-in-Publication Data

Catholicism in the American West : a rosary of hidden voices /
edited by Roberto R. Treviño and Richard V. Francaviglia ; intro-
duction by Steven M. Avella ; contributions by Anne M. Butler . . .
[et al.]. — 1st ed.
    p. cm. — (The Walter Prescott Webb memorial lectures ;
no. 39)
   Includes bibliographical references.
   ISBN-13: 978-1-58544-621-6 (cloth : alk. paper)
   ISBN-10: 1-58544-621-1 (cloth : alk. paper)
    1. Catholic Church—West (U.S.)—History. 2. West (U.S.)—
Church history. I. Treviño, Roberto R. II. Francaviglia, Richard V.
III. Butler, Anne M., 1938–
   BX1406.3.C39 2007
   282'.78—dc22
                                                    2007013217

To Dana Dunn

Contents

Preface

In recent years, two very productive arenas in the study of U.S. history have emerged. The first has been a renewed focus on the American West, and the second has included new ways of examining the role of religion. One of the prominent features shared by these recent trends in historical scholarship is the recovery of minority voices, especially those of women and people of color. In the spirit of this new scholarship, the University of Texas at Arlington history department chose "A Rosary of Hidden Voices: Catholicism in the American West" as the theme of its annual Walter Prescott Webb Memorial Lectures held on March 11, 2004. The present volume is the result.

From the outset, we recognized that substantial literature existed about Spanish Catholicism in the early Southwest. However, we wanted to update the record on multiple Catholic traditions and experiences in the West as a whole, especially with regard to the recent past. As the book's title implies, the following essays present little-known stories about a religion whose traditions and adherents had until recently remained largely at the periphery of U.S. history narratives. And yet, however marginal they may have seemed to fellow contemporaries or subsequent historians, Catholic individuals and organizations made important contributions to the history of the trans-Mississippi West in the nineteenth and twentieth centuries. These essays, then, represent some of the scholarship that is currently reshaping how historians understand the role of Catholicism both in the development of the West and in the broader history of the nation.

A volume such as this cannot be comprehensive, of course, but our contributors' essays clearly reveal the breadth and excellence to be found in recent scholarship on western U.S. Catholicism, as well as some of its future directions. The collection is expertly set in context with an introduction by Professor Steven M. Avella of Marquette University. Arranged chronologically, the essays begin with Anne M. Butler's incisive overview of Catholicism and the American West, which provided a lyrical yet provocative keynote for the conference. Dr. Butler, professor emerita, Utah State University, is currently in very active "retirement" after a rich career that garnered wide recognition for her many notable contributions in the fields of U.S. western, religious, and women's history. The diverse essays constituting the rest of the book unveil some of the historical impact of Catholicism in the development of the West during the nineteenth and twentieth centuries. Those essays include (not in this order) the other three Webb Lectures presented at the conference by Michael E. Engh, S.J., associate professor of history, Loyola Marymount University; Gina Marie Pitti, Ford postdoctoral scholar; and Roberto R. Treviño, associate professor, University of Texas at Arlington. Also included are essays by Professor William Issel of San Francisco State University and Matthew Pehl, a student in the Ph.D. history program at Brandeis University, who were the co-winners of the Webb-Smith Essay Competition held in conjunction with the lectures.

We gratefully recognize the support of the organizations and individuals who institutionalized the Webb Memorial Lectures and made possible the publication of this volume, especially the generosity of the late C. B. Smith Sr. of Austin, Texas; Jenkins and Virginia Garrett of Fort Worth, Texas; and the Rudolf Hermann Endowment for the Liberal Arts. Our thanks also go to James Spaniolo, president of the University of Texas at Arlington; Provost Dana Dunn; dean of the College of Liberal Arts Beth Wright; and history department chair Don Kyle for their participation and unflagging support. We also appreciate Manuel García y Griego, Stephanie Cole, and Father Robert Wright for taking time from their busy schedules to introduce our speakers. Joyce Goldberg, our colleague and chair of the Webb Lectures Committee, facilitated a highly successful conference; many thanks to her and her "volunteer" army of graduate students, ably led by Ronnie Hall, and to the history department staff for the energy and attention to detail that made it all happen. Lastly, for her continuing strong and visible support of the Webb Memorial Lectures, we dedicate this volume to Dana Dunn, provost and vice president for academic affairs.

—*Roberto R. Treviño and Richard V. Francaviglia*

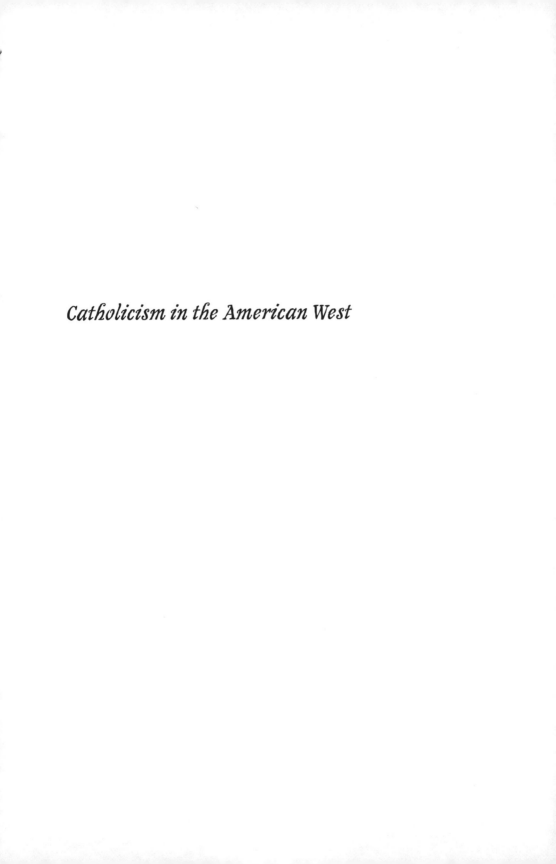

Catholicism in the American West

Introduction

Steven M. Avella

T he rosary has always been the prayer of the people. It is the "poor person's breviary," a more accessible version of the complicated monastic Divine Office, its 150 *Aves* and *Paters* replacing the 150 Psalms. The rosary is also a very adaptable medium of prayer—suitable for every time and circumstance. Rosary beads mark the rites of passage in a Catholic person's life. They are given to young children making their first Communion, they are looped around Filipino and Mexican couples at their nuptial Mass, and they are wrapped around the hands of deceased Catholics whose last words may have been, "Holy Mary, Mother of God, pray for us sinners, now and at the hour of our death. Amen." Rosary beads are fingered during times of stress and trial, and by family members who still drop to their knees to recite the rosary after dinner. It passes away the hours for the homebound; it rests on nightstands, *altarcitos,* and prie-dieux for moments of quiet prayer. For many centuries the rosary has been both a public and private prayer. Tradition holds that thousands of Catholics prayed the rosary to secure the Christian victory over Muslims at the Battle of Lepanto in 1571. Over the centuries, Catholics have also joined large public rosary crusades to keep the family together and to bring about the conversion of Communist Russia. Pro-life activists recite it in front of abortion clinics. But more often than not, the rosary is prayed individually or in small groups.

As an expression of Catholic identity and as an emblem of the power of personal faith, the rosary is an apt metaphor for this collection of essays generated by the 2004 Walter Prescott Webb Memorial Lectures. For, like the rosary, the reality of Catholicism in the American West has been both visible and hidden. The power of personal faith has been a force that has changed lives and communities. Indeed, Catholic life and experience in the West has adapted to the realities of time and place. At the same time, the demands of this diverse region have also affected the scope and nature of religious life and expression. These essays accentuate the agency of religiously motivated men and women who helped shape the American West. Sometimes they have done this publicly and vocally and at other times in quiet and obscurity. But at the end of the day, the American West was qualitatively different for their presence and labors.

To better understand the wider field of American Catholic history and some of the methodologies employed by our essayists, a brief overview of the historiography of American Catholic history and of American Catholic study of the West follows.

Religion and the American West

Historians such as Ferenc Szasz have lamented the exclusion of religion in both traditional and "new western" history.[1] In accounting for this, Szasz accentuates the tendency of historians to privatize the sphere of religion in a manner reminiscent of the constitutional separation of church and state. He points also to the complicating diversity of the West, noting that the variety of geographical locations alone has produced a bewildering medley of religious institutions, movements, and experiences that defy the construction of a coherent master narrative. He further notes the sometimes-militant secularism of western historians, both of the old and new schools, who regard religion as secondary to more important issues of territorial expansion, economic development, and, of course, the triad of race, class, and gender. One might also argue that historians of religion, with their excessive preoccupation with denominational development in the Midwest and East, have given short shrift to conditions in the West. In Catholic circles, western bishops have often complained about the lack of attention to Catholics in the West by joking that the old acronym for the lobbying arm of the American hierarchy, the National Catholic Welfare Conference (NCWC), meant "Nothing Counts West of Chicago."

In fact, if even unwittingly, it has been the new western historians, who regard the West as a distinct region rather than a "frontier process," who integrate religion into the wider cultural life of the American West.[2] Certainly Szasz's (and Margaret Connell's) contribution to the *Oxford History of the American West* accentuates the distinct regional realities that have formed the framework for religious realities.[3] Szasz's small, but significant, *Religion in the Modern American West* (2000) lays bare the richly textured and localized nature of western religious development through an amazing variety of examples of religious diversity. The new "Religion by Region" series, sponsored by the Leonard E. Greenburg Center for the Study of Religion in Public Life at Trinity College in Hartford highlights "how religion shapes, and is being shaped by regional culture in America."[4] Notable as well are the suggestions by scholars such as Laurie Maffly Kipp and

Eldon Ernst who suggest that the time might be suitable to challenge the existing master narrative of American religious development, which moves from East to West, with a new framework that more accurately depicts the nature of American religious development by moving from West to East.[5] The essays in this collection suggest that the general field of religion and the American West will continue to interest scholars.

The Historiography of American Catholicism

Critical shifts in American Catholic historiography also provide a context for these essays.[6] The putative father of U.S. Catholic history was the nineteenth-century chronicler, John Gilmary Shea, a former Jesuit seminarian who began writing a series on American Catholic history in the 1850s.[7] Shea's writing resembled the work of "gentlemen" scholars like Francis Parkman. Shea's example notwithstanding, church history through much of the nineteenth and early twentieth century was often apologetic or filiopietistic in nature. Historical accounts were generally produced to validate some earlier theological position or heavily embellished to edify pious readers.

Modern research methods and archival-based scholarship came to the fore in the early twentieth century through the efforts of Catholic University historian Monsignor Peter Guilday. Guilday was the mentor to a generation of young clerics, laypersons, and nuns who attended Catholic University for advanced degrees. In the 1940s, Monsignor John Tracy Ellis succeeded Guilday. Ellis was even more insistent on the need for solid Catholic history, based in primary sources and subject to rigorous peer review. His own magnum opus, a massive two-volume biography of America's most prominent churchman, Cardinal James Gibbons, was a tour de force of research scholarship.[8] For many years, both Guilday's and Ellis's students (mostly priests and nuns) turned out a series of parallel biographies and institutional histories that lifted Catholic scholarship out of the morass of filiopietism into which it periodically sank.[9] These historians of the Guilday/Ellis school held sway for many years until advances in the historical profession, along with important changes within the Catholic Church, provided a new paradigm for the writing of U.S. church history.

A Paradigm Shift

The new social history burst on the scene in the late 1960s and had important repercussions for American religious history. New social historians, inspired by the work of Fernand Braudel and the Annales School, urged a new emphasis on history "from the bottom up." Soon, studying the realities of "ordinary" daily life, for example, work, family life, sexuality, provided a freshet of new material for historical research, and the findings soon began to alter long-held understandings of important areas of American life, such as race, class, and gender. Later emphasis on cultural history probed even more deeply into the complex and dense realities of human experience. Postmodern theory has provided yet another methodology to uncover new depths of religious agency. Any serious study of "ordinary life" in America soon runs into the reality of religious belief and the agency of religious people and institutions. Social and cultural history and postmodern theory have, on the average, been a boon to scholars of religion. Likewise, this new paradigm has challenged the sometimes-unrelenting secularism of some subfields of U.S. history that have regarded religion as peripheral to more "real" concerns such as economics, status, and power.

Within the Catholic Church itself, an important transformation of the Church's self-understanding emerged in the aftermath of Vatican Council II (1962–65). After centuries of strong emphasis on the clerical and institutional aspects of its identity, Vatican II promoted a more broad-based ecclesiology that was summed up in the succinct aphorism of priest-sociologist Eugene Kennedy: "the people are the church." To be sure, the Catholic hierarchical tradition still remained intact, and the organizational structure of dioceses and formal church institutions still remained significant—Catholics did not become Congregationalists. However, Vatican II energized a new sense of empowerment among Catholic laity and insisted on the "full, active, and conscious" participation of all believers (not just priests and nuns) in every aspect of the Church's mission—even the traditional clerical preserve of public prayer and liturgy.

Inspired by these impulses, a new generation of U.S. Catholic historians began to remake the face of Catholic historiography in America.[10] Key among them was Jay P. Dolan, a former priest and graduate of the University of Chicago.[11] Mentored by veteran church historian Martin Marty, Dolan produced a series of important monographic studies in the 1970s on the ordinary lives and religious experiences of Catholic believers, culminating in a new general history of Catholics in the United States significantly titled *The American Catholic Experience*.[12] In these works, Dolan sought to integrate earlier Catholic historical work into the wider framework of social and cultural realities. He eschewed clerical and episcopal biography and institutional studies and used new sources such as baptismal records, parish bulletins, and popular devotional literature to unearth the experience of the "believer in the pew." Inspired by the "history of religions" approach popular at the University of Chicago, he made important connections between Catholic experiences and similar phenomena in Protestant denominations. For example, his landmark study *Catholic Revivalism* (1978) drew important parallels between Catholic "missions" (i.e., week-long parish-centered religious exercises) and their counterparts in the Protestant revivals of the nineteenth century.

Dolan's scholarship helped reconfigure the Catholic historical landscape, creating a new framework for studies of heretofore-neglected aspects of Catholic life, and even imposing new perspectives on older subjects.[13] For example, Marquette University theologian Patrick Carey revisited the long-maligned lay trustee movement, often depicted by clerical historians as a threat to the divinely ordained hierarchical nature of the Catholic Church. By placing the actions of lay trustees against the backdrop of American Republicanism and also of European theories of lay control, Carey provided a new context for understanding a group long written off by clerical historians as disobedient rebels.[14] Dolan also was able to promote his approach through the creation of the Cushwa Center for the Study of American Catholicism, headquartered at the University of Notre Dame. There he brought scholars, graduate students, and a myriad of interested social historians for conferences, seminars, lectures, and other venues, at which a common enthusiasm for the study of religion "from the bottom up" could find an outlet. Dolan's mark on U.S. Catholic history continues to be felt.[15] Scores of additional works could be added to this list that reflect the influence of both the Ellis and Dolan schools of thought. Good episcopal biographies have been written by historians Thomas Shelley and James O'Toole and excellent diocesan histories by Leslie Tentler Woodcock and Thomas Spalding.[16] Interesting studies of the American Catholic experience that proceed along some of the same lines laid out by Dolan include works by Robert Orsi, John McGreevy, and the aforementioned Leslie Tentler.[17]

The History of the Catholic Church in the American West

The Catholic historiography of the West reflects the trends mentioned above. The Guilday/Ellis school of American Catholic historiography has produced serious studies of the role of religion in the American West as that frontier has developed. Sister Mary Aquinas Norton's *Catholic Missionary Activities in the Northwest* (1930) and Sister M. Ramona Mattingly's *The Catholic Church on the Kentucky Frontier* (1936) are but two examples.[18] An older work that has not yet been surpassed in excellence of research and style is Carlos Eduardo Castañeda's seven-volume *Our Catholic Heritage in Texas, 1519–1936*. A *Supplement* moved the story to 1950. Castañeda, a librarian and historian on the faculty of the University of Texas at Austin, produced in these volumes "the seminal work on the Spanish period of Texas history."[19] Ellis's students, Francis Weber and James Gaffey, have written important accounts of Catholic life in California. The prolific Weber penned hundreds of articles and scores of books on his beloved Los Angeles, including a two-volume study of Cardinal James Francis McIntyre.[20] Gaffey's studies of Archbishop Patrick Riordan of San Francisco and a smaller monograph on the history of St. Patrick's Seminary in Menlo Park are two excellent contributions to Catholic understandings of the West. His two-volume study of Catholic Church Extension founder, Francis Clement Kelley, provides important insight into a man whose organizational efforts literally built the Catholic presence in some of the most remote areas of the West. Although not tied to either Guilday or Ellis, there exist various diocesan histories, such as Thomas Noel's history of the Archdiocese of Denver, and regional studies like Jesuit Henry Casper's three-volume study of the Catholic Church in Nebraska and Jesuit Wilfred Schoenburg's work on Catholicism in the Pacific Northwest.[21]

However, like all historians who have studied the American West, American Catholic scholars had to contend with the Frederick Jackson Turner thesis. Already debate about the nature of the frontier and its supposed "savagery" had been tempered by historians such as Edward G. Bourne and Ruben Gold Thwaites who pointed out the presence of Catholic missionaries in New Spain and New France long before the arrival of the Anglo-Americans.[22] University of California historian Herbert Bolton's studies of the borderlands insisted that the Roman Catholic missions were frontier institutions.[23] In fact, Jesuit students of Bolton formed the Jesuit Institute of History at Loyola University in Chicago and began a program of document collection and publication on the pages of the journal *Mid-America* to not only remedy defects in knowledge about Jesuit missions but also to place a Catholic "marker" in the ongoing study of the frontier.[24] In a paper titled "The Significance of the Frontier to the Historian of the Catholic Church in the United States," which was delivered to the annual meeting of the American Catholic Historical Association in December 1938, Marquette Jesuit historian Raphael Hamilton summed up these efforts and heralded ongoing Catholic interest in the study of the frontier.[25]

Peter Guilday's students soon accommodated this call with studies of Catholic missionary activity in frontier Kentucky, Indiana, Illinois, and Nebraska. Other Catholic scholars pointed to the heroic frontier work of men like Father Stephen Badin, Bishop Benedict Joseph Flaget, Father Gabriel Richard, Father Samuel Mazzuchelli, and others who plunged into the seemingly undeveloped wilderness to establish Catholic outposts.[26] These works tempered the "savagery versus civilization" motif of the Turnerian school, but only by moving back the time frame of "civilization" to the advent of Catholic missionaries. Like the Turnerians, they emphasized the transforming power of white clerics, nuns, and institutions of the Catholic Church in molding the frontier.

Assessing how the frontier shaped U.S. Catholic life fell to another clerical historian of the day, Holy Cross Father Thomas T. McAvoy, professor of history at the University of Notre Dame. The Columbia-trained McAvoy devoted a significant portion of his scholarly career to determine what exactly made American Catholicism "American." Taking a page from Turner, he suggested that the West held some answers to this question. In a 1943 article in Notre Dame's *Review of Politics*, McAvoy noted the tendency of Catholic clerics in the West to soften doctrinal and confessional boundaries. He pointed to the strong emphasis on personal experience and action required by frontier conditions—again clashing with the communitarianism of Catholic life—and singled out the Catholic tendency to modify the practices of devotion and faith to adapt to new circumstances.[27] If McAvoy asked what is "American" about American Catholicism, our scholars in this volume explore what is "western" about western Catholicism. The rosary of voices highlighted by our scholars also reflects the conditioning elements of western time and space, ethnicity, urban politics, and demography that refracted universal Catholic principles. In this dynamic interplay they help advance a new approach to understanding Catholicism in the American West.

Stepping into the Stream

Anne Butler's essay draws on many of the historiographical themes alluded to in this introduction. She also echoes the laments of other scholars of western American religious history and speaks of "the invisible flock." This refers to the lack of scholarly attention paid to Catholics who left their "mixed and dusty footprints" in the American West. However, she also reveals a double invisibility imposed on American Catholic nuns, whose ministry in the West has often been ignored, not only by secular historians, but even by American Catholic historians. Butler's essay seeks to move religious sisters from the margins of western Catholic history and move them more toward the center of the narrative. Few people can capture in words the challenges and opportunity that the West brought to women better than Anne Butler. The religious women she discovers in the rich (and often untapped) archives of religious congregations are anything but the Lilies of the Field types, but rather they were indomitable women from France, Germany, and Ireland, motivated by the highest aspirations of their congregations, and often undaunted by the aridity, desolation, and hostility of the unforgiving western environment. As Butler observes, "They slept in hotels and boarding houses, took their meals with strangers . . . endured public insults, seasickness, lack of privacy, fleas and the howl of coyotes."

Butler's work is amplified by Jesuit Michael Engh, whose earlier work on religion in early Los Angeles was one of the first studies of the impact of religion in a western city.[28] In his essay, Engh singles out the work of Catholic laywomen Mary Workman and Verona Spellmire in creating a Catholic social and educational presence in evolving Los Angeles in the early twentieth century. Workman created the popular Brownson Catholic settlement house, which helped the city's large Japanese and Mexican communities adjust to the challenges of their new home. Workman's efforts were successful at first, but were eventually thwarted by the meddling of Father William Corr, a rather eccentric Los Angeles priest who claimed the social welfare "turf" as his own. Clashes between laity and clergy are a mainstay of U.S. Catholic history, and in this the West is no different from other regions. However, Engh's other subject, Verona Spellmire, enjoyed a positive and cooperative relationship with Father (later bishop) Robert E. Lucey, who drew on her prodigious organizational skills.

Spellmire's work was at the forefront of the popular Confraternity of Christian Doctrine, a highly successful religious education program, promoted effectively by Bishop Edwin Vincent O'Hara in the 1920s and 1930s. Keenly sensitive to the plight of the Mexicans whom she gathered for catechetical instruction, Spellmire migrated to Catholic social work and even followed her friend Lucey to San Antonio when he was appointed bishop. Workman and Spellmire were for many years names known only on a local level, mentioned in religious newspapers and newsletters, and perhaps destined to pass into oblivion. By retrieving their memory and their work, Engh pays them a long overdue homage. He also points out areas of "ordinary" life, that is, catechetical instruction, that might have passed unnoticed even though they had a powerful impact on the transmission of faith, gender issues, religious life, and race relations.

Although Engh does not mention it, Verona Spellmire's work with the Confraternity of Christian Doctrine was part of a larger Catholic organizational revival that took root in the United States after World War I called "Catholic Action." Inspired by papal encyclicals and warmly endorsed by activist bishops, Catholic Action was formally defined as "the cooperation of the laity in the apostolate of the hierarchy." Even though moderns may cringe at such a paternalistic definition, the disparate ventures of lay activism spawned by Catholic Action found many willing and active lay Catholics anxious to "Christianize the social order." William Issel's essay elaborates on how the same spirit that motivated Verona Spellmire also played a role in San Francisco city politics. Although difficult today to imagine the City by the Bay as a bastion of Catholicity, it was once the strongest Catholic redoubt on the Pacific Coast. Issel highlights the work of two Catholic laypersons, Sylvester Andriano and James Hagerty, who brought Catholic interests to bear on city issues (e.g., opposing the proliferation of pornography and energizing anti-Communist elements in labor organizations). They also quickened the devotional and liturgical life of the heavily Catholic city. Andriano and Hagerty relied on the support of their curmudgeonly but socially alert archbishop, John Joseph Mitty, and helped to promote Catholic interests in the public sphere.

Mitty's role does not receive such favorable treatment in Gina Marie Pitti's examination of national parishes and Catholic racial politics. The prelate's refusal to allow Mexican Catholics to have a national parish in San Jose (a traditional grant to most ethnic groups in the diverse San Francisco Archdiocese) is the point of departure for Pitti's insightful examination of the question of race as applied to Mexican Californians. Here we see a case study of otherwise astute church leaders who worked with the rising tide of Latino/a immigrants falling behind the curve of fast-changing social conditions. Pitti notes in particular the resistance of Catholic clergy who worked with Latino/a Catholics who refused to surrender their deeply held belief in interracialism and integration to identity politics and ethnic separatism. Unfortunately, as it turned out for the interracialists, the times had changed and the former advocates of Latino/a Catholics now became part of the problem. In a connection with Issel's work, Pitti's essay notes the breakdown of the liberal consensus that once undergirded the urban activism of Andriano and Hagerty.

Roberto Treviño's account advances some of the same themes as Pitti. He also unpacks the complex relationships between Catholic leaders and the increasingly more militant and aggressive Latino/a proponents of social justice. Here, however, the issue moved beyond the question of separate parishes, and engaged broader issues of social justice. Treviño records that the lines of division between church and people are now less distinct. Priests and nuns join the ranks of the social justice advocates and echo their calls for better social services, an end to racism, higher wages, and improved working conditions—even if this means antagonizing powerful members of the Catholic Anglo community. Treviño notes the ambivalence and occasional harsh authoritarianism of bishops who tread softly on these economic demands. But, before a permanent rupture can sever the bonds between Latino/a Catholics and their church, a prominent clerical social activist Father Patricio Flores becomes a bishop and later an Archbishop of San Antonio, thereby bridging a dangerous gap.

If Latino/a Catholics at times felt isolated and marginalized by church leaders in their quest for social justice, their plight was nothing compared to what Matthew Pehl describes in his essay as the "industrial island" of Italian Catholics in heavily Mormon Carbon County, Utah. However, for all its vivid detail about pastoral difficulties and the daunting challenges of space and resources, Pehl's Italian Catholics are survivors. The interlocking realities of ethnicity and religion provide the matrix for Catholic survival and religious persistence.

Family, home, religion, matriarchy—all helped Catholic identity persist. Pehl's account of adaptation and survival is really the undercurrent to all the other essays. Whether it is the cities of California, the barrios of San Antonio or Houston, or on an "industrial island" in largely Mormon Deseret, Catholicism has often been able to grow, and sometimes flourish, where it has been planted.

As with all good scholarship, these essays tease us a bit. They leave us hanging and hankering for more. Likewise, those who read them carefully will not only perceive fresh lines of inquiry but also rich new sources in the archives of religious institutions that have yet to be tapped. A whole library on the social and cultural history of the West can yet be written using these methodologies and sources that have long been overlooked or unavailable. If these essays do nothing else, they will bring the reader to a more vivid awareness of the agency of religious people and institutions in the American West. They remind religious historians of the malleability of traditions and institutions that often portray themselves as changeless and immutable. In keeping with the rosary metaphor, Catholicism has been both a public and private force for those living in the West. And like the rosary, whether prayed aloud or in whispers, these Catholic voices join themselves to the wider chorus of diversity that has created the American West.

Notes

1.   Both Szasz and his coeditor Richard Etulain make this assertion in the introduction to *Religion in Modern New Mexico* (Albuquerque: University of New Mexico Press, 1997). He repeats this same critique in his introduction to *Religion in the Modern American West* (Tucson: University of Arizona Press, 2000).

2.   See Patricia Nelson Limerick, "Believing in the American West," in *The West: An Illustrated History*, ed. Geoffrey C. West, 207–13 (New York: Little, Brown, 1996).

3.   Ferenc M. Szasz and Margaret Connell Szasz, "Religion and Spirituality," in *The Oxford History of the American West*, ed. Clyde A. Milner, II, Carol O'Connor, and Martha Sandweiss, 359–92 (New York: Oxford University Press, 1994).

4.   Patricia O'Connell Killen and Mark Silk, eds., *Pacific Northwest: The None Zone* (Walnut Creek, Calif.: Alta Mira Press, 2004), 5.

5.   Laurie Maffly Kipp, "Eastward Ho! American Religion from the Perspective of the Pacific Rim," in *Retelling U.S. Religious History*, ed. Thomas A. Tweed, 127–48 (Berkeley: University of California Press, 1997); Eldon Ernst, "American Religious History from a Pacific Coast Perspective," in *Religion and Society in the American West: Historical Essays*, ed. Carl Guarneri and David Alvarez, 366–78 (Lanham, Md.: University Press of America, 1987).

6.   J. Douglas Thomas, "A Century of American Catholic History," *U.S. Catholic Historian* 6 (1987): 25–49.

7. Peter Guilday, *John Gilmary Shea: Father of American Catholic History, 1824–1892* (New York: United States Catholic Historical Society, 1926).

8. John Tracy Ellis, *The Life of James Cardinal Gibbons, Archbishop of Baltimore, 1834–1921,* 2 vols. (Milwaukee: Bruce Publishing, 1952).

9. H. J. Browne, "American Catholic History: A Progress Report on Research and Study," *Church History* 26 (1957): 372–80.

10. Moses Rischin, "The New American Catholic History," *Church History* 41 (1972): 225–29.

11. Two brief articles highlight Dolan's place in American Catholic historiography: Martin E. Marty, "Locating Jay P. Dolan," *U.S. Catholic Historian* 19 (Winter 2001): 99–108; and R. Scott Appleby, "Historicizing the People of God: The Cushwa Center and the Vision of its Founder," *U.S. Catholic Historian* 19 (Winter 2001): 93–98.

12. Jay P. Dolan, *The Immigrant Church: New York's Irish and German Catholics* (Baltimore: Johns Hopkins University Press, 1975); Dolan, *Catholic Revivalism: The American Experience, 1930–1900* (Notre Dame: University of Notre Dame Press, 1978); Dolan, *The American Catholic Experience: A History from Colonial Times to the Present* (Garden City, N.Y.: Doubleday, 1985).

13. Two important Dolan-inspired projects include volumes edited on the Pacific and Intermountain West in his history of American Catholic parishes. *The American Catholic Parish from 1850 to the Present: The Pacific, Intermountain West, and Midwest States* (New York: Paulist Press, 1987); also his three-volume *Notre Dame History of Hispanic Catholics in the United States* (Notre Dame, Ind.: University of Notre Dame Press, 1994). He co-edited these latter volumes with Jaime Vidal, Gilberto Hinojosa, and Allen Figueroa Deck.

14. Patrick W. Carey, *People, Priests, and Prelates: Ecclesiastical Democracy and The Tension of Trusteeism* (Notre Dame, Ind.: University of Notre Dame Press, 1987).

15. Dolan's most recent book, *In Search of an American Catholicism: A History of Religion and Culture in Tension* (New York: Oxford University Press, 2002) carries forward many of the themes of his 1985 *American Catholic Experience.*

16. Thomas J. Shelley, *Paul J. Hallinan: First Archbishop of Atlanta* (Wilmington, Del.: Michael Glazier, 1989); James O'Toole, *Militant and Triumphant: William Henry O'Connell and the Catholic Church in Boston* (Notre Dame: University of Notre Dame Press, 1993); Leslie Woodcock Tentler, *Seasons of Grace: A History of the Catholic Archdiocese of Detroit* (Detroit: Wayne State University Press, 1990); Thomas W. Spalding, *The Premier See: A History of the Archdiocese of Baltimore* (Baltimore: Johns Hopkins University Press, 1989).

17. Robert Orsi, *The Madonna of 115th Street: Faith and Community in Italian Harlem* (New Haven, Conn.: Yale University Press, 1988); John T. McGreevy, *Parish Boundaries: The Catholic Encounter with Race in the Twentieth-Century Urban North* (Chicago: University of Chicago Press, 1996); Leslie Woodcock Tentler, *Catholics and Contraception: An American History* (Ithaca, N.Y.: Cornell University Press, 2004).

18. M. Aquinas Norton, *Catholic Missionary Activities in the Northwest* (Washington, D.C.: Catholic University of America Press, 1930); M. Ramona Mattingly, *The Catholic Church on the Kentucky Frontier, 1785–1812* (Washington, D.C.: Catholic University of America, 1936).

19. Carlos E. Castañeda, *Our Catholic Heritage in Texas,* 7 vols. (Austin: Von Boeckmann-Jones, 1936–58). Felix D. Almaraz Jr. has written the following articles about this series, "Carlos E. Castañeda and *Our Catholic Heritage:* The Initial Volumes (1933–1943)," *Social Science Journal* 13 (April 1976): 27–37; and "Carlos E. Castañeda, Mexican-American Historian: The Formative Years, 1896–1927," *Pacific Historical Review* 42 (August 1973): 319–34.

20. Weber's published corpus is too large to recount here. Two important works include *Century of Fulfillment: The Roman Catholic Church in Southern California, 1840–1947* (Mission Hills, Calif.: The Archival Center, 1990); and his two-volume biography of Cardinal James Francis McIntyre, *His Eminence of Los Angeles* (Mission Hills, Calif.: St. Francis Historical Society, 1997). Gaffey's works include *Citizen of No Mean City: Archbishop Patrick Riordan of San Francisco, 1841–1914* (New York: Consortium Books, 1976); and his two-volume study, *Francis Clement Kelley and the American Catholic Dream* (Bensenville, Ill.: The Heritage Foundation, 1980).

21. Thomas J. Noel, *Colorado Catholicism and the Archdiocese of Denver, 1857–1989* (Denver: University Press of Colorado, 1989); Henry W. Casper, S.J., *History of the Catholic Church in Nebraska,* 3 vols. (Milwaukee: Bruce Publishing, 1960); Wilfred P. Schoenberg, *A History of the Catholic Church in the Pacific Northwest, 1743–1983* (Washington, D.C.: Pastoral Press, 1987).

22. Edward G. Bourne, *Spain in America, 1450–1580* (New York: Harper Brothers, 1904); Ruben Gold Thwaites, *France in America, 1497–1763* (New York: Harper Brothers, 1905).

23. Herbert E. Bolton, "The Mission as Frontier Institution in the Spanish American Colonies," *American Historical Review* 23 (October 1917): 42–61.

24. Bolton gave the inaugural address for the new institute accentuating the importance of the Jesuits on the American frontier. Herbert E. Bolton, "The Jesuits in America: An Opportunity for Historians," *Mid-America* 18 (October 1936): 223–37.

25. Raphael N. Hamilton, "The Significance of the Frontier to the Historian of the Catholic Church in the United States," *Catholic Historical Review* 25 (July 1939): 160–79.

26. J. Herman Schauinger wrote two of these studies; the life of Flaget is recounted in *Cathedrals in the Wilderness* (Milwaukee: Bruce Publishing, 1952); Stephen T. Badin, *Priest in the Wilderness* (Milwaukee: Bruce Publishing, 1956). Richard's life was written by Frank Woodford and Albert Hyma, *Gabriel Richard: Frontier Ambassador* (Detroit: Wayne State University Press, 1958); for Mazzuchelli, see Mary Ellen Evans, *The Seed and*

the Glory: The Career of Samuel Charles Mazzuchelli, O.P., on the Mid-American Frontier (New York: McMullen Books, 1950).

27. Thomas McAvoy, "Americanism and Frontier Catholicism," *Review of Politics* 5 (1943): 292–301.

28. Michael Engh, S.J., *Frontier Faiths: Church, Temple, and Synagogue in Los Angeles, 1846–1888* (Albuquerque: University of New Mexico Press, 1992).

The Invisible Flock
Catholicism and the American West

Anne M. Butler

On March 25, 1634, sea-weary travelers, long weeks confined to the pitching and yawing of two small ships, the *Ark* and the *Dove,* gazed across the gray and choppy waters of the Chesapeake Bay to the welcoming sight of land. Four months earlier, the group had set sail from England, crossing the Atlantic Ocean for this distant place that would become Maryland, a tobacco-bearing, slave-holding colony among the original thirteen. The majority of passengers—gentleman or vagabond, servant or farmer, wife or child—professed religious fealty to the Anglican Church of England—no separatists here like those peculiar Pilgrims to the north; these settlers came as Protestant Englishmen for Protestant England.

On board the *Ark* was Leonard Calvert, chosen by his brother Cecil Calvert to govern the new settlement. The Calverts were, of all things, Catholic—a most distasteful characteristic in seventeenth-century England. Odd fortunes gave the Calverts this chance to escape to a more bountiful and profitable New World, but Leonard Calvert looked around his ship at a sorry assortment of coreligionists. All fled an atmosphere of social scorn, economic limitation, and political danger that translated into unmitigated daily persecution in England.

The sea voyage did not much alter these unpleasant realities and the uneasy shipboard relationships between Catholics and Protestants quickly morphed into open hostility in the new colony. The anti-Catholic sentiments of England transferred seamlessly to Maryland, where confident Protestant landowners flexed their New World political and economic muscle. The few Catholics enjoyed only thin protection from the Calvert family and learned it best not to draw attention to themselves in early Maryland, widely touted for a religious tolerance more written about than realized.[1]

As these ocean-tossed British Catholics and Protestants hunkered down on cold Atlantic shores, eyeing one another with equally cold suspicion, to the north, the earthy and unabashedly Catholic colony of New France had been carving a zesty New World identity for over twenty-five years. In fact, in the very year of 1634, as this handful of English Catholics faced an uncertain future in Maryland, the ruling lord and exuberant spirit of Quebec, Samuel de Champlain, grandly sent his thirty-six-year-old associate Jean Nicolet to the west, in search of a rumored water route that connected North America and China.

Nicolet, who pursued his exploratory charge dressed in elegant flowing Asian robes, halted his search around Lake Winnebago, Wisconsin, and turned back to Quebec. Had he pushed on but another two hundred miles or so Nicolet could have crossed the mighty Mississippi River, that traditional dividing point between the East and the West of the continental United States. Standing on the western bank of that great waterway, would Nicolet, failed in his Asian searches, have been cheered to consider how his presence linked Catholic frontiers over one hundred years in the making? Spanish and French—these were Catholic frontiers that stretched across North America's mountains and valleys, rivers and streams, prairies and deserts—Catholic incursions had laid a European religion on the hearth of Native homes and draped a cloak of Native spirituality over the European newcomers. Neither belief system would ever be completely free of the other again.

Indeed, in 1630, four years before the sortie of Jean Nicolet, a Franciscan missionary had written to Spain that 35,000 Catholic Indians were living around twenty-five New Mexico missions.[2] This was only a fraction of the actual tally. Some estimates suggest the number of Native people baptized in the western hemisphere soared into the millions.[3]

With the sandals of friars, the boots of conquistadors, the moccasins of fur trappers, and the footprints of indigenous men and women, a complex Catholic presence permeated the deep reaches of the American West long before those shivering Papists aboard the *Ark* and the *Dove* dropped anchor in the Chesapeake Bay. The makings of cultural plurality—based on region, language, ritual, tradition, and vision—marked this Catholic West. Given this legacy, one might expect the modern church, with its concerns about inclusiveness and diversity, to gaze back to these early models, eschew their mistakes, and extract their best elements. But Catholicism in the American West has been both misunderstood and underappreciated. Western Catholicism—with its textured Native/Mestizo/Hispano/Tejano/Californio fabric and despite its longevity, stability, and sophistication—appears to be regarded as a second-place component in the American Catholic Church, one that views the Catholics of the West as followers, not builders, of the faith.[4]

Clearly, the national religious narrative of American Catholicism is a lateral account, geographically and institutionally grounded on the windswept and bitter shores of a minor English colony, staunchly Anglican in its preferences, a place where Catholicism survived through a hardscrabble anonymity. Granted, Maryland, with its *Ark* and *Dove* history is entitled in many aspects to its "Cradle of Catholicity" label. After their inauspicious beginnings around St. Clement's Island, Maryland Catholics claimed advances with Charles Carroll of Carrollton, a signer of the Declaration of Independence, and native son Bishop John Carroll who, in 1784, was named overseer for the whole New World church, a domain the prelate had never seen in its entirety.

True, in Maryland in 1829, during the grim days of slavery, four courageous free women of color formed the Oblate Sisters of Divine Providence, fearless educators of slave and nonslave children alike.[5] Yes, the city of Baltimore, with its Benjamin Latrobe–designed cathedral, basked in its prominent clerics, plenary councils, and the omniscient *Baltimore Catechism,* teaching tool of the American parochial school system. But does everything we understand by the term "American Catholicism" trace itself to the shores of the Atlantic Coast? Has the history of American Catholicism acquired legitimacy solely because it has identified itself as a crucial ingredient in the English colonial system?

To place the origins of American Catholicism exclusively with the thirteen colonies grafts the religion onto secular events—most especially the waging of the American Revolution and the writing of the U.S. Constitution. Cultivating this hybrid relationship between church and civics creates for Catholicism a respectable place in the framework of the Republic. By extension, in declaring kinship with our modern democratic institutions, American Catholicism lays claim to a so-called distinctive character, one that sets it apart from other practitioners of the same faith.

This eastern bias suggests that Catholics of the British colonies were the "real" Catholics, the standard bearers of a true Catholicism. Like early pioneers in general, they turned away from the towns and farms of the East Coast, picked up their American-shaped heritage, and led their English-speaking families west to opportunity. In a Catholic context, this settlement movement is seen to have carried the faithful away from eastern oppression and into regions that encouraged the essentially democratic nature of the religion to emerge.

This puts a Catholic spin on the widely known "frontier thesis," associated with that champion of agrarian settlement history, Frederick Jackson Turner. Turner, of course, argued that the meeting place of "civilization" and "wilderness" in an area of free land explained the emergence of democratic institutions of government and a distinctive American personality. When Catholicism is added to the Turnerian view, it places a religious mantle over our national obsession with and distortion of a frontier story that so often highlights, to the exclusion of other experiences, the European march across the continent by white pioneers.[6] At the very least, as the Turner thesis did for the Natty Bumpos and Daniel Boones of yore, this perspective privileges Anglo foundations—in this instance, those of the American Catholic Church.

In much of the historical literature, scholars have treated western Catholicism as an aside. The Catholic chronicle of western people, with its French or Spanish influences, seems to be an inconvenient "prequel" to the arrival of the "authentic" American Catholics.[7] Western Catholics—their skins perhaps too dark, their religious ideas too intimidating, their faith too shaped by local culture, their first priests too often autocratic Europeans—receive an obligatory historical nod, so the narrator can delineate American Catholic identity by returning the narrative to its "proper" eastern environment.

At the very utterance of the words, "Roman Catholic Church," American scholars in the past and the present turn their historic lens toward the Atlantic Corridor of the United States. For example, in 1941, the literary historian Theodore Maynard, in a work of unshaded hagiography, planted his Catholics firmly in the thirteen colonies and declared, "had it not been for the galvanizing effects of the Revolution . . . American Catholicism would soon have become virtually extinct."[8] In 1969, the widely regarded Catholic historian John Tracy Ellis further connected Catholicism and the rise of democracy by identifying the Catholic Church as an Americanizing institution.[9] Thus, for Ellis, as for the western historian Frederick Jackson Turner, that which was essentially European rearranged itself in the English colonies until it became the catalyst for producing the American character. In 1999 and 2000, the historian Robert E. Burns, in a two-volume study detailing the rise of Indiana's University of Notre Dame, pointedly titled the work, *Being Catholic, Being American*.[10] For Burns, the weakening of anti-Catholic sentiment in the United States was, not surprisingly, explained by the rise of football prominence at the South Bend campus.

One of the premier Catholic historians of the University of Notre Dame, Jay P. Dolan, wrote forcefully in his work, *In Search of an American Catholicism: A History of Religion and Culture in Tension*, about the early efforts of Catholics to center their church within the democratizing atmosphere of a new nation sustained by the ideals of the Enlightenment.[11] And finally, Charles R. Morris, in his fascinating study, *American Catholic: The Saints and Sinners Who Built America's Most Powerful Church*, stated that "the roots of the modern American Catholic Church are found not in Rome, or in the early Spanish missions, but in nineteenth century Ireland."[12]

To be sure, these twentieth- and twenty-first-century scholars could draw from the writings of several Catholic defenders, including John Ireland, the eloquent archbishop of St. Paul, Minnesota. Ireland's 1884 oration, *The Church—and the Support of a Just Government,* outlined the natural alliance the archbishop saw between the Roman Catholic Church and the institutions of America.[13] Some, though not all, American clerics agreed with Ireland, looking to build religious strength through civic nationalism and church unity. Ireland, who fell from grace in his quest to link his church to American thought, continued to argue for the place of Irish immigrants in the emergence of an American Catholic Church with an American personality.[14]

Loving and proud granddaughter that I am of two of those Irish immigrants, who as children, aged six and ten, made the grueling voyage from County Cork to Boston Harbor, I find something to challenge in this view that is so grounded in a rousing tale of the Fitzgeralds, the Ryans, and the McNamaras, their Catholicism sanitized and Americanized through contact with Protestants, institutions of democracy, and the game of football. In no way do I trivialize my family's account of bitter poverty and religious persecution, suffered in both Ireland and Massachusetts. Much of the deprivation they endured stemmed from their unflagging adherence to a deeply cherished and carefully practiced Catholic faith; they paid dearly for it in a Protestant community that had no use for these Irish interlopers. Indeed, I believe that the painful, angry stories I heard around the Sunday dinner table prodded me, as a historian, to look beyond my own family's misfortunes and think about what has occurred because of the unleashed villain of discrimination marauding through the annals of American religion.

Accordingly, I am intrigued by the fact that in modern America the Catholic Church in the West appears to be lesser known and lesser valued. Across the country, Americans seem only vaguely aware and perhaps a tad suspicious of anything or anyone of western Catholicism. On reflection, Catholic history, Catholic conversation, and real Catholics, it seems, can only be found with the schools and cathedrals, theologians, clergy, and laity of the East.[15]

Yet, what about this Catholicism of the West? Today, it is among Latino/a Catholics that church membership is most vibrant. Almost 40 percent of the over 65 million Catholics in this country are Spanish-speaking people, representing a variety of national cultures. All projections indicate that in less than twenty years, the U.S. Census "Hispanic" category of the country will mushroom far beyond its present approximately 35 million, reaching toward 52 million. At present, almost 73 percent of Hispanic/Latinos in the United States identify themselves as Roman Catholic.[16]

Among Native Americans, it has been harder to make an accurate count of the Catholics. The tally certainly approaches five hundred thousand persons, but they are widely dispersed across the country.[17] Still, as any U.S. population map shows, the religious identity of Latino and Native remains deeply embedded in the states of the Far West.[18]

With these rich histories and sweeping demographics, why are these communities still Catholics "at the edge," clinging to their faith out there in the wide open spaces, where the deer and the antelope roam, somewhere unknown and unknowable? Why, as Theodore Maynard insisted, would we accept a notion that without the impact of a 1776 revolution by British colonists, American Catholicism would now be extinct? How can that be, when, for over four hundred years, Catholicism—with its virtues and flaws, its strengths and weaknesses—has been as West as the desert and the canyon? And Catholics, from town or country, reservation or barrio continue to sketch the seasons of their lives with the sacraments of their church?[19] What explains this paradox of a region with mature, broad, and ongoing connections to a religious institution that seems to have returned the loyalty with cool indifference and slim respect?

I suggest turning to the nineteenth-century West in searching for some answers to this complex and thorny question. At best, it will only be a partial explanation, for the West is not called a "contested terrain" for naught. Nowhere is that term—contested terrain—more applicable than in the religious history of the West, and perhaps nowhere do the bitter legacies of cruelty and callousness touch us with more sorrow than in the arenas of spiritual life.[20]

The Catholic history of the West provides an unusual way to examine how the expectations of differing peoples mixed and melded across cultural chasms. We know only too well that Europeans saw triumph in changing the prayer and practice of a Native, while Native people counted victory in holding tight to sacred words and ways. No surprise that the tensions descended into scenarios of torture, bloodshed, and death.[21] At the same time, in this fierce battle between abstract faith and daily life, in this war between and among cultures, some events unexpectedly reveal a time when joy countered sorrow, or insight overcame inhumanity. This is a story as filled with tears as with laughter, but it is also one that illuminates landscapes of race, class, and gender and brings marginalized people to the center of the narrative. Ultimately, it may help us to understand if the West will ever fit comfortably into the standard description of the American Catholic mosaic.

As the nineteenth-century political and economic potential in the West shifted, especially for Europeans, Roman Catholic administrators hoped to be a part of the growing regional opportunities. Additionally, Catholics could look on several hundreds of years of experience in the American Southwest, seeing where and why they had failed and how they had prevailed. A core of Catholicism, sustained in the cultures of Native American and Mexican American people, suggested the West could yet be more Catholic: Indian and Mexican bases could be increased, European and Canadian immigrants supported, and, above all, Protestant advances thwarted. Temporal and spiritual ambition, thus, fueled the desires of cleric visionaries to expand the influence of Catholicism.[22]

However, the Catholic church of Europe, under the aegis of the Society for the Propagation of the Faith, had neither the program nor the personnel to respond in an orderly, reasonable, or informed manner to these challenges. A few foreign bishops left European Catholic strongholds and came to unknown places in the American West, charged to be both ambassadors and administrators for the Catholic Church. They were sent off with well wishes, many prayers, and slim pocketbooks. For the most well intended, the tasks were daunting.

It was the West itself that proved to be the most formidable adversary. Distance, distance, and more distance—a bishop's district could cover two, three, or four hundred thousand square miles. Moreover, all bishops did not blend well into this North American world of great space, nomadic people, and many languages. Some, of course, pushed themselves to engage the environment, extend themselves in new cultures, and accept this place as they found it.[23] But others—inexperienced as frontier travelers, unaccustomed to camping under the sky, afflicted with problematic health, intimidated by the rough feel of the land, uncertain about strategies—often floundered in all these areas. Language differences blocked relationships with the bishops' constituencies; conversations and proclamations were not always graced by civility.[24] Opportunities for disagreement lurked at every turn, and many of these western rookies tripped over their assignments in one fashion or another.

For example, the French priest Jean Baptiste Lamy and his associate Joseph P. Machebeuf, after a staggering trip through the Southwest of 1851, arrived to an enormous and effusive reception in Santa Fe. But the two misread the temper of the community, believing a joyous welcome meant acquiescence to an outsider's authority. Their ecclesiastical directives, assigned by the American bishops and endorsed by the Vatican, reduced the power of well-known local priests, trained in the seminaries of Santa Fe and Durango. The stage was set for the strained relations that developed, as the two Frenchmen projected an unappealing chauvinism and nationalism—not mitigated when Machebeuf stumbled through a Sunday homily in such mangled Spanish that one parishioner concluded, "the preacher must be a Jew or a Protestant."[25]

If the bishops hoped that European clergy would carry the Catholic word into the West, their own rocky performance was not the only indicator that such was not to be. French-, Spanish-, Prussian-, Italian-, Irish-, Polish-, or American-born—the priests needed for the overly spacious West could not be rallied.[26]

From among the ordained, those willing to undertake the physical hardship, relentless poverty, and crushing loneliness of western life, compounded by the social aloofness implied by celibacy, remained few. One embittered French missionary retreating from the frontier wrote that he found it disagreeable to travel by horseback, could not find a cook, feared for the salvation of his own soul, and summed up his complaints by remarking, "I hate the long dreary winters of Iowa."[27]

Increasingly, bishops and priests saw that they must look elsewhere for individuals willing to accept the rigors of a ministry to frontier Catholics—Native people, Mexicans, Mexican Americans, recent European immigrants. The church wanted to aid its members and collect its converts, but there was also a clamor from local ethnic populations, who hoped that a mission station meant better food, medicine, education, or general assistance than would be forthcoming from an ungenerous U.S. government.[28]

The obvious untapped source of Catholic labor for these vineyards was to be found in the monasteries of women—nuns, those secret, mysterious veiled figures, living out their commitments to poverty, chastity, and obedience behind the bolts and grilles of thick-walled convents, seemingly unaware of the day-to-day hurly-burly of a rapidly changing world. An odd choice one might say—to select women to carry the canon of a masculine church into the far reaches of America's mountains and deserts. Odd to expect a collection of white women to bring the story of a Jewish carpenter to the West and odd to think the people of color who lived there would be inclined to accept these religious messengers or what they had to say.

Perhaps it was odd—but there were so many of those nuns and their vows and traditions trained them to yield to the wishes of their church superiors. To be sure, there were obstacles, not the least of which was that most nuns lived inside European monasteries, where they knew little about the American West. However, local political unrest, power struggles inside convents, and a desire to convert "the heathen, the savage" prompted women's monastic orders to listen favorably to mission bishops and to look toward New World opportunities.[29]

A major hurdle concerned enclosure, a practice that bound European nuns to a life totally separated from society and permanently confined to the monastery of one's original religious profession.[30] Transporting nuns from Europe to far western communities, weakened—indeed violated—the concept of enclosure.[31] The trip itself marked the first suspension of the rule. The second came in the poverty of the locations to which the nuns would travel, places where poor people had no way to support a locked house filled with holy but unemployed women. Additionally, the American bishops of the West, unlike their European

As this Shrine of St. Ignatius demonstrates, Native American converts
added to the landscape with places
of worship that integrated accessible
building materials, symbols of local
culture, and images of Roman
Catholicism. Courtesy Denver Public
Library, Western History Collection,
Photo #X-310433, by Benjamin Stone.

Although the subjects of mission photos are usually glum, this group of Sisters of Providence
and Kutenai children shows that nuns and students could find common merriment in a kitten
and a dog with a hat. Courtesy Northwest Museum of Arts and Culture, Eastern Washington
State Historical Society, Spokane, Washington, Accession Number L97-2442.

Sisters of the Holy Spirit gather with more than 125 students at Our Lady of Guadalupe School in Laredo, Texas, in 1905, little more than a decade after Mother Margaret Mary Murphy founded the order for the education of children of color. Courtesy Archives, Sisters of the Holy Spirit, San Antonio, Texas.

In the nineteenth century, the Oblate sisters of Providence, under the leadership of Mother Petra, extended their educational ministry to African American children with an orphanage in St. Louis, Missouri. Courtesy Archives, Oblate Sisters of Providence, Baltimore, Maryland.

In 1954 Texas, young Latinas of the Missionary Catechists of Divine Providence, still associated with the larger Congregation of Divine Providence, prepared for a life of religious service to Mexican American Catholics. Photographer Eddie Hinojosa, Courtesy Archives, Missionary Catechists of Divine Providence, San Antonio, Texas.

The First Communion class of nearly one hundred children from the Río Grande Valley shows the magnitude of the rural Mexican American Catholic population cared for by the Missionary Catechists of Divine Providence in the modern West. Courtesy Archives, Missionary Catechists of Divine Providence, San Antonio, Texas.

peers, lacked enthusiasm for enclosed monasteries. They wanted religious women to be workers, taking up public ministries to address the many needs of varied western constituencies, most of whom lived in almost unbelievable destitution.

For example, Bishop John William Shaw of San Antonio, who had been educated in Ireland and Italy, bargained with a small congregation of European Carmelites who wished to open a foundation in the southern Texas city.[32] Shaw, nearly overwhelmed by the poverty in the area of San Antonio and frantic to provide some church response, encouraged the nuns to come to Texas. Shaw, however, imposed conditions on the new convent: first, he would only consent to a Carmelite active ministry among Tejano families, strongly urging the mother superior to send Spanish-speaking nuns or those who could learn the language quickly; second, Shaw expected the nuns would accept intense personal poverty, for, as he asked their bishop, "I should especially like to know if they would be ready to put up with very simple quarters"; third, Shaw emphasized that he would give zero financial support to the new convent.[33] Shaw's message to the nuns echoed a common refrain among priests and bishops across the West—"come here, work diligently, and do good, but do not expect one farthing from me."[34]

Despite the implied hardships, the invitations struck a strong chord among many religious orders. And so, once-cloistered women, in clusters of five or ten, bowed to the order of a mother superior to become American immigrants. They packed their meager belongings into trunks, said farewell to their sisters in religion, and headed for the seaports of Europe. Standing on the decks of creaking, lurching, rat-infested ships, dressed in their improbable and impractical habits, the women watched the horizon of home slide away, braving the storms of the Atlantic Ocean to try themselves in a new country.[35]

Hardly pausing for Catholic hospitality in the East, these nuns headed to the West, taking passage on trains and steamboats, in carriages, stagecoaches, canoes, and dogsleds. They slept in hotels and boarding houses, took their meals with strangers, and forded rivers in open wagons. They ignored public insults, seasickness, lack of privacy, fleas, and the howl of coyotes. They rode horses and mules, struggled through rain and snow, heat and cold, fell into mud ditches, crawled across corduroy bridges, stumbled down canyon rock; battered and weary they made their way to the nooks and crannies of the American West. Through such epic travels came the Sisters of Mercy from Ireland to California, the Sisters of Saint Mary from Germany to Missouri, the Sisters of Charity of the Incarnate Word from France to Texas.[36]

With every year after 1850, Catholic nuns—or sisters, as they are correctly called—built a presence among the people of the West, immersed themselves in a region utterly foreign to their earlier lives, and surprised themselves with their ability to meet the out-of-doors, culturally different, demanding West on its own terms.[37] They came to places in New Mexico, Montana, or Colorado filled, however, with confidence that once at a frontier destination, their physical peril would end. The mission sisters' quickly learned promises smoothly made in a motherhouse parlor did not always translate into reality. Despite the bishop's assurances that a little white house with a tidy picket fence awaited the sisters, the new convent was more likely to be an abandoned shack, an old chicken coop, or an unheated loft above the church.[38]

Additionally, the bishop usually guaranteed there would be a resident priest at the new mission, so that the sisters could be certain they would have masculine support for labor, protection in a strange environment, and spiritual sustenance for their prayer routines. Time and again, however, no priest lived at a small mission and, if he did, he stayed at home infrequently as he moved endlessly about a large territory, trying to reach his scattered flock. In more than one mission, the sisters were astonished when a congregation of priests withdrew entirely, leaving the nuns indefinitely without help or the sacraments of their church.[39]

Yet, there was an unexpected outcome to this turn of events. Religious women and indigenous western people were thrown together in ways that neither had anticipated. These two unlikely groups—people of color and white women—found themselves alone, far from the nearest town, and removed from various church authorities, as was the case with the Sisters of Charity of Leavenworth at St. Stephen's Indian Mission in Wyoming, the Benedictine Sisters at White Earth, Minnesota, and the Sisters of Divine Providence in Castroville, Texas.[40] Disparate neighbors of disparate heritage began living in an unprecedented intimacy.

Nuns, housed in shabby one-room cabins, faced daily lives quite contrary to the enclosed routines of those cloistered castlelike monasteries of recent memory. No grilles and grates here. No secluded courtyards, silent corridors, ancient chapels, and sweet sounds of the Angelus bell. Here there was work and more work—garments to sew, gardens to plant, cows to milk.

In addition, in the midst of cramped sleeping quarters and tiny kitchens, the sisters began the lessons that introduced the principles of American education and the ways of the Catholic faith.[41] Mission nuns launched their schools determined to hold high the banner of their own culture—and they did; but Indians and Mexicans were equally determined to do the same—and they did. Thus, the actual lived experience did not necessarily follow perfectly the design of either group.

Almost immediately, lay people and nuns initiated the delicate process of building cultural bridges. Teachers became pupils, students became instructors—

the distinctions blurred as information flowed in two directions. Adults and children formed their tongues around the sounds of an alien language, everyone tried meals cooked with foreign ingredients over foreign fires, each group entertained with the songs of its own—music and speech, food and drink—modest but lasting gifts from each society to the other. Within both camps, bold persons curious enough to run their fingers and their minds across the culture of strangers learned about sameness and difference. And they especially learned about faith—as practiced in one's own home, as well as the homes of others. As a result, culture bumped into culture and exchange—spontaneous and surprising—occurred in remote locations throughout the West. As Mother Amadeus of the Ursuline Sisters of Toledo, Ohio, commented about her life in Montana, "Everything out here is far different than we expected." [42]

With the passing of time, Catholic religious women, from Europe and the American East, ventured to this western space of cultural overlay with greater knowledge about the life ahead. They became more comfortable in the West and they articulated an increased confidence in the values of those with whom they lived and worked. People of the West also changed, negotiating their relationships with the nuns according to their own expectations for themselves and their children.[43] Although there may be no way to know exactly the conversations indigenous people had among themselves about the sisters, one nun writing about the families of her students remarked, "I would tremble to disregard their rights as parents." [44]

This is a statement that could be said to underscore the educational philosophy of Mother Katharine Drexel. Born to a wealthy banking family in Philadelphia, Katharine Drexel, at the age of twenty-four, inherited a multimillion-dollar estate, which she used almost exclusively for the education of Native Americans and African Americans.[45] By 1886, she was convinced that if Native people worked and learned in their own communities, they might then enter fully into American society, where racism, she believed, could be eradicated through marriage across ethnic lines.[46] Accordingly, Drexel, who saw the West through a Catholic prism, funneled her investments into specific projects that included construction of educational facilities, long-term employment for Indian families, fire insurance for mission compounds, groceries for students, and salaries for teacher/nuns.

Although much has been made of the Drexel fortune and the manner in which she dispersed at least 25 million dollars to the direct benefit of children of color, there was another compelling aspect to Katharine Drexel's life. Intense Catholic fervor always fueled Drexel's initiatives, and in 1891 she entered the convent, with the intention to organize her own religious congregation, the

Sisters of the Blessed Sacrament for Indians and Colored People. After her initial religious formation with the Sisters of Mercy, Mother Katharine and fourteen young women withdrew to the Drexel family summer home outside of Philadelphia to build a sisterhood entirely dedicated to service among African American and Native American people.[47]

Hers was not a particularly well received program in segregated America. Even with administrators of the Catholic Church, Katharine Drexel, her fortune, and people of color sparked little enthusiasm. One priest friend, commenting about the attitude of the American bishops, remarked, "They waited too long . . . and for the last six years treated the Indian missions indifferently. . . . When favorable opportunities presented themselves, they kicked them away like a football and told each other, 'Don't bother. Mother Katharine will take care of the Indian schools.'"[48] Nonetheless, with her ideal of devotion to people of color, regardless of the price—financially, intellectually, or spiritually—Katharine Drexel effected a unique social interaction.

Most particularly, she brought together communities of western people and the young white women of religious congregations, insisting that they confront one another's humanity, thus, changing the cultural landscape for all involved. For example, in 1894 several Sisters of the Blessed Sacrament moved from Pennsylvania to St. Catherine's Convent in Santa Fe, New Mexico, where they opened a boarding school for Indian children. Quickly adopting an active ministry in keeping with Mother Katharine's directives, the sisters mingled in the crowds at local festivals, inviting their new acquaintances to a convent hospitality program. Within a short time, the nuns hosted at least a dozen Indians each night, preparing and serving their Native guests an evening meal, and providing camping spaces for traveling families on the convent grounds.[49] By 1895, a year after their arrival in New Mexico, the sisters routinely attended parish worship services and participated in religious processions of the laity. One of the nuns trained a choir of Indian boys in the Latin music of Catholicism and the group received a steady flow of requests to sing for mass, evening vespers, and holy day celebrations at churches or in street processions.[50] When deadly epidemics swept across the area, stricken families sent for the sisters to come into their homes to nurse the sick and prepare the dead for burial.[51] Each Sunday, the one free day in their busy week, the sisters volunteered at the penitentiary in Santa Fe, making the nine-mile trek from their convent in a mule-drawn cart driven by a trustee inmate. Through the morning, the nuns went to the cellblock or the chapel to sing and pray in Spanish or English with both men and women prisoners.[52]

Thus, over several years, the Blessed Sacrament Sisters established a multifaceted public presence in the Mexican, Indian, and Anglo communities in the area. Their congregation was widely known in Santa Fe and the nearby towns and pueblos. The Blessed Sacrament Sisters circulated among the poor and the privileged. They had access to the governor and the warden, conversed with physicians and prisoners, and interacted with nuns of other religious congregations; they knew Hispanics, African Americans, Native Americans, Anglos, Catholics and non-Catholics, the clergy and the laity.

In 1906, three of the sisters left St. Catherine's, traveling by wagon into the mountains to recruit eligible Indian children for the coming academic year.[53] After a rough and perilous trip of nearly twelve hours, they reached Abiquiú. Surrounded by the sounds of four different languages, taken by the unique architecture of the Hispanic hacienda, and surprised that clothing styles blurred between the Indian and Hispanic communities, these three sisters stepped into a world of even greater cultural plurality than they witnessed in Santa Fe. They found ethnic segregation weaker here, with Hispanic and Indian families worshiping and working together. The Hispanic community, employers of the Indians, clearly had the economic advantage, with large, well-furnished homes, many trained servants from the pueblo, and perhaps a daughter or two educated at the Santa Fe academy of the Sisters of Loretto. Nonetheless, here, in the mountains, Hispanics and Indians acted out together the routines of life and shared Catholic rituals. Hispanic families, with no church of their own, entered into the pueblo for religious services, which on this day included a high mass and a street parade.

Not these traditional activities, however, but an informal encounter illuminated the larger religious élan of the West for the sisters. Ameliana Chávez, Santa Fe educated daughter of a local wealthy Hispanic family, secured permission for the Blessed Sacrament nuns to enter the *morada*, a locked building of the local brotherhood of Penitentes.[54] Although the priest had cautioned the sisters that the Penitentes were "ignorant" and had been ordered to cease their rituals of blood penance, such as having "bundles of cactus tied to their naked backs," the sisters themselves reacted somewhat differently to the brotherhood. The sisters, despite nervousness on entering the darkened morada, saw, not ignorance, but a religious space, one they did not fully understand, but perceived as sacred. The chapel-like aura, wooden altar, figures of the Mother of Sorrows and Doña Sebastiana, skeleton of death, huge crosses, and instruments of penance, including a wide "leather belt, thickly studded with wire points," struck them as unusual, but powerful indicators of personal faith. Ameliana explained the use of each artifact, especially during Good Friday, when the Penitentes invited those outside the brotherhood into the morada. After the Stations of the Cross, everyone followed the men performing various self-mortifications to a mountain place for a mock Crucifixion.[55]

Clearly, this was not exactly Catholicism as the nuns practiced it, nor did they endorse the extreme flagellations, the bloodletting. But neither did they patronize, scorn, or ridicule.[56] It seemed that, as religious women often challenged for promoting their own agency within Catholicism, they identified with the brotherhood's difficult position in the church. Perhaps for these nuns, the refusal of the Penitentes to abandon deeply held spiritual and social values, despite church censure, echoed their own determination to create a self-defined spirituality in an institution that dismissed the theological legitimacy of women.[57]

This rich moment—a young Hispana and three European/Anglo nuns standing in the holy space of indigenous men and believing in the promotion of worldly good through faith—speaks over time to the tenor of western Catholicism. Similar scenes, brushed with the crisscrossing of spirituality, the stretch for religious commonality, and the fellowship of blended faith, washed across the canvas of western landscapes, breaking through the angry skies of many frontier horizons. These other images might be remembered in brighter and bolder colors, for they recall lives often forgotten in the Catholic chronicle.

For example, in 1893, Margaret Mary Murphy, an Irish widow, formed a sisterhood devoted to the education of African American and Mexican children and wrote the congregation's original constitution in both English and Spanish, reflecting her intent to build an ethnically mixed convent.[58] At White Earth, Minnesota, a Benedictine sister who worked for thirty-one years at this Chippewa mission, used her spare time as a cobbler for the poor, mending over three thousand shoes, and each December sewed until two or three in the morning, making dresses for the seventy-five boarding students. She remembered, "I wished each child to have something new [at Christmas]."[59] In 1914 at the New Mexico penitentiary, an African American woman prisoner was placed in solitary confinement on a diet of bread and water when the authorities learned she was pregnant. Through the intervention of the nuns who made weekly prison visitations, this young inmate was removed to the hospital of the Daughters of Charity, where she remained with her newborn son until he was adopted. Nearly forty years later, the former prisoner, who had found and reunited with that son conceived under prison circumstances, stopped a Blessed Sacrament sister on a Santa Fe street, inquired about her benefactor of the past and said, "Tell [Sister Ligouri] I send her my love."[60] In Houston, Texas, two Sisters of Divine Providence, commuting from their Anglo convent to a barrio school, inspired some of their Mexican pupils to request training as teachers of catechism. The outgrowth of this initiative was the Missionary Catechists of Divine Providence, Mexican women who began as students of white nuns, then affiliated with them as professed sisters, but ultimately achieved an autonomous identity as a religious organization.[61] In Arizona, an outspoken nun commenting on local politics wrote, "Washington will have a . . . problem on its hands . . . to keep these poor people from starving if the Whites come in and get the best of their land and of everything else worth having." [62]

Are these anecdotes clues to why western Catholicism sinks into a lacuna in the history of American Catholicism? Is this how the West became a giant monolithic parish with its communicants outside the power structures of church building? Were there just too many women who carried the message of faith from this decidedly male-controlled church?[63] Were their associates, students, and friends just too often people of color? Were all the Catholics of West, regardless of national origin or ethnicity, just too scattered across a vast geography to constitute a critical mass for the church? Was the religious expression of western cultures just too frightening—the sense of faith too ethereal, too exciting, too exuberant, and too challenging for those of a European tradition?

Moreover, was Catholicism in the American West burdened by its early designation as a mission zone, suggesting distant poorly staffed outposts, small reserves where mean-spirited friars herded reluctant and not terribly bright Natives into the bosom of the church? Did that unhappy image from the nineteenth century evolve into a romantic one in the twentieth, but one where the word "mission" still connoted a place ancillary to the power centers of the religion? Have the old adobe churches, once in collapse, now restored for tourists, taken on the rosy shades of yesterday, giving a muted tint to religious practices we can fondly identify as "folk," or "colorful," or "quaint," but not as "essential, powerful, important, or theological?"

Whatever the answers to these uncomfortable questions, one thing is certain. In the nineteenth century, the religious women and lay Catholics of the West lacked the spiritual and temporal power to reshape their place within the Roman Catholic Church. Yet, theirs was a Catholicism that endured across landscapes of physical, intellectual, and spiritual pain and grief. At the same time, cultural borders, even those that seemed impenetrable, weakened and shifted. By plan and by chance, remarkably different people exchanged values and rituals, merging faiths and forging relationships in which the Catholic religion, with good and ill, played a significant and permanent role.

By 1900, a unique Catholicism had emerged in the American West. This was not the "unique" Catholicism so bonded with the East and the American Revolution. This Catholicism increasingly turned on the axis of politics and was carried in the choices and faith of people of color, ethnic communities, and European immigrants from across a spectrum of nations—urban and rural Catholics frequently poor beyond description—who found their advocates in those nuns, brothers, and priests who allowed themselves as individuals to learn and grow in western places. It was a Catholicism that in its best form practiced the best ideals of Mother Katharine Drexel, of whom one Native American student wrote, "Hers was a flaming desire to dream lofty dreams . . . a vision of what you and I should be."[64] It was a Catholicism that had its roots in the very essence of cultural pluralism, when such a term had no existence. It was and is a Catholicism that has no single definition, no simplistic agreement, no one face, no one color, no common explanation, and no agreed upon vision. That is, after all, what diversity means.

Still, one cannot travel the roads of the West without seeing and feeling the lingering traces of those mixed and dusty footprints of a Catholic past shaped by the neglected and the powerless. Today, those neglected and powerless—Catholics of the West—energized by political liberation, gender awareness, and cultural validation raise their voices in a chorus of new hymns. It is holy music that celebrates an American West where there lives no longer a silent and invisible flock. Rather, now are heard the clear sounds of articulate and active Catholics, driven by a quest for the social justice, theological recognition, and spiritual fulfillment promised in the tenets of their faith.[65] Certainly, it is time, especially among those East-centered faithful, to hear the hope-filled anthems, reminding everyone of those more than four hundred years that Catholicism has reverberated through the magnificent mountains and deep valleys, across the arid flats and lofty mesas of the West. Here, Catholicism placed its signature on people often hard pressed into receiving the message, but, nonetheless, through their courageous perseverance, adding strength, plurality, and originality to the American Catholic Church.

Notes

1.   While Catholic loyalties meant a rocky road in this mid-Atlantic Protestant-dominated outpost, at least the followers of Rome, literally driven from neighboring colonies, carved a niche in the Calverts' colony. Eventually, a general suppression of Catholics became the norm in colonial Maryland. Jerome R. Reich, *Colonial America,* 5th ed. (Upper Saddle River, N.J.: Prentice-Hall, 2001), 69–71; John Tracy Ellis, *American Catholicism,* 2nd ed., rev. (Chicago: University of Chicago Press, 1969), 22–25.

2.   Ellis, *American Catholicism,* 6.

3.   Robert Ignatius Burns, S.J., "Roman Catholic missionaries," in *The New Encyclopedia of the American West,* ed. Howard R. Lamar, 983 (New Haven, Conn.: Yale University Press, 1998).

4.   There is a growing awareness in American society that self-identification labels have produced a complicated conversation among people of color. Self-identity may vary

according to national origins, political circumstances, social perspective, as well as other personal factors. In this paper, the use of Mexican or Mexican American is intended to reflect the voice of the nineteenth-century documents. Latino/a is applied to modern America, where the term has acquired political and scholarly currency. Indian, Native, and Native American are used interchangeably for literary variation. For a discussion of self-identification terminology that informed this paper, see Timothy Matovina and Gerald E. Poyo, eds., *Presente!: U.S. Latino Catholics from Colonial Origins to the Present, American Catholic Identities: A Documentary History*, Christopher J. Kauffman, gen. ed. (Maryknoll: Orbis Press, 2000), xx–xxi. According to David J. Weber, the term *mestizo* was used in a general way to mean people of a racially mixed background. David J. Weber, *The Spanish Frontier in North America* (New Haven, Conn.: Yale University Press, 1992), 8. Benjamin Keen agreed with that assertion, but added that mestizos were rejected by both Spanish and Indian society, a circumstance that sometimes led to instability within their communities. Benjamin Keen, *A History of Latin America,* 4th ed. (Boston: Houghton Mifflin, 1992), 110–11.

5. The founding members of the Oblate Sisters of Providence came to Baltimore, Maryland, as refugees from political revolts in Saint-Domingue in the Caribbean. Thus, these women, African in family ancestry, French in lived culture, and American in race experience brought complex identities to Catholicism and sisterhood in Maryland. See Diane Batts Morrow, *Persons of Color and Religious at the Same Time* (Chapel Hill: University of North Carolina Press, 2002), esp., 1–12.

6. Turner presented his ideas in an address to the 1893 American Historical Association meeting, and his remarks were printed in the proceedings. Frederick Jackson Turner, "The Significance of the Frontier in American History," *Annual Report of the American Historical Association, 1893* (Washington, D.C.: Government Printing Office, 1894), 199–227. A voluminous literature responds to this presentation. For a traditional explanation, see Ray Allen Billington, *Westward Expansion: A History of the American Frontier,* 4th ed. (New York: Macmillan, 1974), 1–11. For a longer, more current analysis of the Turner ideas, see Allan G. Bogue, *Frederick Jackson Turner: Strange Roads Going Down* (Norman: University of Oklahoma Press, 1998). Also important is Richard White, "Frederick Jackson Turner," in *Historians of the American Frontier: A Bio-Bibliographical Sourcebook,* ed. John R. Wunder, 660–81 (New York: Greenwood Press, 1988).

7. Robert E. Wright, O.M.I., argues that much historiography of Catholicism places the mission at the center and ignores the general population of faithful in the Southwest. As a result, Catholicism as a force and composed of more than just European friars has been greatly underestimated. Robert E. Wright, O.M.I., "The Hispanic Church in Texas under Spain and Mexico," *U. S. Catholic Historian* 20 (Fall 2002): 15–33.

8. Theodore Maynard, *The Story of American Catholicism* (New York: Macmillan, 1941), 128.

9.   Ellis, *American Catholicism*, 41–83.

10. Robert E. Burns, *Being Catholic, Being American: The Notre Dame Story, 1842–1934* (Notre Dame, Ind.: University of Notre Dame Press, 1999 and 2000), 1: x, 265–305, 443–44; 2: ix–x.

11. Jay P. Dolan, *In Search of an American Catholicism: A History of Religion and Culture in Tension* (New York: Oxford University Press, 2002), esp. 13–45. For a discussion of the complexity of Dolan's many ideas, see Thomas W. Jodziewicz, review of Jay P. Dolan, *In Search of an American Catholicism: A History of Religion and Culture in Tension*, *Catholic Historical Review* 89 (October 2003): 807–12.

12. Charles R. Morris, *American Catholic: The Saints and Sinners Who Built America's Most Powerful Church* (New York: Vintage Books of Random House, 1997), preface, n.p.

13. Marvin R. O'Connell, *John Ireland and the American Catholic Church* (St. Paul: Minnesota Historical Society Press, 1988), 192–95; Dolan, *In Search of an American Catholicism*, 96, 99–101. Charles R. Morris details the intensely political networking that was connected to Ireland's agenda for the American church. Morris, *American Catholic*, 96–110.

14. Bishop John Ireland was involved in a complicated political and theological debate concerning the need for the Catholic Church to respond to modern change versus those who perceived of the church as immutable. Jay P. Dolan places Bishop Ireland within the general context of the struggle between the conservatives and the "modernists," showing the complexity of the intellectual and faith issues involved. See Dolan, *In Search of an American Catholicism*, 99–117.

15. The administrative center of the American Catholic Church is situated in the East, as the United States Conference of Catholic Bishops, with its labyrinthlike offices, is located in Washington, D.C., and at least eight of its twelve presidents have been from the East or Midwest. The prototypes for the United States Conference of Bishops date to 1917 and 1919. In July 2001, the U.S. Conference of Catholic Bishops and the National Conference of Catholic Bishops merged into one agency (U.S. Conference of Catholic Bishops Web site, www.usccb.org). The intellectual and theological center of the American Catholic Church is considered to be at The Catholic University of America. Aside from the University of Notre Dame, the common Catholic names that resonate with the American public are such as Dorothy Day, St. Patrick's Cathedral, and the Joseph P. Kennedy family—all persons and places with Catholic identities, eastern roots, and broad recognition on the boulevards of America. There are not equally instant responses to the 1878 intellectual defense of the Colegio de Las Vegas, New Mexico, knowledge of La Sociedad Folklórica, or in a political context, the Catholic lineage of the social activist César Chávez, or the emergence of Las Hermanas. For documents concerning these subjects, see Matovina and Poyo, eds., *Presente!*, 73–6, 206–209, 217–18.

16. Religion journalist David Gibson asserts that the Latino community, through immigration and birthrate, has accounted for more than 70 percent of the growth in the American church since approximately 1960. David Gibson, *The Coming Catholic Church: How the Faithful Are Shaping a New American Catholicism* (New York: HarperCollins, 2003), 73–75. The Conference of U.S. Bishops through surveys of its Hispanic Affairs division indicated that between 1990 and 2000 the U.S. Hispanic population increased by 13 million people and that projected estimates are that by 2020 the total number will increase to 52.7 million (U.S. Conference of Catholic Bishops, www.usccb.org/hispanicaffairs/).

17. Presentation of Bishop Donald E. Pelotte, S.S.S., to the spring assembly of the U.S. Conference of Catholic Bishops, June 19, 2003 (U.S. Conference of Catholic Bishops, www.usccb.org/education/).

18. U.S. Conference of Catholic Bishops, Hispanic Affairs, U.S. (Conference of Catholic Bishops, www.nccbuscc.org/hispanicaffairs/).

19. Michael P. Carroll argues that among Hispano and Pueblo communities participation in life-cycle rituals of faith were and remain the process by which participants made important social and economic connections. Michael P. Carroll, *The Penitente Brotherhood: Patriarchy and Hispano-Catholicism in New Mexico* (Baltimore: Johns Hopkins University Press, 2002), 47–48.

20. Jacqueline Peterson has written about the sensitivities and sadness within Native/Catholic history and the resulting spiritual legacies in the Northwest. Many of her observations can be applied generally to the West. See, Jacqueline Peterson "Sacred Encounters in the Northwest: A Persistent Dialogue," *U.S. Catholic Historian* 12 (Fall 1994): 37–48.

21. Weber, *The Spanish Frontier in North America*, 122–46.

22. Certainly Protestants feared these goals of Catholics for the West. In 1846 Edward Beecher, brother of Harriet Beecher Stowe, suggested in a speech to the Ladies Society for the Promotion of Education at the West that Catholics intended to extend their conversion efforts into western states by opening many schools for young women. See Thomas Woody, *A History of Women's Education in the United States*, 2 vols. (New York: Octagon Press, 1966, repr. ed.), ii, 456–57.

23. For a readable account of the travel demanded of engaged western priests and bishops, see Paul Horgan, *Lamy of Santa Fe: His Life and Times* (New York: Farrar, Straus, and Giroux, 1975), 98–110, 132–39, 305–14, 382–86.

24. See Wilfred P. Schoenberg, S.J., "Frontier Catholics in the Pacific Northwest," *U.S. Catholic Historian* 12 (Fall 1994): 65–84.

25. Lynn Bridgers, *Death's Deceiver: The Life of Joseph P. Machebeuf* (Albuquerque: University of New Mexico Press, 1997), esp. 81, 108, quote on 91.

26. An opposing view would be that of the scholar of the history of Catholic education Timothy Walch, who details the western frontier initiatives as a masculine undertaking, with nuns providing an auxiliary but admirable service role in the parochial school system. Timothy Walch, *Parish School: American Catholic Parochial Education from Colonial Times to the Present* (New York: Crossroad Publishing, 1996), 7–12. Timothy M. Matovina, however, argues that the absence of priests in the Southwest gave rise to an activist laity, including women, accustomed to taking responsibility for its worship services. Timothy M. Matovina, "Lay Initiatives in Worship on the Texas *Frontera*, 1830–1860," *U.S. Catholic Historian* 12 (Fall 1994): 107–20.

27. Rev. Jean C. Perrodin to Rt. Rev. Bishop Mathias Loras, April 10, 1851, Rev. Jean Perrodin Papers, Archives of the Archdiocese of Dubuque, Iowa. Around 1883 an anonymous Jesuit missionary priest wrote, "You cannot imagine how much it consoles me to know that I am not here of my own choice. If this were the case, I could not hold out three days." Gertrude Bush Papers, Sister Eustella, Folder 8, Box 3, Series P 1384, Archives, School Sisters of St. Francis, Milwaukee, Wisconsin.

28. When the Ursuline Sisters of Toledo opened their convent in Miles City, Montana, frequent visitors were men of the Northern Cheyenne tribe, who insisted on knowing how soon the sisters could move to the reservation. Sister Sacred Heart to Dear Mother, April 27, 1884, Miles City, Letters, January 1884–May 1884, Folder 8; Sister of the Sacred Heart of Jesus to Dearest Mother, June 14, 1884, St. Labre's Mission, Letters, Folder 7, Archives of the Ursuline Convent, Toledo, Ohio (hereafter, AUC). Also see the 1877 requests of the Lakota Sioux to President Rutherford B. Hayes for teachers, as quoted in Marie Therese Archambault, O.S.F., Mark G. Thiel, and Christopher Vecsey, eds., *The Crossing of Two Roads: Being Catholic and Native in the United States*, American Catholic Identities: A Documentary History (Maryknoll, N.Y.: Orbis Books, 2003), 118.

29. In 1872, the foundress of the Sisters of Saint Mary wrote from Germany, "The present state of affairs with regard to religious and convents especially is so discouraging that we feel inclined to cross the ocean." Mother Mary Odilia to Dear Mr. Wegman, August 11, 1872, printed in Sister Mary Gabriel Henninger, S.S.M., *Sisters of Saint Mary and Their Healing Mission* (St. Louis: n.p., 1979), 4. For sisters for whom the mission aspect of the call was an imperative, see Sister Margaret Shekleton, S.D.S., *Bending in Season: History of the North American Province of the Sisters of the Divine Savior, 1895–1985* (Milwaukee: Bulfin Printers, 1985), 34–49. Not all missionary sisters came from Europe. For example, the Cordi-Marian Missionary Sisters emigrated from Mexico to Texas, following religious suppression in their country. See Thomas P. McCarthy, C.S.V., *Guide to the Catholic Sisterhoods in the United States* (Washington, D.C.: Catholic University of America Press, 1952), 180.

30. Enclosure, codified by Pope Benedict VIII in 1283, proved to be an awkward and costly arrangement, one that made cloistered women totally dependent on outsiders for

every sort of assistance. James R. Cain, *The Influence of the Cloister on the Apostolate of Congregations of Religious Women* (Rome: Pontifical Lateran University, 1965), 28–37.

31. Once situated in small western convents, the nuns themselves saw that the imposition of strict enclosure was not only impractical, it was also impossible. For example, Benedictine nuns in Minnesota had no means of support in a cloister because the local families did not have the funds to send children inside the convent for music lessons. The nuns decided they had to suspend enclosure to do public begging through the community. Sister M. Grace McDonald, O.S.B., *With Lamps Burning* (Saint Joseph, Minn.: Saint Benedict's Priory Press, 1957), 60.

32. John William Shaw was born in Alabama, educated in Europe, and then served in his home state until 1910, when he was transferred to San Antonio, Texas. James Talmadge Moore, *Acts of Faith: The Catholic Church in Texas, 1900–1950* (College Station: Texas A&M University Press, 2002), 32–35.

33. This protracted correspondence also demonstrated the bargaining that often occurred when bishops wanted to avoid making financial commitments to a congregation and the nuns wanted to negotiate for the most favorable arrangements. Mother Marie-Teresa of the Heart of Jesus to Rt. Rev. J. A. Forest, May 2, 1913, to J. W. Shaw, May 11, June 14, July 26, August 13, October 15, November 6, November 10, November 25, December 17, 1913; J. W. Shaw to Most Rev. S. G. Messmer, May 8, 1913, to Most Rev. Neil McNeil, May 8, 1913, to Mother Marie-Teresa, July 12, July 30, August 23, September 10, November 6, November 13, 1913, Religious Orders of Women, Carmelite Sisters of the Divine Heart of Jesus, Chancery Office, Archdiocese of San Antonio, San Antonio, Texas.

34. Florence Deacon, O.S.F., examines the various economic ventures, investment resources, and imagination four different women's congregations of the Midwestern United States used to support their foundations. Florence Deacon, O.S.F., "More than Just a Shoe String and a Prayer: How Women Religious Helped Finance the Nineteenth-Century Social Fabric," *U.S. Catholic Historian* 14 (Winter 1996): 67–89.

35. The religious habit was often a lightning rod for drawing anti-Catholic sentiment. For this reason, many nuns dressed in secular attire while traveling, reverting to the habit in the privacy of the convent. In addition, as American democracy took shape in the early nineteenth century, the sight of nuns dressed in habits caused some in the United States to be unfavorably reminded of the Catholic allegiance to the Vatican. The rise of several anti-Catholic societies, such as the American Protective Association, further exacerbated problems for women wearing religious habits. See Elizabeth Kuhns, *The Habit: The History of the Clothing of Catholic Nuns* (New York: Doubleday, 2003), 119–21.

36. For examples, see Sister Adeline Jonas, Sister Ambrosia Layer, Sister Antoinette Loth, Sister Barnabas Siebenhor, and Sister Mary Bona Reiff, "Memoirs of Pioneer CDP Sisters, 1868–1926," typescript, Archives, Congregation of Divine Providence, San Antonio, Texas (hereafter, ACDP); "Introductory Epoch, 1859," *Chronicles, St. Mary's*

Academy, Portland, Oregon, vol. 2, 1859–1885, 11–21, Archives, Sisters of the Holy Names of Jesus and Mary, Portland, Oregon; *Annals, 1890–1923,* 44–46, Archives, Sisters of Saint Dominic of the Congregation of the Holy Cross, Edmonds, Washington; P. J. DeSmet to Rev. and dear Father, September 24, September 30, 1869, in Sister Julia Gilmore S.C.L., *Come North: The Life Story of Mother Xavier Ross, Valiant Pioneer and Foundress of the Sisters of Charity of Leavenworth* (New York: McMullen Books, 1951), 280–81.

37. In 1884, an Ursuline nun wrote, "one who has never traveled over mountains has a very faint idea of the difficulties and dangers." Sister of the Sacred Heart of Jesus to My dear Mother, April 7, 1884, St. Labre's Mission, Letters 1884–1885, Folder 7, AUC. By canon law, in general, nuns take perpetual vows and follow the rule of enclosure. Sisters take simple vows and have no enclosure. Albert J. Nevins, M.M., *The Maryknoll Catholic Dictionary* (New York: Grosset and Dunlap, 1965), 408. For purposes of literary variety, the two are used interchangeably here.

38. Records of Schools, St. Mary's Academy, Beeville, Texas; for additional examples, see Sister Adeline Jonas, Sister Antoinette Loth, Sister Barnabas Siebenhor, "Memoirs of Pioneer CDP Sisters, 1868–1926," ACDP.

39. When Bishop Brondel crossed Montana to visit St. Labre's mission at the Cheyenne reservation, in August of 1884, he found the Jesuits and the hired hand had departed and the Ursuline nuns were without support for their domestic and spiritual needs. B. Brondel to Rev. Canon Ad Ducles, February 16, 1885, Folder 10. Several years later, one nun reported that between 1897 and 1914 secular priests were sent to the Northern Cheyenne tribe, but frequently there was no priest available. Earlier, the Jesuits had completely withdrawn from the area. Sister Eustella to Rev. Mother, January 26, 1958, p. 5, Gertrude Bush Papers, Sister Eustella, Folder 9, Box 3, Series P 1384, Archives, School Sisters of Saint Francis, Milwaukee, Wisconsin.

40. Sister Mary Buckner, S.C.L., *History of the Sisters of Charity of Leavenworth, Kansas* (Kansas City, Miss.: Hudson-Kimberly Publishing, 1898), 408–21; Sister M. Grace McDonald, O.S.B., *With Lamps Burning,* 232–8; Sister Mary Generosa Callahan, C.D.P., *The History of the Sisters of Divine Providence, San Antonio, Texas* (Milwaukee: Bruce Publications, 1955), 56–57, 80–81.

41. For examples, see *Annals, Sioux Falls, South Dakota, St. Joseph [St. Michael's],* 5, *Annals, Eagle Grove, Iowa, Sacred Heart,* 1, Archives, Dominicans of the Congregation of the Most Holy Rosary, Sinsinawa, Wisconsin. One nun politely noted of the 1896 convent in Beeville, Texas, "The residence of the sisters and school building were found too incommodius." Records of Schools, St. Mary's Academy, Beeville, Texas, ACDP.

42. Sister Mary Amadeus to My dear Mother, March 29, 1884, Miles City, Letters, January 1884–May 1884, Folder 8, AUC.

43. Your Mother in the Blessed Sacrament, to My dear Daughters in the Blessed Sacrament, October 1902, *Annals, Sisters of the Blessed Sacrament, 1894–1908;* Sister M. Agatha

to My dear Sisters at St. C's, St. E's, and St. F de Sales, October 1902, Mission Records, St. Michael's, Arizona, Archives, Sisters of the Blessed Sacrament, Saint Elizabeth's Convent, Cornwalls Heights, Pennsylvania (hereafter, ASBS).

44. Mother Evangelist to Mother Katharine Drexel (?), n.d., n.m. 1897, *Annals, Sisters of the Blessed Sacrament, 1894–1908*, ASBS.

45. For a more detailed account of Katharine Drexel, see Anne M. Butler, "Mother Katharine Drexel: Spiritual Visionary for the West," in *By Grit and Grace: Eleven Women who Shaped the American West,* ed. Glenda Riley and Richard W. Etulain, 198–220 (Golden, Colo.: Fulcrum Publishing, 1997).

46. Mother in the B. S. to My very dear daughters in the B. S., October 15, 1902, Writings of Katharine Drexel, vol. 1, no. 144, ASBS.

47. It was not a proposition necessarily greeted warmly within a fiercely segregated American society of the day, and the convent did not want for abuse and threat. J. A. Stephen to Reverend dear Mother, September 29, 1899, *Annals, Sisters of the Blessed Sacrament, 1894–1908*, ASBS. About threats at the dedication of the motherhouse, see Sister Consuela Marie Duffy, S.B.S., *Katharine Drexel: A Biography* (Bensalem, Pa.: Mother Katharine Drexel Guild, 1966), 178–79.

48. J. A. Stephens to Dear Mother Katharine, January/February 1901 (?), *Annals, Sisters of the Blessed Sacrament*, ASBS.

49. Sister M. Evangelist to My dear Mother & Sisters, August 12, 1894, November 4, 1894, July 15, 1895, *Annals, Sisters of the Blessed Sacrament, 1894–1908*, ASBS.

50. Sister M. Evangelist to My dear Mother, July 15, 1895, Sister M. Ignatius to My own dear Sisters, Feast of St. Josaphat, July 1896, *Annals, Sisters of the Blessed Sacrament, 1894–1908*, ASBS.

51. The Blessed Sacrament sisters lived at the Cochiti Pueblo for five weeks during one epidemic. Their letters of their experiences were published in the convent annals at the motherhouse. Sister M. Perpetua to Dear Mother and Sisters, August 21, 1901; Sister M. Perpetua to Dear Mother and Sisters, September 10, 1901; Sister M. Loyola to Dear Mother, n.d.; Sister M. Perpetua to Dear Mother and Sisters, September 12 and 13, 1901; Sister M. Loyola to Dear Mother and Sisters, September 10, 1901; Sister M. Perpetua to Dear Mother and Sisters, n.d.; Sister M. Loyola to Dear Mother and Sisters, n.d.; Sister M. Perpetua to Dear Mother and Sisters, September 12, 1901, *Annals, Sisters of the Blessed Sacrament, 1894–1908*, ASBS.

52. "Memoirs of Sister M. Ligouri, S.B.S., 1895–1952," written at the Request of Sister Mary Lourdes, S.B.S., Records of St. Catherine's, Santa Fe, New Mexico, ASBS.

53. Mother Katharine Drexel would only permit full-blood Indian children to be enrolled in schools she supported. Mother to My dear daughters in the Blessed Sacrament one and all, October 1902, Writings of Katharine Drexel, vol. 2, no. 133, typescript, ASBS.

54. The brotherhood formally known as Hermandad de Nuestro Padre Jesús Nazareno has been the subject of considerable scholarly writing. One major interpretation argues that the organization traces its roots to the early missionaries and actually builds on the themes of mysticism and social service found in the medieval Franciscan way of life. See Thomas J. Steele, S.J., "Cofradía," in *Folk and Church in New Mexico* (Colorado Springs: Hulbert Center Press of Colorado College, 1993), 9. Another view states that the Penitentes emerged out of modern circumstances that prompted Hispano action designed to respond to various forms of dispossession. Michael P. Carroll, *The Penitente Brotherhood*. In Abiquiú there were two moradas, apparently the result of a splinter group that separated from the main brotherhood.

55. All details and quotes about the trip to Abiquiú are from a twelve-page letter printed in the annals. Sister M. Evangelist to My dear Mother, March 7, 1906 (?), *Annals, Sisters of the Blessed Sacrament, 1894–1908*, ASBS.

56. This is not an unqualified statement about the relationships of Catholic nuns to the cultures of western people. There are many accounts that show the language of convent records and letters to reflect the biases and racism of the era. These sisters, however, did not include negative descriptors in the reporting of this event.

57. The process by which women were excluded from areas of scientific thought and the role of the Catholic church in that process are explored by David F. Noble, *A World without Women: The Christian Clerical Culture of Western Science* (New York: Oxford University Press, 1992).

58. Constitutions and Rule, 1896, typescripts, one in English, one in Spanish, Box 8, Envelope 1.1, Archives, Sisters of the Holy Spirit, San Antonio, Texas.

59. "Memories of Sister Ladislaus Twardowski, O.S.B.," mss., Indian Mission Records, White Earth, Record Group 24, Archives, Sisters of Saint Benedict, Saint Joseph, Minnesota.

60. "Memoirs of Sister M. Ligouri," written at the request of Sister Mary of Lourdes, S. B. S., p. 10, Records of St. Catherine's, Santa Fe, New Mexico, ASBS. For a more complete account of the inmate Alma Lyons, see Anne M. Butler, *Gendered Justice in the American West: Women Prisoners in Men's Penitentiaries* (Urbana: University of Illinois Press, 1997), 120–21, 137–38.

61. Records of Schools, Our Lady of Guadalupe, Houston, Texas, and Immaculate Conception, Houston, Texas, 1912, ACDP. Also see, Anita de Luna, M.C.D.P., "*Evangelizadoras del Barrio:* The Rise of the Missionary Catechists of Divine Providence," *U.S. Catholic Historian* 21 (Winter 2003): 53–71; Sister Mary Generosa Callahan, C.D.P., *The History of the Sisters of Divine Providence: San Antonio, Texas*, 266–8.

62. S. M. B. to [Mother Katharine Drexel?], letter fragment, n.d., St. Michael's, Arizona, ASBS.

63. In his discussion of gender, Jay P. Dolan examines the emergence of the "new" Catholic woman at the turn of the century. He points out that this woman was clearly defined within the Catholic laity and that the place of a vocation and the role of the nun were not expected to be revised. Although Catholics continued to honor the concept of the religious vocation for women, it seems that the male hierarchy retained its vision of women's religious congregations as a source of cheap labor that should be subservient to church authority. Dolan, *In Search of an American Catholicism,* 117–25. Deirdre M. Moloney further develops this discussion concerning the role of laywomen and laymen in charitable undertakings, particularly as influenced by the philanthropic record of congregations of sisters. "Divisions of Labor: The Roles of American Catholic Lay Women, Lay Men, and Women Religious in Charity Provision," *U.S. Catholic Historian* 20 (Winter 2002): 41–55.

64. Sister Consuela Marie Duffy, S.B.S., *Katharine Drexel: A Biography,* 361.

65. Jay P. Dolan argues that in modern America, clergy and laity alike continue to wrestle with what the future Catholic Church in the United States will be, with the understanding that a reshaped religious identity should not fracture along cultural divides. He also employs the term "pastor barons" to refer to ranking clergy prior to Vatican II. This phrase aptly explains much of the church atmosphere for the nineteenth-century topics of this paper. Dolan, *In Search of an American Catholicism,* 195–98, 206. Charles R. Morris, in a chapter titled "Theological Visions," considers the many different perspectives in the modern church that have resulted in extreme camps among the discussants and a growing response from the Vatican. Morris, *American Catholic,* 322–51.

From the City of the Angels to the Parishes of San Antonio
Catholic Organization, Women Activists, and Racial Intersections, 1900–50

Michael E. Engh, S.J.

T he first time I flew from Los Angeles to San Antonio, the rising sun illuminated broad deserts and painted deep purple hues across the distant mountains. Viewed from the air, the vast terrain fell flatter and stretched farther than I recalled from driving the interstate. Proportions and distances had changed for me, and I read the land differently from a plane than I did from a car. The landscape had not altered, but my new position allowed me to recognize the connections and distances between familiar sites. Similar changes in perception and relationship occur when we view the history of the Catholic Church in the American West from the perspective of women.

The landscape of western history has long revealed evidence of Franciscan missionaries, pioneer bishops, and other clerical leaders. Their stories have formed landmarks along the trails by which historians have guided readers through the region's religious past. In recent years, however, investigators have discovered and claimed neglected trails blazed by women—both nuns and laity. Writing western Catholic history from the perspective of women, these historians have lifted us higher in order to see farther and to discern networks of relationships and patterns of participation and exclusion. A different Catholic history is appearing, one that includes alternative issues, forgotten leaders, and numerous achievements missing from familiar trails of interpretation. These emerging vistas reveal connections between cities and regions, as well as the conflicts and cooperation that tell a fuller story of women in the American Catholic Church.[1]

One case study provides an example of two women, Mary Julia Workman and Verona Miriam Spellmire, who responded to the massive problems of urbanization and immigration, but whose stories have slipped into obscurity. Their efforts began in Los Angeles, expanded across southern California to Texas, and involved participants from across the United States, as well as from Japan, Mexico, Spain, France, and Italy. The time period was the dawning of the twentieth century, when cities, railroads, and agriculture boomed in the American West. Los Angeles, which in 1900 counted just over one hundred thousand residents, prided itself on being one of the five most-homogeneous (Caucasian) cities in the nation.[2] Within ten years, its population had tripled. Vast numbers of Japanese, Mexicans, and Europeans arrived in search of jobs in newly built factories and in the vast fields and orchards surrounding the city. Angelenos vigorously debated how the foreign-born ought to fit in civic society, and these clashes about Americanization divided the city.[3]

Mary Workman and Verona Spellmire participated in these debates and gained the attention of Roman Catholics and other residents in Los Angeles. Workman, born in 1871, when Los Angeles counted six thousand inhabitants, lived until 1964, when her native city numbered more than 2.4 million residents. Defending immigrants, she challenged Angelenos to reexamine their understanding of justice, citizenship, racial prejudice, and government's responsibilities to the poor.[4] Missouri-born Spellmire (1889–1975) first volunteered alongside Workman, and then chose to serve immigrants through the religious education of their children. Both women belonged to that first generation of American Catholics who began articulating what social justice meant for their church and for wider society.

Workman and Spellmire capitalized upon the advantages that cities afforded women in the early twentieth century. Urban centers permitted them to develop a "unique religious creativity" in which they utilized their church and spirituality to negotiate changing social circumstances.[5] Women developed new urban religious practices, imitated contemporary social reformers, pursued advanced education, and engaged in civic affairs beyond the traditional domestic sphere. Like many of their Protestant sisters, Catholic women believed that they had a distinct role to play as "municipal housekeepers." In the loose nationwide coalition known as Progressivism, they joined men to combat government corruption and to improve education, housing, public health, and working conditions.[6] Workman in particular used her religion to reimagine American society as more inclusive, more just, and more democratic.

In her socially prominent family, Mary Workman's Protestant father, William Henry Workman, served as mayor of Los Angeles and developed the eastside area of the city known as Boyle Heights. Maria Boyle, her Catholic mother, had grown up with the town's elite Mexican families (with whom she spoke Spanish) and led women's charitable works for the church. Mary's parents educated her locally with the Daughters of Charity of St. Vincent de Paul and then in a convent academy of the French-Canadian Sisters of the Holy Names of Jesus and Mary in Oakland, California. Following the customs of the time, she returned home after her schooling, aided her mother, and volunteered in the local Catholic Truth Society and Catholic Ladies' Aid Society. Later she attended the state normal school (now the University of California at Los Angeles) and then began teaching kindergarten in the Los Angeles public schools.[7]

During her normal school years (1898–1901), Workman also volunteered at the city's first settlement house, the Casa de Castelar, in Sonoratown, the established Mexican barrio northeast of the center of the city. There she met Protestant women whose social activism differed from the traditional charitable works in which most Catholic women were involved. Providing a center for immigrants to study and to recreate, the Casa also served as a base for investigations into social problems. Among other initiatives, the women of the settlement conducted a housing survey, promoted public health measures, lobbied to establish a juvenile court system, advocated kindergartens in public schools, and campaigned for women's suffrage. Workman credited the Casa's leaders for demonstrating how active and intelligent women could exert powerful leadership in the civic community.[8]

Many Catholics considered such social reform by women, and the larger movement known as Progressivism, to be distinctly Protestant phenomena. Often antagonistic toward Roman Catholics, most Progressives were white, middle- and upper-class Protestants born in this country.[9] Catholics, particularly pastors, recalled that, despite Los Angeles' Spanish and Roman Catholic origins, by 1900 the social, business, and government leadership rested in the hands of native-born Protestants. Although Roman Catholicism remained the largest single religious denomination in the city, its congregations included the less prosperous working class and many of the newly arrived immigrants.[10] Workman's experiences at the Casa de Castelar prepared her to introduce new models of activism within her own church when few Catholic leaders supported such roles for women.

The Catholic world in which Workman was raised in Los Angeles faced immense change at the turn of the twentieth century. In 1899, the year when the most accurate statistics are available, Catholics numbered more than nineteen thousand souls, approximately 19 percent of the city's population. Catholics worshipped in six parishes where pastors encouraged them to join church-sponsored organizations and to avoid "mixed" societies that included "non-Catholics." Every parish supported a school or academy for the education of the young, and the diocese boasted St. Vincent's College for young men. Parish sodalities, confraternities, and altar societies existed along with local branches of the Young Men's and Young Ladies' Institutes, the League of the Sacred Heart, the Ladies of Charity, and the Society of Our Lady of Guadalupe.[11] None of these traditional

Catholic social and devotional organizations, however, addressed the growing social and economic injustices that Mary Workman had encountered while working at the Casa de Castelar.

In 1901, the young associate pastor of the Cathedral, Rev. John J. Clifford,
urged the members of the Ladies' Aid Society to undertake the religious instruction of immigrant children crowding the southern portion of the parish.
Responding to his call, the women organized themselves as an association and
named it for the nineteenth-century American convert to Catholicism, Orestes
Brownson. Mary Workman's friends recruited her to accept the presidency of the
newly formed Brownson House Settlement Association. Together they began to
teach Sunday School classes in a rented cottage located across the street from
one of the city's largest breweries, only a few blocks from the city's Chinatown.
Within the first ten months, they had enrolled over eighty children.[12]

At first, the Brownson House women followed the model of a four-year-old
project, El Hogar Feliz, founded by the bishop, George Montgomery. At this
"Happy Home," female volunteers provided religious education, as well as a small
day-care center for the children of women working outside the home. El Hogar
Feliz was located in the city's oldest parish, Our Lady of the Angels, on the edge
of the Sonoratown barrio.[13] As the numbers of Brownson House volunteers grew
under Workman's leadership, they offered a wider range of services than El Hogar
Feliz, and attracted broader outside support and neighborhood participation.

Brownson House was an immediate success. It soon expanded its outreach
to immigrant Italians, Armenians, Russian Jews, and others in its neighborhood.
The settlement sponsored a women's club, sewing classes for mothers, recreation
for children, and activities for adolescents. In 1905, the new bishop of the diocese,
Thomas J. Conaty, donated a shingle-sided building on Jackson Street, one block
from the Los Angeles River. In this district of packinghouses, soap factories, and
other polluting industries, thousands of people crowded the boarding houses and
small cottages along unpaved streets. Workman and her volunteers, sometimes
termed "settlers," redoubled their efforts in response to the bishop's support. They
recruited new members to the settlement association and expanded their activities into a weeklong schedule for the women and children living in the city's
infamous "bloody Ninth" ward.[14]

Each new facility at Brownson House developed out of the women's conversations with local residents about the neighborhood's greatest needs. As a result, the settlement added a playground, bathhouse, clothing dispensary, medical
and dental clinics, a lending library, woodworking shop, and meeting room for a
Boy Scout troop. The women also organized more clubs for children, classes for
adults, and group excursions to the beach and to the mountains. Nearby they

Mary Julia Workman stands at center, second row from the top. Photo courtesy of Workman Family Papers, Center for the Study of Los Angeles Research Collection, Loyola Marymount University.

opened a day nursery to care for the children of workingwomen. Catechism classes expanded to include first communion and confirmation preparation, and a chaplain appointed by the bishop in 1912 began offering Mass every Sunday.[15] With his arrival, however, came further changes at the settlement, ones that unexpectedly challenged Workman and her followers.

The priest, Rev. Albert Breton, a thirty-year-old French missionary, had worked five years in Japan until he was sent to California to serve Japanese Catholic immigrants.[16] Once Breton was in Los Angeles, his base for a west-coast ministry, Workman escorted him down the streets of the "Japanese quarter" adjacent to Jackson Street. Over 4,200 Japanese resided in the city and worked in manual labor, domestic service, and agriculture.[17] Brownson House volunteers welcomed the priest and his congregants with a reception and concert. Breton began offering two Sunday Masses at Brownson House; the first was for the settlement's Mexican neighbors, and the second for fifty or so Japanese Catholics, mostly men. "On Christmas Day," Workman wrote a long-time friend, "you would have been so edified to see the Japanese who came to receive the sacraments, and to hear Mass."[18] Few Angelenos, though, shared her positive regard for the Japanese.

Except for church-sponsored centers in Los Angeles, seldom did elite white women meet under the same roof as immigrants from Japan, many of whom were single working-class men. Virulent anti-Japanese prejudice festered throughout California. The year following Workman's welcome of the Japanese to Brownson House, the state legislature passed the Alien Land Law that prohibited Japanese and others from owning real estate in California. Subsequent laws further targeted immigrants from Japan, legislation that Workman opposed as "a dangerous approach to a very complex question." [19]

Workman's surviving letters do not explain the reasons for her resistance to widespread anti-Asian feeling. But her father, William Henry Workman, had long opposed prejudice against the Chinese in Los Angeles. And Bishop Conaty had welcomed Breton and praised the members of his flock.[20] Finally, among Breton's congregation in Brownson House, Workman found fellow Catholics, Asians who lived in the poorest of part of the city. Whatever her feelings toward immigrants from Japan, every Sunday she welcomed the single laborers and the small families who arrived at the settlement for Mass.

Workman also met Breton's Catholic recruits from Japan who joined him to evangelize immigrants in the city's emerging "Little Tokyo." In a series of four trips across the Pacific, Breton invited pious women from Japan to teach catechism and to offer basic charity to the Japanese in Los Angeles. The first women—Sue Matsumoto, Toi Oe, Eki Fujisawa, and Tsui Yamano—arrived in March 1915.[21] Trained as nurses, midwives, or sewing teachers, the women ranged from twenty-four to forty-six years in age. The leader, Matsumoto, had twenty years' experience as a catechist and in preparing young women to evangelize for the Roman Catholic Church in Japan.[22]

In subsequent years, seven more women from their homeland joined this initial band working with Father Breton. Forming an order as the Sisters of the Visitation, they soon experienced poverty in their convent and suffered insults and verbal abuse on the streets of Los Angeles. Undeterred, they opened an orphanage, a kindergarten, and a school for the children of the city's Japanese residents, and local Franciscan Sisters aided them by handling the English classes.[23] Breton also enlisted at least one man to assist him, Henry Haison Yoni, and soon he sent for his family to join him.[24] Workman welcomed these Catholic immigrants whom fellow Angelenos scorned. Her encounters forced her to ponder how to reconcile prevailing attitudes on race with her deeply held religious beliefs.[25]

Workman noted that besides the Japanese, the neighborhood increasingly attracted Mexican immigrants. Beginning in 1910, the turmoil of the Mexican Revolution drove thousands to flee their homeland for safety in the United States. Like the Japanese, immigrants from Mexico received a hostile welcome from Angelenos. Long recruited for work on the railroads and in agriculture and construction in the Southwest, Mexicans alarmed Californians as their

新メンバーを迎えシスターズホームで子供たちに囲まれるブルトン神父

Rev. Albert Breton, with Japanese Catechists (the future Sisters of the Visitation of Japan), Los Angeles, 1920. Photo courtesy of the Sisters of the Visitation of Japan, Kanagawa, Japan.

numbers increased. In 1901, when Brownson House opened, Los Angeles counted few Mexicans among its one hundred thousand residents. By 1919, the city numbered more than 570,000 people, of whom thirty thousand were newly arrived Mexicans.[26]

The accelerating migration frightened many Angelenos, and a virulent "Brown Scare" raged between 1913 and 1917. Mexican radicals, such as the socialist Ricardo Flores-Magón, had also fled to Los Angeles and established a base to agitate for their partisans in Mexico. Their arrival horrified the city's business leaders, and the Los Angeles *Times* fanned fears of a border invasion by bloodthirsty "reds" and "*cholos.*" When Francisco "Pancho" Villa attacked Columbus, New Mexico, in March 1916, the *Times* believed Los Angeles lay in imminent danger of invasion. The chief of police prohibited the sale of liquor and guns to Mexicans, tripled police patrols in Mexican neighborhoods, and recruited special militia to handle "a possible insurrection of Villa's supporters."[27]

Brownson House stood in the midst of the swelling population of immigrants of color at a time when Angelenos grew shrill in their denunciations of Mexicans and Japanese. Across the country, most middle- and upper-class white volunteers abandoned the areas they served when people of color came to predominate in the neighborhoods surrounding those settlements. Settlers typically moved or closed their centers when confronted with a change in racial composition of the local population.[28] In Los Angeles, the Brownson House women were aware as early as 1910 that growing numbers of Japanese and Mexican laborers were displacing European immigrants in the settlement neighborhood.[29] Yet these Catholic settlers remained.

Brownson House welcomed the Mexicans as they had the Japanese, and both groups recognized that Workman and her associates could assist them in their community projects. "Our Mexican neighbors," Workman wrote in 1917, "are forming a league for mutual benefit and have asked us to co-operate and assist." The trust of these men and women affected her: "it seemed to me the most impressive moment in the career of Brownson House."[30] The officers of the Liga Mutualista Mexicana invited her to join them as second vice president. They wanted Workman to enter their world and to participate in an organization they led that served their people in Los Angeles. Not only did they see how she could be useful to them in achieving their goals, but they also trusted the settlers who lived among them.[31]

In August of 1919, thirteen Mexicans arrived at Brownson House to celebrate the feast of their patron, San Lorenzo, according to the customs of their native city of Durango. Wearing "tall feather head dresses" and "bright red and cerise suits trimmed with beads and fringe," the visitors entered the chapel on their knees. The dozen men and one woman carried bows and arrows, painted gourds or tin cans filled with pebbles, and religious pictures and crucifixes. After the Mass, they pushed back the chairs, formed two lines, and bowed solemnly to the altar before they began to dance. Accompanied by a violin and a guitar, they kept time with the pounding of their feet and with the rattle of gourds and cans. They then knelt, sang a hymn to the Virgin Mary in Spanish, and left as they entered, on their knees, facing the altar.[32]

Over breakfast, the Brownson House settlers learned that the dancers desired to celebrate other important feasts, such as the Virgin of Guadalupe (December 12), Christmas, and Saint Joseph (March 19). "They were invited to return," Workman, later wrote, "whenever they wished." The settlement workers, who were "delighted" with the presence of the dancers, saw more than an exotic religious spectacle. Workman believed that all those present had advanced "a little further toward mutual understanding and spiritual ideals."[33] Knowledge gained through personal contact and acquaintance corrected the misperceptions among both immigrants and settlers.

The formation of the *mutualista* and the introduction of Mexican forms of worship offer two examples of immigrants reestablishing familiar forms of self-help and spirituality. Workman and the settlement workers witnessed Mexicans reorganizing their lives, customs, and associations in Los Angeles *barrios* and outlying *colonias*. Religious societies and *cofradías*, such as the Apostolado de la Oración, Hijas de María, Santo Nombre, and the Asociación Guadalupana, emerged to lead communal devotions.[34] Rural Mexican society had long provided women leadership roles in spiritual matters, and these customs also crossed the borders with the immigrants. Recognized for their wisdom and piety, older women known as *rezadoras* counseled the young and led traditional prayer, such as the rosary. Focusing on significant Catholic beliefs, the rosary was the "oral Bible" of the poor, and the rezadoras informally instructed the young in their faith.[35]

Regardless of how they understood these religious expressions, Workman and her corps of seventy volunteers opted to remain on Jackson Street amidst the immigrants. Surviving records do not explain how they reached this decision, or even if there was a serious discussion about moving to avoid the growing presence of Mexicans and Japanese. Two factors, however, loom large in determining the reasons for the women's commitment to their neighbors. The settlers drew upon their spiritual beliefs to develop a flexible approach to their new neighbors. "The ideal of Christian brotherhood," Workman wrote, "was raised aloft by the Divine Savior of mankind, and through the centuries men have striven to approach it. The inspiration has ever been the same, but the form of expression and method of approach must be adapted to the special necessities of the period." She specifically noted the challenges to society posed by industrialization, labor strife, and class conflict.[36] The settlers shared a common religious faith with immigrants, a bond that Protestant volunteers in other settlements lacked. Citing the Old Testament injunction, "Thou shalt love thy neighbor as thyself," the settlers welcomed as their neighbors the ever-increasing numbers of often-destitute Mexicans.[37]

A second influence to remain on Jackson Street appears in Mary Workman's writings over the course of nineteen years in leading the settlement association. In her first decade at Brownson House, Workman emphasized the charitable and philanthropic nature of the work. She was aware that she was engaged in a project that most Catholics avoided as Protestant in its origin and ethos, yet she urged Catholic women to take up the cause. Dedicated to the people of the inner city, she urged Catholics to accept their responsibilities as citizens to promote a more just city.

After 1911, when Socialists almost elected a mayor in Los Angeles, Workman's public statements increasingly emphasized themes of justice and responsible citizenship. She challenged Angelenos to demonstrate by their actions what it meant to be an American, so immigrants could see the living principles of democracy. "The first step," she wrote, "is for us to Americanize ourselves, to determine what kind of a person an American should be, what sort of ideals our country should uphold." [38] Workman grew impatient with advocates of Americanization who advocated rapid assimilation of immigrants, yet neglected the dire circumstances in which most of them lived. After long years of personal acquaintance with struggling people, she saw the institutional causes of poverty, juvenile crime, inadequate housing, and high infant mortality.

What Workman witnessed on Jackson Street altered her understanding of the duties of citizenship and the demands of justice. Los Angeles looked far different to her from the battered doorway of Brownson House than it did from the elegant entry to her parents' estate. "When a man or woman is hungry, overworked, or exploited," Workman wrote a former teacher, "you cannot teach Catechism to him [sic], you must first remedy his condition. When children live eight or nine people in one room, you cannot expect the grace of First Communion to perform a miracle in every single case and keep them decently moral." [39] She increasingly denounced the economic structures that exploited the poor and social movements that stigmatized the immigrant. "The people must live!," she wrote. "Food, shelter and [the] right condition of labor and recreation must be considered as elemental human necessities." [40]

In Workman's spiritual life, the meaning of Christianity underwent gradual but dramatic change. Precepts that urged Catholic women to focus their efforts on domestic duties held little appeal to her. In an address to local Catholic women in 1939, she revealed the activist spirituality that she had developed over forty years. Denouncing isolationism, she urged her listeners to lobby for efforts on behalf of international peace. "Good desires are important," she continued, "prayer is necessary, but peace will come only when we use appropriate means to make it a reality by the establishment of just and peaceful procedure." Most important, she noted, "The world needs builders. There are too many destroyers." [41]

In the first twenty years of its existence, Brownson House attracted over two hundred women who heeded Workman's example as a builder. They taught catechism, staffed the clinics, ran night classes, raised operating funds, and organized popular events such as street dances and train excursions to the beach. Many volunteers were teachers employed in the inner-city public schools who devoted their free hours to the settlement house programs. One woman in her early thirties, Verona Spellmire, assisted at Brownson House in 1918, but wrestled with the question of how best to serve her church and the immigrants beyond Jackson Street. Trained at the state normal school in Santa Barbara (now the University of California at Santa Barbara), she was—like Workman—also fluent in Spanish. She shared her dreams with several Brownson House friends and cast about for an outlet for her energy. [42]

Workman's supporter, Bishop Thomas Conaty, died in 1915. His successor committed the diocese to efficiency in charity in coordinated operations run by trained social workers under the guidance of the clergy. Bishop John J. Cantwell arrived in Los Angeles from San Francisco, where he had been a chancery official for more than a dozen years. He centralized charitable operations in a diocesan bureau that he entrusted to Rev. William E. Corr, a priest with graduate training in social work. When Corr attempted to direct the women of Brownson House, however, Workman and her followers resisted politely yet firmly. Tensions increased, and Workman protested to the bishop. "We pleaded for the development of Catholic women for public service through the bearing of responsibility," she wrote to a friend. "We pleaded for liberty under law, with full recognition of lawful authority. . . . As a consequence of the 'autocratic regime,' our Catholic women are losing interest and going into non-sectarian organizations."[43] When the bishop refused to intervene, Workman and her fellow officers resigned and walked quietly away from the settlement they had founded and operated for nearly two decades.

After leaving Brownson House, Mary Workman turned her energies to social, civic, and political causes. From the League of Women Voters and the League of Nations Association to the Democratic Party and the Catholic International Association for Peace, Workman served as a dedicated leader and activist. Realizing his loss and seeking to make amends, Bishop Cantwell nominated her for a major papal award in 1926. Pope Pius XI honored Workman with the medal, Pro Ecclesia et Pontifice (for service "For the Church and for the Pope"), the first time that this papal recognition had been granted in the Los Angeles diocese.[44]

While tensions were building at Brownson House in 1920, Verona Spellmire had consulted with Father Corr about other locales where children needed religious instruction. Little evidence survives about Spellmire's background and what inspired her to volunteer. She was born in Kansas City, Missouri, one of eight children of Anthony and Theresa (Marshall) Spellmire. They relocated the family to California in 1892 and resided in Los Angeles by 1899. Verona attended the state normal college at Santa Barbara, and then taught in the Los Angeles public schools. Like Workman, Spellmire was assigned to the Utah Street public school, in one of the poorest neighborhoods of the city near the east bank of the Los Angeles River. Active in her parish sodality, she volunteered to teach catechism on Sundays at Brownson House, but saw needs for such instruction in other immigrant neighborhoods.[45]

Father Corr directed her to a parish several miles east of Los Angeles with a Mexican *colonia* whose residents labored in Simon's Brickyard. In the summer of 1919, Spellmire enlisted ten friends to teach with her on a weekly basis. When the settlement association began to dissolve in the following year, Spellmire left

Los Angeles and relocated to Carmel, California. There she undertook religious education of children and social work in the parish of Mission San Carlos. The pastor, Rev. Ramón Mestres, had long years of experience in religious pedagogy in his native Barcelona, Spain. After a year with Mestres, Spellmire returned to Los Angeles and found employment in the Americanization program at the Bridge Street public school in the inner city.[46]

Still searching for a way to address the needs of children for religious instruction, Spellmire met with Rev. Robert Emmet Lucey, the energetic new director of the diocesan Catholic Welfare Bureau. A native of Los Angeles, Lucey had grown up in a working-class Irish Catholic family, entered the seminary, and studied theology in Rome where he was ordained a priest. He possessed a passion for social justice that stemmed from a personal tragedy: his father was killed while working on the Southern Pacific railroad. The railroad deemed the death due to negligence by the elder Lucey, so the family received no compensation and faced severe financial hardship. For the rest of his life, Lucey championed the rights of workers, no matter the nationality of the laborer.

When Verona Spellmire met with Lucey early in 1922, she proposed that the diocese form an association of volunteers to teach catechism to children not receiving instruction in their faith. She suggested a centuries-old European model, known as the Confraternity of Christian Doctrine (the CCD). Only two American dioceses, New York and Pittsburgh, had founded branches of this organization. Familiar with the Pittsburgh confraternity from her reading, Spellmire saw the possibilities it offered laypersons like herself to engage in active service to the church. She believed that the CCD offered women opportunities for meaningful service in an independent organization that permitted significant female leadership.

Spellmire and six friends broached the topic of the CCD with Lucey in March 1922, and he quickly recognized its possibilities. He left the women sitting in his office and walked down the hall to obtain the bishop's approval. He returned with Bishop Cantwell's warm but qualified endorsement. The bishop was not as trusting of women's leadership as Father Lucey. Cantwell approved the CCD, but appointed a diocesan "spiritual director," Rev. William J. Mullane. This young assistant pastor at the cathedral parish was charged to guide the work of the women and to ensure the cooperation of the CCD with the Catholic Welfare Bureau.[47]

Encouraged by the endorsement of their idea, Spellmire set her sights on the Belvedere district on the east side of Los Angeles, beyond the city limits.[48] She and a friend, Anna McGarry, located an empty theater and persuaded the owner to give them the use of the building without cost. They returned a week later with seven or eight volunteers. McGarry and several women "drove up and down

Verona Spellmire, pioneer of the
Confraternity of Christian Doctrine
in Los Angeles and in San Antonio.
Photo courtesy of the Office of Reli-
gious Education, Archdiocese of Los
Angeles.

the streets honking the horn," Spellmire recalled, and "the children flocked to
the car and were given cards and told to ask their parents for permission to come
to classes that afternoon." Named the Santa Maria Center, fifty-eight children
attended the first day, and two hundred were present within a few months. When
four Sisters of the Holy Family arrived from San Francisco in 1920, they took
over the direction of the center, and McGarry drove the nuns to and from the
east side. Soon a priest, Rev. Rafael Grajales, began offering Mass on Sundays
in the theater. Later a church was built in the district, and finally a parish was
established under the title of Our Lady of Guadalupe.[49]

   For reasons that are not clear, after two months of this work, Spellmire left
Los Angeles to join the Sisters of the Holy Family, the nuns she had met at the
Santa Maria Center. Founded in San Francisco in 1871, this religious order consisted of women who dedicated themselves to social work and to the religious education of children who could not attend Catholic schools. Bishop Cantwell had
known the order during his years in northern California and had requested that
they send several sisters to teach immigrant children in Los Angeles. Spellmire
admired the dedication of these nuns, and applied to be trained as a member of
their order. However, she discovered within eight months that she did not find
convent life congenial. By January 1923, she was on the train again, this time to
Los Angeles, still in search of her calling in life.[50]

Father Lucey welcomed Spellmire's return. Impressed with her organizational skills, Lucey hired Spellmire to work as supervisor of the immigrant welfare division of the Catholic Welfare Bureau. Spellmire announced, however, that she would only accept half of a salary so that the rest of her time could be devoted to the CCD. This arrangement suited Lucey's vision of his office because he believed that social welfare activities, the preaching of social justice, and religious education were closely linked. Spellmire and Lucey worked well together, though she eventually resigned from the Catholic Welfare Bureau to concentrate all her energies on the CCD.[51]

Spellmire later recalled that the successful experience at Santa Maria Center became the pattern for Catholic work in all the immigrant districts in Los Angeles. Volunteers would establish a teaching center, then a chapel was built, and later a parish was organized. Ten to twelve parishes developed out of the initiative of the religious educators who first gathered the children, and then attracted the adults. Funds for the construction of chapels came from various sources. Some of Spellmire's female volunteers generously financed several churches, while pastors of wealthier parishes contributed costs for others. When sufficient numbers gathered for worship, Bishop Cantwell then assigned priests to staff these new parishes, usually located in the poorest neighborhoods of the diocese.[52]

With Lucey's encouragement, Spellmire, McGarry, and Mullane decided to expand the CCD. They called a meeting for April 16, 1923 to organize and to extend the work. Forty-five people attended and elected Spellmire as chair and McGarry as vice-chair, along with a secretary and an advisory board. Most who were present that evening volunteered to serve. They set out to work alongside nuns who were already engaged in religious education, such as the Sisters of the Holy Family, and the Missionary Sisters of the Sacred Heart, who had been working with Italian immigrants in Los Angeles since 1905. The addition of numerous laypeople led by Spellmire and McGarry, however, expanded tenfold the instruction that the sisters offered.[53]

Witnessing the enthusiasm of the laypeople, Bishop Cantwell announced his own meeting five months later. Cantwell issued a letter that was read from the pulpit of every church in the diocese inviting priests and laity to organize a diocesanwide religious education program under the CCD. Four hundred laypeople and thirty priests attended, and three hundred volunteered to participate. Cantwell organized the outreach as a parish-based program, directed by the local pastor and a CCD board comprised of parishioners. The bishop expanded the central office in Los Angeles to coordinate efforts, train teachers, and supply information and textbooks. This headquarters continued to function as a branch of the Catholic Welfare Bureau, headed by Lucey.

Spellmire and her colleagues labored throughout the diocese that then stretched about three hundred miles from the Mexican border to northern Santa Barbara County, and from the Pacific Ocean to the Nevada state line.[54] Despite the distances, the early volunteers achieved impressive results. Within the first year as a diocesan operation, nearly 3,600 children were under the instruction of 280 CCD teachers. By 1927, over seven hundred volunteers in 120 local catechetical centers ("not including regular Sunday Schools") were instructing fourteen thousand children across the diocese, each modeled on the original Santa Maria Center.[55] The new venture had quickly gained the support of generous lay Catholics interested in serving their church.

Spellmire and Father Mullane, the official director, offered practical advice based on growing experience. They suggested that pastors select sites close to public schools in order to be near children leaving campus at the end of the day. Volunteers were to be divided into three groups. While one person remained at the center to receive the children, two others spread the word from door to door in the vicinity of the center. Two more people went by automobile through the streets to attract children to the car and tell them of the classes. As Spellmire explained, "We needed not only teachers to conduct the classes but home visitors or 'Fishers' to bring the children from far and near to the Catechism Center."[56]

The door-to-door visits revealed other needs besides instruction in catechism. Volunteers learned of illness, unemployment, legal difficulties, and other problems, which they reported to the Bureau of Catholic Charities. Social workers and volunteers followed up these notices and provided either church aid or a referral to public assistance. Other benefits resulted from these neighborhood visits. "Many real leaders were discovered or developed," Spellmire noted, "through the formation of mothers' societies. . . . At the club meetings they report[ed] families in need of help or friendly visiting."[57]

One example reveals how the CCD and the Catholic Welfare Bureau coordinated their efforts on behalf of Mexican immigrants. In 1925 a woman volunteered to instruct children in a two-room house in Watts, south of central Los Angeles. The following year, the Bureau of Catholic Charities hired her as a social worker and, with the aid of a volunteer, she began organizing clubs and activities for Spanish-speaking residents of the area. The bureau later erected a four-hundred-seat community center, where large groups of women met weekly for sewing, nearly five hundred children gathered for sports teams and clubs, and residents of all ages enjoyed dramas, musicals, and social events. Following the Santa Maria Center model, a Catholic church was erected in 1929 across the street from the hall and a parish was later established.[58]

The CCD program continued to burgeon, even amidst changes in leadership. Father Mullane resigned due to ill health and, in November 1924, Bishop Cantwell appointed an Irish-born priest, Rev. Thomas O'Dwyer, to head the CCD office and to assist Father Lucey in Catholic charities. Spellmire again demonstrated her organizational skills when she proposed coordinating the multiplying parish-based CCD groups. She drafted a constitution for a Diocesan Union of Confraternities. The bishop approved the plan, appointed the diocesan officers, and named Spellmire as president. Pastors selected local officers, called for volunteers, and reported results to the central office. This simple organizational scheme soon attracted notice from other bishops. Within the amazingly short time of a single decade, the Los Angeles plan became the national model for CCD religious instruction in the United States.[59]

In 1926 Bishop Cantwell reorganized responsibilities in the chancery offices. Father Lucey received oversight of Catholic hospitals, while Father O'Dwyer assumed leadership of the Catholic Welfare Bureau. The bishop separated the CCD as a distinct operation and placed it under the leadership of Rev. Leroy Callahan. Twenty-six years old, recently ordained, and highly energetic, the tall, blond-haired priest was fluent in four languages. Within a year of his appointment, Callahan had written a booklet for the use of CCD teachers, titled "Model Lessons in Cathechism," that was intended to appeal to children. He also introduced summer vacation schools, based on the example developed by Bishop Edwin V. O'Hara, in the diocese of Great Falls, Montana.

Callahan asked Spellmire to devise a curriculum for the summer vacation schools, and she compiled the "Handbook of Suggestions on Religious Vacation Schools." The four-week-long course of instruction organized each day into a series of activities that included doctrinal instruction, hymn singing, recreation, handicrafts, and stories from the Bible and the lives of the saints. Although Spellmire admitted that she borrowed liberally from instructional techniques in Protestant summer Bible schools, her manual soon was in use in CCD programs across the United States.[60]

Callahan and Spellmire collaborated in making improvements in instruction, developing textbooks, and directing the expansion of CCD centers across the diocese. The 1929 summer vacation schools, for example, enrolled over eleven thousand children who were mostly Mexicans in 116 schools conducted by 505 volunteer teachers. Callahan recruited additional assistants to write a graded series of textbooks to offer twelve years of instruction. With the aid of a lay volunteer, Alice Vignos, Callahan promoted these volumes to bishops across the country at the annual meetings of the National Catholic Rural Life Conference. The enthusiasm of the bishops led to the establishment of a national CCD office in Washington D.C. Soon these volumes from Los Angeles were in use across the United States and in several foreign nations.[61] In 1932, Spellmire re-signed her position as president of the diocesan union of the CCD. By then, the number of children enrolled in the diocesan CCD program had grown to 28,500 who gathered in 305 centers under the instruction of 1,525 volunteer teachers.[62] Joining the staff of a public welfare organization, Spellmire remained active in religious education work throughout the 1930s.[63]

It is here that the broad view across the Southwest sheds more light on women in the Church. Our focus shifts to Texas, where in 1934, Pope Pius XI named Lucey as bishop of Amarillo, Texas, a vast diocese with limited personnel and a huge debt. Lucey "hit the diocese like a bombshell. He had a clear idea of what he wanted to do and the will to proceed." One stunned chancery official recalled that having Lucey "as bishop of Amarillo was like having the president of General Motors running the corner gas station."[64] Lucey refinanced the dioc-esan debt, spoke out vigorously about the rights of labor, attacked anti-Semitism, involved himself in civic affairs, and ultimately gained widespread attention. He recruited a social worker from Los Angeles to reorganize the Catholic Welfare Bureau. He also established the CCD in northern Texas, again based on a Los Angeles model. His constant activity kept his name before ecclesial superiors, and in 1940 Pope Pius XII appointed Lucey archbishop of San Antonio.[65]

As in Amarillo, Lucey turned to Los Angeles for assistance from trusted laywomen for organizations that he was founding in the Archdiocese of San Antonio. Since his departure from the Catholic charities bureau in Los Ange-les, Lucey had maintained contact with Spellmire and other Catholics, such as Mary Workman.[66] In 1941 he recruited Verona Spellmire as executive director of the archdiocesan Confraternity of Christian Doctrine, and Helen Montegriffo to head the Catholic Welfare Bureau. Lucey appointed Rev. Anthony F. Drodz as moderator of the Catholic Action program, of which the CCD was a major component. Nine months after his arrival in San Antonio, Lucey summoned pastors and lay leaders to a four-day institute to launch the CCD. He convened smaller gatherings in various sections of the archdiocese so that 2,300 Texans learned firsthand what their new shepherd envisioned. Lucey, Spellmire, and one CCD official from Washington, D.C. introduced the new program. "Everyone is a leader," Spellmire explained, whether they are teachers, "fishers," helpers, or members of discussion clubs. She urged her audience to work alongside priests and nuns in the mission of spreading the message of Jesus Christ.[67]

Lucey alerted his audience to his high expectations of the laity of the arch-diocese. "I feel sorry for the people of this Archdiocese," he announced, "because the dear, dead days are certainly gone beyond recall. . . . The laity must get away from the idea of letting the priest do it all. They too must do their share."[68] The new archbishop believed that the local church needed to be revitalized, both spiritually and materially, and he saw it as his duty to initiate this renewal. To carry out this revival, Lucey ordered his priests to cooperate with the two women he brought from Los Angeles to assist him in this mission.

Spellmire and Helen Montegriffo found that in 1941 the archdiocese of San Antonio included 195,000 Catholics, whom chancery officials tallied as "Mexicans" (130,000) and "non-Mexicans" (65,000).[69] Montegriffo surveyed the needs of poor Catholics and, after only a few months, concluded that, "It is impossible to picture the conditions that have been revealed" in San Antonio. "Hunger, nakedness, pain, disease, despair, ignorance, filth, and crime," she wrote, "these are the problems in ever increasing numbers, which the Catholic Welfare Bureau has to contend with, day in and day out."[70] Lucey supported Montegriffo's efforts and repeatedly struggled to obtain funds for Catholic charities to benefit the poorest members of his flock.

For Lucey, religious education and social justice were fundamental elements of the Gospel message. He believed that a just society required active Catholic efforts in civic affairs to implement equitable social policies for all residents. Catholics, however, had a responsibility to educate themselves in the beliefs of their faith and in the teachings of the popes on social issues. These themes, which Lucey first announced in 1941, were ideals to which he would return throughout his tenure as archbishop. To emphasize the relationship between religious training and social action, he declared that CCD teachers "may not teach catechism if they are not familiar with the social doctrine of the church."[71]

Verona Spellmire familiarized herself with the problems she faced. Among her first discoveries was the absence of what she considered adequate educational materials in Spanish. When she wrote to the national CCD office in Washington D.C. for workbooks and manuals, she learned that the national organization did not provide such instructional literature. After consulting the archbishop, Spellmire began compiling and printing a set of books. As she had done in Los Angeles with Father Callahan, Spellmire filled the void by supervising the creation of needed instructional materials in Spanish.[72] Spellmire's publications attracted the interest of the Washington office of the CCD, the first time a local effort had stimulated the national leaders to consider the needs of Spanish-speaking Catholics.

In her travels, Spellmire learned that religious education of the young, as in Los Angeles, had largely been left in the hands of several groups of nuns. San Antonio, however, was home to Sister Benitia Vermeersch, a Belgian nun who had recruited Mexican American young women as catechists affiliated with her religious order, the Sisters of Divine Providence. In 1941, Sister Benitia and ten assistants were teaching 1,359 children in eleven centers. They also taught at the Boys' Reform School and at the County Home for the Aged. Spellmire and Lucey quickly recognized the importance of Spanish-speaking educators, and the archbishop actively lobbied to obtain full Church recognition of these catechists as a new religious order, the Missionary Catechists of Divine Providence.[73] As they grew in numbers, the Missionary Catechists embraced the CCD wholeheartedly and promoted its programs with great success.

One of Spellmire's unpleasant discoveries, however, was the cold reception she experienced from certain pastors. More than a few priests resisted taking orders from a woman—and a Californian at that. These clerics "resented Lucey's importing 'outsiders' to spearhead his pet programs." Targeting Spellmire and Montegriffo as the new archbishop's "biggest mistake," one cleric later recalled that "the priests were very bitter that he put lay people to give orders to priests!"[74] Lucey, however, was not a leader who tolerated opposition, even from his clergy. He issued a stream of directives to his priests, mandated the establishment of the CCD in every parish, and ordered annual reports about the CCD from every pastor. His letters left little room for misunderstanding his intentions.

Every September Lucey set the date for "Catechetical Day," a Sunday when pastors were to preach on the CCD and to enroll new members. Catechism classes were to begin, along with adult discussion clubs, for which Lucey set the theme and mandated the training of discussion leaders. Lucey reminded pastors that a correspondence course was available to train religious educators in each parish. He also required pastors to provide him with the list of officers (elected or appointed) of every parish's CCD executive board. Lest any pastor misunderstand how active these groups ought to be, the archbishop demanded that these parish boards "hold regular monthly meetings."[75]

While Spellmire launched the educational project, Lucey lobbied the nation's bishops to address the spiritual and material needs of the nation's Spanish-speaking Catholics. He believed that few of the hierarchy were adequately serving the growing Hispanic population, and in July 1943 he chaired a meeting of bishops and Catholic leaders to consider what to do. For Lucey, immediate action was imperative. "All of us," he proclaimed, "Catholics and non-Catholics, must think and plan and live like Christians" in order to provide a just economy, better social legislation, and the training of Hispanic leaders.[76] Those attending returned the following year; this gathering evolved into the Bishops' Committee for the Spanish Speaking. The committee later relocated to Washington D.C., and evolved into one of the major offices of the United States' bishops.

With Lucey promoting social justice and religious education for Mexican Americans, Spellmire recruited increasing numbers of volunteers for the CCD.

In 1941 when she arrived in San Antonio, Spellmire found limited religious education programs. By 1945, however, she had organized parish efforts to operate 208 religious vacations schools in the archdiocese that enrolled almost fifteen thousand students (out of a Catholic population of 232, 975). By 1950, she reported a year-round system of religious instruction operating in 623 centers, with some twenty-six thousand children in regular attendance. In contrast to these figures, all the parochial schools, high schools, and academies in the archdiocese only instructed twenty thousand pupils. In eight years' time, Spellmire had created a CCD network that surpassed the decades-old parish school system.[77]

Lucey's pride in Spellmire's accomplishments and his steadfast belief in the value of the CCD prompted him to convene a Regional Inter-American Congress of Confraternities of Christian Doctrine in 1947. In October, more than six thousand people attended and, including "five Archbishops and twenty bishops from the United States, Mexico, and Central America." Speakers from a variety of nations addressed the sessions on the best developments in catechetical instruction. In what became an annual gathering, Lucey promoted the San Antonio model of CCD for imitation in other parts of the Spanish-speaking world. In later years he invited speakers from nations south of the Rio Grande to share their ideas and to enrich the practices in the Southwest.[78]

By 1950, Spellmire had retired from her post in San Antonio and returned to California. Taking her leave of Archbishop Lucey, she rejoined relatives in the Los Angeles area and continued her work in the CCD. She first taught in nearby Altadena, where her old-time friend and first director of the CCD, Rev. William Mullane, was pastor. Later she volunteered to assist with catechetical work at St. Andrew's parish in Pasadena. Not until February of 1972, at age eighty-three, did she receive recognition for her labors when the Los Angeles CCD celebrated its fiftieth anniversary at a religious education "congress" attended by almost ten thousand people. Two years later, on the nomination of Cardinal Timothy Manning of Los Angeles, Pope Paul VI bestowed on Spellmire the medal, Pro Ecclesia et Pontifice—the same award received by Mary Workman almost a half-century earlier.[79]

Conclusion

Both Mary Workman and Verona Spellmire outlived most of their friends. Their passings in 1964 and in 1977, respectively, attracted small articles in the local press and little notice except from mourning relatives. Subsequent historians seldom gave either woman recognition for her labors, a fate not uncommon for women in general, and particularly true for laywomen in the American Catholic Church. As early as 1927, for example, one writer had explained that the CCD in

Los Angeles originated "at the suggestion of one of the laity." Nameless, without gender, and deprived of her history, Spellmire fell into the shadow of the priests and bishops who received credit for her accomplishments.

When we survey the historical terrain of the Catholic Church in the American West from the perspective of women, Workman and Spellmire loom large. One might wonder what the Catholic Church would have accomplished among immigrants without the labors of Workman and her two hundred volunteers at Brownson House, or Spellmire and her horn-honking driver, Anna McGarry. How would religious instruction have developed without the Japanese volunteers in Los Angeles and Sister Benitia Vermeersch and the Missionary Catechists of Divine Providence in San Antonio? How could Archbishop Lucey have integrated his message of social justice with the training of the young if hundreds of volunteers—most of them women—had not donated their time and energy? How would the Catholic Church have expanded and opened new parishes for immigrants without these women?

When viewed from the perspective of women, the history of the Catholic Church in California and the Southwest displays a richer and more interesting topography. Themes emerge that include lay initiative and leadership, innovative religious pedagogy, ethnic and racial interaction, creative programs, political participation, social justice activism, and the international exchange of ideas and personnel. Because they asked different questions, developed their own organizations, and faced obstacles from a clerical and patriarchal church, Catholic women responded in ways that we have yet fully to know and to understand. These women have left an unexplored legacy of immense importance for a religious institution recently plagued by failures in leadership by the hierarchy and by the moral behavior of certain of its clergy.

Significantly, Workman, Spellmire, and other women of their era were attracted to convent life. Workman's Protestant father impeded her efforts and persuaded her to return to duties at home, a situation that college-educated women frequently faced in the late nineteenth century. Like many college graduates, Workman on the one hand channeled her idealism into teaching in the public schools, working in a settlement house, and participating in municipal government. Spellmire, on the other hand, entered a religious order, but found that this form of service to God was not the outlet she sought for her altruism. Instead, she accepted positions among the first generation of salaried lay employees in the chancery office in Los Angeles. Both women and many others actively pursued alternative forms of lay participation in the Catholic Church, efforts that were novel for the time and subsequently overlooked.

Mary Workman provides an example of those women who resisted clerical control of the organizations they founded. Given her class standing and social position in Los Angeles society, she could challenge the priest-director and the bishop when they imposed their will on her settlement work. When she found herself rejected, she turned to other avenues of activism and remained committed to progressive causes until her death in 1964. She did not forget what she had seen at Brownson House, whom she had met, what she had heard. Those early encounters fanned the flames of her passion for justice, civic responsibility, and an activist spirituality first enkindled by her reading of Pope Leo XIII's *Rerum Novarum*. Drawing on Protestant women's example of social involvement, Workman adapted their model of service for Catholic women. For Mary Workman, the place of "conversion" was the muddy, pot-holed lane of Jackson Street, deep in the Ninth Ward. The city's despised Japanese and Mexican immigrants opened her eyes and moved her heart so that Los Angeles—and the world—never again looked the same.

Verona Spellmire offers a different example, but one equally important. She represents the many Catholic women who accepted the church structure they found and who cooperated with the clergy and bishops. She focused on the work she wished to accomplish for immigrants and their children, and she served under the direction of priests appointed to supervise her efforts. Spellmire's significant skills in organization and pedagogy enabled the CCD to take root and to flourish, first in southern California and then in south-central Texas. She left no record of protest against the ecclesial structure in which she worked. On the contrary, her presence in leadership roles within chancery offices reassured women of their traditional importance to Catholic efforts to educate and to pass on the faith to younger generations.

Workman and Spellmire were leaders among educated Catholic women born in this country who helped to create new roles for women in the Catholic Church beyond those of marriage, motherhood, and the convent. They were western women, comfortable in cities and willing to meet immigrants from Asia and Mexico. They were often the first faces of the American Catholic Church that the foreign-born saw, as well as the first voices heard on behalf of social justice. Lacking models for the roles they wished to play, they drew from the example of Protestant women's social and political organizations. By adapting elements from these sources, women like Workman and Spellmire helped to Americanize the Catholic Church and to demonstrate that democratic principles could benefit the church of their birth.

Much more remains to be discovered about laywomen's history in the Catholic Church in the American West. We need to recall that Roman Catholics in the United States have erected "thousands of churches, the world's largest private school system, the nation's largest private social welfare agencies, and the nation's largest chain of private hospitals." Who remembers, however, the women who dreamed of, funded, organized, and ran so many of these institutions?[80] When we search the history of the Church from their perspective, we can better chart the diverse landscape of women's roles and accomplishments, both in the Church and in the American West.

Like the great wagon trains that cut deep but now overgrown ruts on the overland trails, women have carved out paths across the religious terrain of the American West. These forgotten routes remain for us to study and to claim so we might make our way and climb to new vistas of understanding. Mary Workman, Verona Spellmire, and their colleagues can inspire present journeys toward reimagining an American society and an American Catholic Church that are more inclusive, more just, and more democratic.

Notes

The author expresses gratitude for assistance received from William Kevin Crawley, Archives of the University of Notre Dame; Kevin Feeney, Archives of the Archdiocese of Los Angeles; Paul Fitzgerald, S.J., Santa Clara University; Brother Edward Loch, S.M., Archives of the Archdiocese of San Antonio; Sister Genevieve Matsuo, Tsu-Kamakura, Japan; Bishop Robert E. Mulvee, Providence, Rhode Island; Sister Michaela O'Connor, S.H.F., Archives of the Sisters of the Holy Family; Suellen Hoy, University of Notre Dame; David Workman, Los Angeles, and Nancy Workman, Sharon, Massachusetts. Special thanks go to my student research assistant, Darcy Pollan, who chased numerous leads in search of the elusive Verona Spellmire.

1.   See, for example, Paula Kane, James Kenneally, and Karen Kennelly, eds., *Gender Identities in American Catholicism* (Maryknoll, N.Y.: Orbis Press, 2001); Carol K. Coburn and Martha Smith, *Spirited Lives: How Nuns Shaped Catholic Culture and American Life, 1836–1920* (Chapel Hill: University of North Carolina Press, 1999); and Anne M. Butler: "Pioneering Sisters in a Catholic Melting Pot: Juggling Identity in the Pacific Northwest," *American Catholic Studies* 114 (2003): 21–39; Butler, "Building Justice: Mother Margaret Murphy, Race, and Texas," *Catholic Southwest: A Journal of History and Culture* 13 (2002): 13–36; Butler, "Mission in the Mountains: The Daughters of Charity in Virginia City," in *Comstock Women: The Making of a Mining Community*, ed. Ronald B. James and C. Elizabeth Raymond, 142–64 (Reno: University of Nevada Press, 1997); and Butler, "Mother Katherine Drexel: Spiritual Visionary for the West," in *By Grit and By Grace: Eleven Women Who Shaped the American West*, ed. Glenda Riley and Richard W. Etulain, 198–220 (Golden, Colo.: Fulcrum, 1997).

2.   The 1900 federal census listed 52.7 percent of the Los Angeles population as "native white" born of Caucasian American parents. The other cities recorded were Kansas

City and St. Joseph, Missouri; Columbus, Ohio; and Indianapolis, Indiana. See U.S. Bureau of the Census, *Twelfth Census of the United States, 1900*, vol. 1: *Population*, Part 1 (Washington, D.C.: Government Printing Office, 1901), cxxii.

3. The literature on Americanization is immense, but important sources include: Frank Van Nuys, *Americanizing the West: Race, Immigrants, and Citizenship, 1890–1930* (Lawrence: University Press of Kansas, 2002); Christopher Jencks, "Who Should Get In?" *New York Review of Books*, 48 (November 29, 2001): 57–63, and Part 2 (December 20, 2001): 94–7, 100–102; Gary Gerstle, "Liberty, Coercion, and Making Americans," in *The Handbook of International Migration: The American Experience*, ed. Charles Hirschman, Philip Kasinitz, and Josh DeWind, 275–93 (New York: Russell Sage Foundation, 1999); James R. Barrett, "Americanization from the Bottom Up: Immigrants and the Remaking of the Working Class in the United States, 1880–1930," *Journal of American History* 79 (December 1992): 996–1020; George J. Sanchez, "'Go After the Women': Americanization and the Mexican Immigrant Woman, 1915–1929," in *Unequal Sisters: A Multicultural Reader in U.S. Women's History*, ed. Ellen Carol DuBois and Vicki Ruiz, 250–63 (New York: Routledge,1990); John Higham, *Strangers in the Land: Patterns of American Nativism, 1860–1925* (New Brunswick, N.J.: Rutgers University Press, 1955); and Edward Hartmann, *The Movement to Americanize the Immigrant* (New York: Columbia University Press, 1948).

4. In reference to Workman's activities in Los Angeles over nine decades of its expansion, Robert A. Orsi offers a valuable insight: "What people do religiously in cities is shaped by what kinds of cities they find themselves in, at what moment in the histories of those cities, and by their life experiences, cultural traditions, and contemporary circumstances." Robert A. Orsi, "Introduction: Crossing the City Line," in *Gods of the City: Religion and the American Urban Landscape*, ed. Robert A. Orsi, 1–78 (Bloomington: Indiana University Press, 1999), 46.

5. "Urban religion is what comes from the dynamic engagement of religious traditions . . . with specific features of industrial and post-industrial cityscapes and with the social conditions of city life." Orsi, *Gods of the City*, 43.

6. See Daphne Spain, *How Women Saved the City* (Minneapolis: University of Minnesota Press, 2001), 14–60; Anastasia J. Christman, "The Best Laid Plans: Women's Clubs and City Planning in Los Angeles, 1890–1930" (Ph.D. diss., University of California at Los Angeles, 2000), 171–223; Gayle Gullett, *Becoming Citizens: The Emergence and Development of the California Women's Movement, 1880–1911* (Urbana: University of Illinois Press, 2000), 151–61; and Suellen Hoy, *Chasing Dirt: The American Pursuit of Cleanliness* (New York: Oxford University Press, 1995), 59–86.

7. Michael E. Engh, "Mary Julia Workman: The Catholic Conscience of Los Angeles," *California History* 72 (Spring 1993): 4–8; and *Tidings* (Los Angeles), June 27, 1896.

8. Mary Julia Workman, "Panel—Social Work in Los Angeles, 1900–1924," type-

script, February 19, 1947, 3; Series I, Box 20, Folder 13, Workman Family Collection, Department of Archives and Special Collections, Charles Von der Ahe Library, Loyola Marymount University, Los Angeles, California (hereafter, CSLA-9).

9. Walter Nugent, "A Catholic Progressive? The Case of Judge E. O. Brown," *Journal of the Gilded Age and Progressive Era* 2 (January 2003): 5–47; and Douglas Flamming, "African-Americans and the Politics of Race in Progressive-Era Los Angeles," in *California Progressivism Revisited,* ed. William Deverell and Tom Sitton, 203–23 (Berkeley: University of California Press, 1994).

10. Bureau of the Census, *Religious Bodies, 1906,* Part 1 (Washington, D.C.: Government Printing Office, 1910), 456–59.

11. Fred L. Reardon, *Catholic Directory and Census of Los Angeles City and Parish Gazetteer of the Diocese of Monterey and Los Angeles* (Los Angeles: Fred L. Reardon, 1899), 12, 26–30, 40, 43–45, 47, 50, 54, 57, 59.

12. *Tidings* (Los Angeles), December 29, 1901.

13. *Tidings* (Los Angeles), April 24 and June 26, 1897, December 16, 1910, February 20, 1920; and Francis J. Weber, *Readings in California Catholic History* (Los Angeles: Westernlore Press, 1967), 117–19.

14. Clementina de Forest Griffin, "Brownson House Dispensary," *Queen's Work* 3 (October 1915): 189–90; "Activities of Brownson House: Calendar of House Activities, December, 1914," *Queen's Work* 2 (April 1915): 216; and *Los Angeles Times,* October 15, 1916.

15. Robert A. Woods and Albert J. Kennedy, *Handbook of Settlements* (New York: Charities Publication Committee, 1911): 11–12.

16. A member of the Paris Foreign Mission Society, Breton remained in Los Angeles until 1921, when he returned to Japan. He served as bishop of the diocese of Fukuoka from 1931 to 1940, and died in Japan in 1954. See Francis J. Weber, "Japanese Apostolate," in *Encyclopedia of California's Catholic Heritage* (Mission Hills, Calif.: St. Francis Historical Society and Arthur H. Clarke Company, 2001), 1004.

17. Japanese sources estimate that there were between six thousand to seven thousand Japanese in Los Angeles. The local Japanese Association counted seasonal agricultural workers prior to their departure from the city and the arrival of federal census enumerators. See William M. Mason and John A. McKistry, *The Japanese of Los Angeles* (Los Angeles: Los Angeles County Museum of Natural History, 1969), 28–29.

18. Breton to "Monseigneur," February 13, 1913, Los Angeles, Breton file, Archives of the Parish Foreign Mission Society, Paris; *Tidings* (Los Angeles), February 7, 1913; Mary J. Workman, quoted in Clementina de Forrest Griffin, "Sociology," *Tidings* (Los Angeles), July 7, 1916, 7; and undated letter from Workman to Sister Mary Leopold Dufresne, S.N.J.M., one of Workman's former teachers, published in Dufresne's compilation, *Golden Friendships: Letters of Friendship, Travel, General Interest* (New York: Louis Carrier and Company, 1929), 217.

19. Dufresne, *Golden Friendships*, 264.

20. For William Henry Workman, see John S. McGroarty, *Los Angeles: From the Mountains to the Sea* (New York: American Historical Society, 1921): 2: 3–8; for Bishop Conaty, see *Tidings* (Los Angeles), February 6, 1914, 12–13.

21. *Reflections of Bishop Albert Breton, Founder of the Sisters of the Visitation of Japan* (Kanagawa-ken, Japan: Congregation of the Sisters of the Visitation of Japan, 2001), 19.

22. Hiromi Hayafune, *Hurrying along Mountains with Mother Mary: The History of the Sisters of the Visitation of Japan, 1915–2001*, trans. Yuko Haga and Jennifer Cullen, (Kanagawa, Japan: Sisters of the Visitation of Japan, 2001), 46–47.

23. "Japanese Mission in Los Angeles," *Tidings* (Los Angeles), February 22, 1918, 5–6.

24. Interview with Bernadette Nishimura, April 12, 2003, Los Angeles. Breton recruited her father, Henry Haison Yoni, to assist the priest when Yoni arrived in Los Angeles from Norioka, Japan, in 1919. Yoni worked at a vegetable stand in Grand Central Market on Broadway to pay for the passage of his family the following year.

25. Breton secured facilities to open a school in 1915, only a few blocks from Brownson House. *Tidings* (Los Angeles), February 6, 1914, 12–13, July 16, 1915, 3–4; selections from Breton's diary, 1912–19, in *Keeping Faith: European and Asian Catholic Immigrants*, ed. Jeffrey Burns, Ellen Skerrett, and Joseph M. White, 248–49 (Maryknoll, N.Y.: Orbis, 2000); Harry Honda, "A Brief History of Maryknoll Los Angeles," in *Sixtieth Anniversary of Maryknoll* (Los Angeles: Maryknoll Center, 1972), n.p.; and *Reflections of Bishop Albert Breton*, 16–24.

26. Census figures found in Robert M. Folgelson, *The Fragmented Metropolis: Los Angeles, 1850–1930* (Cambridge, Mass.: Harvard University Press, 1967; repr., Berkeley: University of California Press, 1993), 78. Workman's figures on the Mexican population in Los Angels appeared in her article, "Brownson House," *Catholic Charities Review* 2 (September 1918): 213. Scholars have long recognized, however, that census enumerators repeatedly undercounted the Mexican population in the city and the state.

27. Ricardo Romo, *East Los Angeles: History of a Barrio* (Austin: University of Texas Press, 1983), 101–102.

28. Judith Ann Trolander, *Professionalism and Social Change: From the Settlement House to Neighborhood Centers, 1886 to the Present* (New York: Columbia University Press, 1987), 22. See also Elisabeth Lasch-Quinn, *Black Neighbors: Race and the Limits of Reform in the American Settlement House Movement, 1890–1945* (Chapel Hill: University of North Carolina Press, 1993).

29. For an extended discussion of local neighborhood demographics, see H. Mark Wild, "A Rumored Congregation: Cross-Cultural Interaction in the Immigrant Neighborhoods of Early Twentieth-Century Los Angeles" (Ph.D. diss., University of California at San Diego, 2000), 27–84.

30. Undated letter, Workman to Dufresne, quoted in *Golden Friendships*, 265. See also

Reverend William E. Corr to Workman, May 6, 1917, Fall River, Massachusetts; Series 1, Box 1, Folder 1, CSLA-9.

31. Mary J. Workman, quoted in the weekly column, "Sociology," by Clementina de Forrest Griffin, *Tidings* (Los Angeles), March 30, 1917, 5.

32. Mary Julia Workman, "A Mexican Indian Feast at Brownson House," typescript, August 15, 1919, in Collection 10: National Catholic Welfare Council/United States Catholic Conference, CSWA—Women's Committee: Community House—Los Angeles, Correspondence 12/9/1919–12/19/1919, Box 34, Folder 7, Catholic University of America Archives, Washington, D.C.

33. Ibid.

34. In 1928, officials of eight Mexican social and religious societies in Los Angeles protested the alleged anti-Mexican bias of Rev. Clement Molony, pastor of St. Agnes Church, Los Angeles; see letter to Bishop John J. Cantwell, May 22, 1928 Los Angeles, in Clement Molony file, AALA. See also Luis Stanford, "The Hijas de Maria," *Password*, 39 (1994): 113–23; and Gina Marie Pitti, "The Sociedades Guadalupanas in the San Francisco Archdiocese, 1942–1962," *U.S. Catholic Historian* 21 (Winter 2003): 83–98.

35. Ana Maria Diaz-Stevens, "Latinas and the Church," in *Hispanic Catholic Culture in the U.S.: Issues and Concerns*, ed. Jay P. Dolan and Allan Figueroa Deck, S.J., 251–52 (Notre Dame, Ind.: University of Notre Dame Press, 1994); Gilberto M. Hinojosa, "Mexican-American Faith Communities in Texas and the Southwest," in *Mexican Americans and the Catholic Church, 1900–1965*, ed. Jay P. Dolan and Gilberto M. Hinojosa, 45 (Notre Dame, Ind.: University of Notre Dame Press, 1994); and Anna Maria Padilla, "Rezadoras y Animadoras: Women, Faith, and Community in Northern New Mexico and Southern Colorado," *U.S. Catholic Historian* 21 (Winter 2003): 81.

36. Mary F. [sic] Workman, "A California Social Settlement," *Queen's Work* 8 (February 1918): 31.

37. *Yearbook* of the Brownson House Association of Los Angeles, February 1909, 4 and May 1911, 3, 4.

38. Mary J. Workman, "The Uniting of Native Born and Foreign Born in the United States," *Catholic Women's Club Bulletin* (Los Angeles), October 2, 1919, 6.

39. Dufresne, *Golden Friendships*, 220. After 1914, Workman became far more critical of social and economic conditions affecting the city's poor.

40. Dufresne, *Golden Friendships*, 272.

41. Workman, "Council of Catholic Women" (1939); Series 1, Box 1, Folder 1, CSLA-9. Workman's actions predate many of the principles later articulated by the pope who honored her labors in social welfare. Long after Workman had begun, Pope Pius XI (r. 1922–39) urged greater lay involvement in a movement known as "Catholic Action."

42. "Verona Spellmire," Weber, *Encyclopedia of California's Catholic History*, 497.

43. Workman to Dufresne, quoted in *Golden Friendships*, 267–68.

44. "Miss Workman Honored by Pope Pius," [Los Angeles] *Tidings* (Los Angeles), November 19, 1926.

45. Death Certificate for Verona Spellmire, #0190–051547, Office of the Registrar-Recorder-County Clerk, County of Los Angeles; Reardon, *Catholic Directory and Census of Los Angeles City*, 191; and Weber, *Encyclopedia of California's Catholic Heritage*, 497.

46. Mrs. R. Calvert Haws, "Early Days of the Los Angeles CCD," *Confraternity Notes* (Los Angeles) 18 (June 1962): 1, 4.

47. Dennis J. Burke, "The History of the Confraternity of Christian Doctrine in the Diocese of Los Angeles, 1922–1936" (master's thesis, Catholic University of America, 1965), 21–22; and Joseph B. Collins, "Religious Education in the United States: Early Years (1902–1935)," *American Ecclesiastical Review* 169 (January 1975): 54–57.

48. For religious life among Mexican immigrants, see George J. Sanchez, *Becoming Mexican American: Ethnicity, Culture, and Identity in Chicano Los Angeles, 1900–1945* (New York: Oxford University Press, 1993), 151–70.

49. Verona Spellmire, "Notes—Re: The Questionnaire," typed manuscript, February 16, 1965, 7, Archbishop Robert E. Lucey Collection, Archives of the Archdiocese of San Antonio, San Antonio, Texas (hereafter, AASA).

50. "Journal" of the San Francisco motherhouse, Sisters of the Holy Family, entries for May 3, 1922 and January 5, 1923, quoted in a letter, Sister Michaela O'Connor (historian for the Sisters of the Holy Family) to author, February 8, 2004, Fremont, California. See also Dennis J. Kavanaugh, S.J., *Sisters of the Holy Family of San Francisco: A Sketch of the First Fifty Years* (San Francisco: Gilmartin Company, 1922).

51. Spellmire to Lucey, February 16, 1965, Los Angeles, AASA.

52. Ibid.

53. *Tidings* (Los Angeles), December 1923 (Christmas annual issue), 111.

54. *Tidings* (Los Angeles), April 27, 7, and September 21, 1923; and Robert E. Mulvee, "The Catechetical Legislation in the Diocese of New England: An Historico-Juridic Study" (Ph.D. diss., Pontifical Lateran University, Rome, 1964), 142.

55. "Los Angeles Confraternity Second Largest Organization of Its Kind," *Tidings* (Los Angeles), December 1927 (Christmas annual issue), 99.

56. *Annual Report*, Bureau of Catholic Charities of the Diocese of Los Angeles and San Diego (Los Angeles: Diocese of Los Angeles and San Diego, 1924), 24; *Tidings* (Los Angeles), October 13, 1924, 40; and Verona Spellmire, "Development of Neighborhood Centers," *Proceedings, Thirteenth National Conference of Catholic Charities 1926* (Los Angeles: National Conference of Catholic Charities, 1927), 189.

57. Verona Spellmire, "Immigrant Welfare Department," in *Annual Report*, Bureau of Catholic Charities, Diocese of Los Angeles and San Diego, 15–16; and Spellmire, "Development of Neighborhood Centers," 190.

58. Clara Gertrude Smith, "The Development of the Mexican People in the Community of Watts, California" (master's thesis, University of Southern California, 1933), 80–81.

59. Burke, "History of the Confraternity," 34–35.

60. Ibid., 52–54.

61. Alice Vignos, "Project Defined," *Proceedings of the National Catechetical Congress of the Confraternity of Christian Doctrine, 1935* (Paterson, N.J.: St. Anthony Guild Press, 1936), 148–51.

62. William E. North, *Catholic Education in Southern California* (Washington, D.C.: Catholic University of America Press, 1936), 194. In describing Spellmire's role, North consigned her to anonymity: "The plan of organizing the Confraternity in Los Angeles was proposed by a lay-woman who possessed an intimate knowledge of the conditions and problems to be met from her experience as a public school teacher in some of the immigrant sections of the city (189)."

63. By 1937, the Los Angeles–based CCD had 36,472 children under the instruction of 1,472 teachers in three hundred centers. *Tidings* (Los Angeles), December 10, 1937, 69.

64. Quoted in Stephen A. Privett, S.J., *The U.S. Catholic Church and Its Hispanic Members: The Pastoral Vision of Archbishop Robert E. Lucey* (San Antonio, Tex.: Trinity University Press, 1988), 120.

65. *The Journey of the Diocese of Amarillo: 75 Years on the Llano Estacado, 1926–2001* (Amarillo, Tex.: Diocese of Amarillo, 2001), 35; James Talmadge Moore, *Acts of Faith: The Catholic Church in Texas, 1900–1950* (College Station: Texas A&M University Press, 2002), 115–19; and Franklin C. Williams Jr., *Lone Star Bishops: The Roman Catholic Hierarchy in Texas* (Waco, Tex.: Texian Press, 1997), 361–5.

66. More than sixty letters between Lucey and Workman exist for the period from 1922 to 1961, and cover a wide range of national and international issues, such a labor laws, papal teachings on social justice, peace and disarmament, and racial desegregation. See Box 1, Folder 4, CSLA-9. See also Verona M. Spellmire, "Helping to Safeguard Their Heritage—The Laity's Part," *Proceedings of the National Catechetical Congress of the Confraternity of Christian Doctrine, 1940* (Paterson, N.J.: St. Anthony Guild Press, 1941), 496.

67. Saul E. Bronder, *Social Justice and Church Authority: The Public Life of Archbishop Robert E. Lucey* (Philadelphia: Temple University Press, 1982), 70–71, 89–91; Miriam Marks to Verona Spellmire, December 8, 1941, Washington, D.C., and December 15, 1941, Apalachicola, Florida; and transcript of the "General Meeting of the Confraternity of Christian Doctrine, January 18, 1942," p. 3, in Box 20, Folder 5, Robert Emmet Lucey Papers, Archives of the University of Notre Dame, Notre Dame, Indiana (hereafter, LUC).

68. Quoted in Privett, *U.S. Catholic Church and Its Hispanic Members*, 120.

69. *Official Catholic Directory* (New York: P. J. Kenedy and Sons, 1942): 237.

70. Quoted in Carlos E. Castañeda, *The Church in Texas since Independence, 1836–1950*, vol. 7 of *Our Catholic Heritage in Texas, 1519–1936* (Austin: Von Boeckmann-Jones Company, 1958), 419.

71. Quoted in Privett, *U.S. Catholic Church and Its Hispanic Members*, 29. See also Lucey, "The Necessity of Religious Instruction for Children Attending Public Schools," *Proceedings, National Catechetical Congress of the Confraternity of Christian Doctrine, 1940* (Paterson, N.J.: St. Anthony Guild Press, 1941), 82–86; and Lucey, "Justice for the Mexicans," *Commonweal*, November 20, 1948, 117.

72. Privett, *U.S. Catholic Church and Its Hispanic Members*, 137.

73. Mary Paul Valdez, M.C.D.P., *The History of the Missionary Catechists of Divine Providence* (San Antonio: Missionary Catechists of Divine Providence, 1978), 68.

74. Quoted in Privett, *U.S. Catholic Church and Its Hispanic Members*, 121.

75. Lucey to "Reverend and Dear Father," September 13, 1949, San Antonio, Box 20, Folder 5, LUC.

76. *The Spanish Speaking of the Southwest and West* (Washington, D.C.: Social Action Department, National Catholic Welfare Conference, 1943), 19; and Bronder, *Social Justice and Church Authority*, 75–76.

77. *Official Catholic Directory* (New York: P. J. Kenedy and Sons, 1945), 266, and (1950), 201.

78. Castañeda, *The Church in Texas since Independence*,113; and Mary Charles Bryce, *Pride of Place: The Role of Bishops in the Development of Catechesis in the United States* (Washington, D.C.: Catholic University of America Press, 1984), 116.

79. Penny Gilpin, "The Confraternity of Christian Doctrine: History in the Making," in the program booklet, "Jubilee Congress: Confraternity of Christian Doctrine, Archdiocese of Los Angeles" (1972), 6–7; and *Tidings* (Los Angeles), June 21, 1974.

80. John T. McGreevy, "Productivity and Promise: American Catholic History since 1993," *U.S. Catholic Historian* 21 (Spring 2003): 121, 124.

"Wherever They Mention His Name"
Ethnic Catholicism on an Industrial Island

Matthew Pehl

The Rev. Monsignor Alfredo Giovannoni liked to regale listeners with the tale of his epic "sick call." One morning in the early 1920s, Giovannoni received a telephone call asking for "the Catholic priest at Price," a small town in the industrialized, east-central district of Carbon County, Utah (named for the abundant coal mines). The caller, a Mrs. Powers, continued, "I am not a Catholic but I believe in Catholicity and I know what your religion means to a dying person. Won't you come down here and minister to a very sick man of your Faith?" Pat Meehan, the gravely ill Catholic, rested nearly two hundred mountainous miles away.

Giovannoni hurried to his car—"still hot from another call to one of the mining camps"—and began the long journey to southeastern Utah. But by five o'clock in the afternoon, still seven miles from his destination and traveling on a rugged, trail-like road, Giovannoni's car died. After a long wait under the afternoon sun, Giovannoni caught a ride on a horse-drawn wagon with an old man who revealed himself to be a retired bishop from the area (though he did not mention from which faith). The two men rode along for another three hours before arriving at LaSal. Giovannoni thanked the bishop, who had offered him "the hospitality of a real westerner," and moved on to the Powers' home.[1]

Giovannoni performed his priestly duties and anointed the dying Catholic, but he had to wait another day before his car was ready to drive. Yet no sooner had he started home than the cleric was caught in a "grand storm," and became stuck in a washout. Stranded for the night, he was forced to lie on the ground for rest; it was the "fourth time I slept on the road somewhere." Later, describing his night in the wilderness in a letter to Bishop Joseph Glass, Giovannoni claimed he waited "until morning listening to the coyote call, and praying for the sun." It is no wonder that, as he confided to the bishop, "one feels this country. It gets into your bones."[2] By the next morning, a passerby helped Giovannoni with his car, and finally the weary priest straggled back to his home in the basement of the unfinished Notre Dame de Lourdes church in Price. Giovannoni cannot be faulted for thinking to himself, "if someone in the big and comfortable cities would try one of these wonderful trips, how much more would he appreciate the things he has and love to help the poor missionary of the wild West." [3]

Giovannoni's misadventure illustrates the difficulty of Catholic life in eastern Utah. The sheer geographic vastness and isolation, combined with a sparse population, created unique conditions that challenged the effectiveness of a young and fragile religious community. Juxtaposed against American urban environments, which teemed with immigrant Catholics both lay and clergy, the small Catholic clusters within the Mormon Zion of Utah demanded spiritual stamina and versatility. [4]

The Catholics of eastern Utah did, however, share something with many other American Catholics of the early twentieth century: the experience of immigration and the challenge of retaining traditional, ethnic folkways. The majority of Catholics in Carbon County were, like Giovannoni, immigrant Italians. As such, they maintained a Catholicism rooted in sacred social gatherings, special familial bonds, and personal relationships with saints or the Virgin Mary—an ethnic variant that often drew the ire of more "mainstream" (or, "Americanized") Catholics. [5] Religion, as a cultural tool, offered American immigrant groups the chance to define themselves as self-conscious ethnic communities and, as the historian Timothy Smith explained, to etch "boundaries of peoplehood" around themselves. [6] Italian Catholics in Utah thus easily fit into the broader patterns of Italian immigrant life in the United States.

However, the local situation in east-central Utah—an industrial frontier in which organized churches could be few and far between—allowed the boundaries of religious identity to stretch with greater ease than in densely settled urban environments. This regional peculiarity allowed believers great permeability, and encouraged participation in a variety of denominational activities. Religious affiliations often acted more as porous membranes than as strict lines of separation. Mrs. Powers, for example, housed a Catholic priest and claimed that she believed in "Catholicity," though she herself was not Catholic. Italians in Carbon County, particularly Italian women, expressed the elastic nature of their religious boundaries by drawing upon the available religious communities—Mormon, Protestant, and Greek Orthodox, as well as Roman Catholic—for their personal spiritual needs.

Religion and ethnicity nonetheless remained closely linked. While Italians lived in a pluralistic social environment epitomized by their fraternization with other religions, they continued to define themselves and their community as

both Italian and Catholic. The initiative of the local laity, more than any con-
centrated attention by the institutional church, immeasurably aided the growth
of the local Catholic Church in Carbon County. Indeed, ordinary people kept
their ethno-religious traditions alive largely in the absence of an elaborate institutional network.

The story of Italian Catholicism in the Utah coalfields thus reveals the nature of human complexity and the contingency of specific circumstances. It rests
in the interplay between the allowance of social exchange and the erection of
social boundaries, between a religious institution and lay agency, between regional uniqueness and transnational upheavals, and between a "lived," experiential religion in the home and an "official" religion in the Church. As such, it
demonstrates new models in both religious history and immigration history.

As it expanded into the American West, the Catholic Church faced challenges that were both geographic and cultural. Scarcity of finances, a shortage of
clergy and nuns, and "(especially) ongoing conflicts over ethnicity" persistently
loomed as daunting problems for the Church.[7] In the mid-nineteenth century,
European Catholics began establishing American parishes west of the Mississippi River. Joseph Machebeuf in Colorado, Jean Baptise Lamy in New Mexico,
and Joseph Alemany in California all deeply colored the character of the western
church, and all aimed to cement clerical authority over cultural idiosyncrasies.
The persistence of Native Americans and Hispanics, each with their own syn-
cretic styles of Catholic worship (or Native Americans' resistance to Christianity
in general), bedeviled these mostly French clerics in their attempts to impose a
Euro-American model of church leadership on an often unwilling population.
This pattern of ethnic heterogeneity and lay autonomy would be further complicated by the rise of mining frontiers, which attracted a variety of Catholic
immigrant groups, primarily those from southern and eastern Europe.[8]

The Italians of Carbon County comprised this latter category. They had
entered the modern, international, industrial workforce to escape the blight of
poverty and to preserve ethnic and family ties. Italian laborers became the "most
ubiquitous," and often the "most mobile of nineteenth-century peoples."[9] Facing
stunted economic growth and grim prospects in their homelands, these mostly
unskilled workers funneled from a rural periphery into an industrial core—dominated by the United States and western Europe—like water down a drain.[10]
The number of Italians flooding into the United States between 1890 and 1920
reflected both the desperation of the immigrants and the tendency of Italians
to move with their countrymen to areas offering new opportunities: between
1891 and 1900, 651,893 Italians entered the United States; from 1901 to 1910,
2,045,877; and from 1911 to 1920, an additional 1,109,524.[11]

The image of the restlessly moving migrant, always hoping to earn enough money to return to his homeland, rang true for many of the Italians who eventually settled in Utah. Mary Angotti Palomi, the daughter of a Utah immigrant, related that her father "went to South America, to Brazil." From there, he moved through industrial jobs in Pennsylvania and West Virginia. Mary was eight when her family settled in Price, Utah, and her father floated between ranch work and wage labor in the mines.[12] Filomena Fazzio Bonacci likewise remembered a father on the move, and the terrible strain it exerted on his family. "My dad used to migrate," Bonacci said, "four or five times," between America and Italy. Bonacci recalled her mother's reaction to this unpredictable home life: "[M]y mother used to say, she said, if you're going to go back again, don't come back anymore. She said, I can't live this—. . . he'd go home and only stay there a year and she'd get pregnant and then he'd leave again and he'd come back and get her pregnant and he'd leave again."[13] Bonacci's family finally resolved the tension when her mother moved to the United States. Her father "said he loved mama too much to leave her there."[14]

Utah's Italian miners relied on informal connections to arrive in Carbon County's coalfields. Tony Priano, a miner of southern-Italian origin, noted that immigrants "used to write each other and say, 'There is coal in Utah and there is work.'"[15] Vito Bonacci found himself in Utah via similar channels. After corresponding with a distant uncle in the Sunnyside mine, Bonacci received a reply: "come over here and you'll get a job."[16] Stanley Litizzette asserted that Italian migration into Utah rested simply on "word of mouth." The total number of Italians in Carbon County as of 1900 was a modest 374, but from these seeds sprouted a full-fledged ethnic community: 798 by 1910, a high of 1,215 in 1920, and a leveling out to 935 in 1930.[17] Most of the first wave of Italian immigrants originated in northern Italian provinces (particularly Piedmont and Lombard), but by the mid-1910s, an ever-increasing number of southern Italian immigrants sought work and community in Utah's coalfields. Although Old World regional animosities continued to simmer in New World soil, the Italians of Utah nonetheless created a remarkably well-defined ethnic identity that incorporated language, foodways, family structure, fraternal organizations, and a unique Catholic heritage.

If the West as a region presented complex challenges to Catholic settlement, Utah as a subregion added even more wrinkles to the mix. In 1906, an overwhelming 87.4 percent of all churchgoers in Utah were Mormon; so dominant were the Latter-day Saints that Catholics, as the second most populous religious group, claimed only 5.3 percent.[18] Mormon hegemony, while not aggressively anti-Catholic in the style of many eastern Protestant strongholds, clearly influenced Catholic settlement in the region. Writing to the Society for the Propagation of the Faith in 1876, Lawrence Scanlan, a priest and soon-to-be bishop of the Salt Lake Diocese, characterized Utah Territory as a "far off and all but pagan land." By 1882, however, Father Dennis Kiely could note the expansion of churches, schools, and hospitals. He also observed that the rise of Catholic institutions, as well as the open spirit of the Sisters of the Holy Cross, had created amenable relations between Catholics and Mormons. He sensed the shifting religious boundaries typical of frontier settings. "Eight years ago," Kiely wrote, "six Mormons would not enter our little church in twelve months. Today many attend regularly on Sundays."[19] Mormon attendance at Catholic services illustrates the diversity of religious experiences available in a frontier community, and Mormon exploration of other faiths resembled the spiritual curiosity and tentative ecumenism characteristic of Carbon County's Italian Catholics.

Institutional Catholic life in Carbon County developed in the context of thin financial resources, scattered clergy, and often a dependence upon the deeper pockets of urban centers. Despite the fact that Catholics in Carbon County created areas where their religion was the majority faith—as in the railroad and mining town of Helper—attention by the archdiocese itself remained parsimonious. In the 1890s, shortly after Catholic immigrants began inundating the coalfields, Lawrence Scanlan arranged for priests to make monthly tours of the camps, in order to perform the mass and provide other sacraments. Scanlan himself made a number of trips into Carbon County for these purposes; Stanley Litizzette, whose grandparents immigrated to Utah, claims that Scanlan personally signed the baptismal record of his uncle, James Bottino. In 1897, Scanlan and his congregation transformed an old company house into the first Catholic Church in the coal camps. It was so small that "only the women and children could attend mass inside, while the men would stand outside during the mass."[20]

The isolation did not end with the nineteenth century but persisted well into the twentieth. Catholics in Helper constructed St. Anthony's Church in 1914, but almost everywhere else, the monthly visits of priests proved the extent of Catholicism's institutional presence. For the most part, institutional Catholicism in such far-flung locales as eastern Utah depended upon the Catholic Church Extension Society, a missionary organization based in Chicago, throughout the 1920s and 1930s. For example, in 1919, Extension Society vice president E. B. Lebvina wrote to Salt Lake City bishop Joseph Glass, announcing a contribution to assist the building of chapels at the coal camp of Sunnyside and in the town of Price. The bishop had contacted the Extension Society in 1917, requesting funds for these chapels. For two years, Glass remained powerless to construct the chapels with local resources. Frontier "mustard seeds" like Utah remained dependent on urban centers. In fact, local residents in Sunnyside and Price did not even have the authority to name their own chapels; that power rested with the donors. "We will take precaution," Lebvina assured the bishop, "that no very unusual name will be selected."[21]

In the same letter of 1917, Lebvina also indicated that the Extension Society was arranging with Bishop Glass for the tour of a chapel car through these same far-off locales. The Catholic chapel car, which took its inspiration from a Protestant example, was essentially a church on wheels—or, more exactly, on railroad tracks. Although similar in exterior appearance to regular railroad passenger cars, the chapel cars' interiors were transformed into little churches. Designed to reach distant locations without a Catholic church, but usually with a few resident Catholics, the church operated two railroad chapel cars: the "St. Paul," which serviced the South, and the "St. Peter," which traveled the West. According to an Extension Society booster:

> When a Chapel Car comes to town everyone soon knows about it, and Catholics begin to spring up all around it. People who had never before been known as Catholics suddenly show interest in the Church, and come to the services. The Chapel Car has a subtle appeal to the pride of even a fallen-away member of the Great Family. . . . The beauty and up-to-dateness of the Chapel Car gives them a sense of sharing in its glory; and they begin to boast, amongst surprised neighbors, of the Church they had never before claimed as their own.[22]

The St. Peter Chapel Car visited Carbon County in 1918. The headline of a front-page article in the diocesan newspaper announced the train's arrival: "Famous Traveling Church Here." The article featured photos of the interior and stated the mission of the tour as carrying "into remote parts of the state the gospel of Jesus Christ."[23] Moreover, a photograph from this trip depicts a class of children receiving first communion in Helper.[24] For many rural Catholics, formal religious life consisted of such ritualistic moments, often enacted outside of a regular church building.

Carbon County and its environs remained, in the eyes of many, a wilderness of spiritual danger well into the twentieth century. As late as the 1920s, clerics were exploring the eastern part of Utah. In a "Report of 1922 Missionary Trip," Father McCarthy from St. Patrick's Rectory in Eureka, Utah, recorded his observations of the rocky desert from Price through Moab. After an informational reconnaissance with Alfredo Giovannoni in Price, McCarthy proceeded to Green River, Utah, which was not a Mormon community but rather one more typical of the western frontier. There, the priest discovered "a scattering of American families and some 30 or 40 Italians." McCarthy expressed dismay with the state of the town. Masons, hostile to Catholicism, held sway over the local business scene and intimidated Catholics. The spiritual situation was even worse than the commercial one: "The Americans are in a bad condition." Italians, likewise, reacted apathetically toward the priest; they "have become extremely indifferent." Green River seemed the epitome of frontier irreligion:

> All these folks had been notified in good time of the coming of the priest. . . . [The priest] spent a few days going around, spreading the good news. He mustered all the forces he could . . . but it seemed like the voice of one crying in the desert. Mass was said Sunday morning, August 13 . . . for some fifty souls. Quite a few non-Catholics came for the services. It would be a better plan to have the services in a private home, as the Italians would probably come. After Mass, [I] spent some time going around making a last appeal to two families for permission to baptize their children, but all being in vain.[25]

Although McCarthy bemoaned the situation, Green River actually displayed many characteristics typical of western and frontier locations where organized religion faced challenges and ambivalence. For example, though McCarthy grimaced at the lack of interest in his services, he nonetheless attracted fifty churchgoers in a remote setting. Further, as McCarthy noted, many of those who attended Mass were non-Catholics. The reticence of families to baptize children, a fact lamented by the priest, stemmed from interfaith marriages, not hostility to the Catholic Church per se. Both the interest of non-Catholics in a Catholic service and the prevalence of interfaith marriage indicate that people in Green River simply responded to the frontier in a typical fashion: they took what they could get, building their community from what was available.

Italians fell into this category like the other residents. Family-centered, the Italians responded to the priest saying Mass in a home—as Giovannoni did for many years in the coal camps—but were reluctant to enter a church. In many ways, because Italians defined their religion through their family, they were uniquely able to endure with a bare-bones institutional church. McCarthy thought the Italians irreligious, but in fact they were adhering perfectly to their own religious customs; a more liturgical immigrant group may have suffered a deeper spiritual rift in the absence of clerical attention. Still, McCarthy's low opinion of Italian religiosity fit perfectly with the views of many in the organizational church.

Yet, despite its small scale, a Catholic presence in Carbon County increased steadily in the early decades of the twentieth century, in large part due to the efforts of the Rev. Monsignor Alfredo Giovannoni. We have seen the effects of

Giovannoni's dedication, but should place him in the larger historical context of Catholicism and the American West. Born on April 13, 1881 in the northern Italian province of Lucca, Giovannoni was ordained in 1904 and taught in Italy until being transferred to the United States in 1911. His first assignment was to an Italian community in Racine, Wisconsin. According to one of his biographers, his stay in Wisconsin molded the priest's "sensitivity to the insufferable conditions under which many Italian laborers [in the United States] lived." In 1916, Giovannoni moved on to Utah, where he was assigned the immense territory of Carbon, Emory, Grand, Wayne, San Juan, Uintah, and Duchesne counties in eastern Utah; Giovannoni estimated that this area comprised forty thousand square miles.[26]

Despite the daunting sprawl of his spiritual terrain, Giovannoni aggressively and energetically worked to build the institutional base of the Catholic Church in eastern Utah. The results of Giovannoni's efforts quickly became visible. After the parish seat was transferred from Helper to Price in 1918, Giovannoni immediately produced his collection plate and actively encouraged people to fill it for the purpose of constructing a new church. His entreaties found particular success among the French sheepherders around Price. Giovannoni responded by naming the new church (which was finally completed in 1923) Notre Dame de Lourdes. Despite French generosity, there does not appear to have been animosity between French and Italian Catholics in the area, and Italians remained the dominant ethnic group within the church.[27] In addition to the Notre Dame church, Giovannoni campaigned for the creation of a Catholic school system. In a heartfelt, if somewhat melodramatic, letter to Bishop Joseph Glass, Giovannoni implored both the bishop and the Extension Society for aid in saving young souls: "[W]hat gets me, and holds me, is the uselessness of my present endeavor, the utter futility of my present method of attack. Why I am just gathering up a few sands of the desert, while the wind blows oceans away. I am not doing anything for the children; those little souls out here alone. I can only pray, and God knows how I have prayed for them." Giovannoni concluded his letter by asserting that "these little children are in danger of losing their souls, and I simply cannot sit idlely [sic] by and see that go on. . . . We have thousands of souls waiting for the bread of salvation. Who will help me in this Holy cause?"[28] The priest's theatrics paid off. In 1927, Giovannoni announced that the Catholic Church would construct an eight-grade school to be run by the Daughters of Charity of St. Vincent de Paul and, on May 4, 1928, Bishop John Mitty dedicated the Notre Dame school.

Residents of Carbon County generally held Giovannoni in high regard. Clara Rugerri felt as much when she told an interviewer, "Father Giovannoni needs to be credited with the building of the church and also the building of the schools." Marian Bonacci Lupo agreed, claiming that a strong, visible Catholic life "really started [with Giovannoni]." On December 4, 1929, Giovannoni celebrated his Silver Jubilee as a priest, and local appreciation ran high. The Price newspaper averred, "They all love him," and described Giovannoni as "a great soul." Nor was admiration limited to locals, or even to Catholics. Among his many congratulatory telegrams, Giovannoni received praise from Utah governor George H. Dern, who wrote, "I know of the good work you are doing and how your broadminded views and genial personality have won the esteem and admiration of all with whom you have come in contact regardless of their religious views and affiliations." [29]

Giovannoni thus stands as something of a watershed figure in the history of Utah Catholicism, but his legacy is not entirely one-dimensional. Ambiguity, not simple triumphalism, shadows Giovannoni's considerable achievements. His own personality, however winning, harbored deeper complexities and inconsistencies than previous commentators have noted. For example, although he fine-tuned his public image as that of the rugged frontier priest ready to endure any discomfort for the grace of God, his own living habits cast such claims into doubt. In the midst of an isolated, working-class, industrial frontier, Giovannoni's "lifestyle was extraordinary for Carbon County. He lived in a five-room rectory south of the church. He loved fine cars and usually drove a Buick or Studebaker. He wore knickers and smoked fine Italian cigars." [30] This dichotomy between the image of the poor priest and the reality of a man who managed to live well also found reflection in Giovannoni's attitude toward class. Although his early days in Wisconsin nurtured his sensitivity to the exploitation of Italian workers, he was perceived by many as discouraging Carbon County's 1922 coal miners' strike and siding with management. This action alienated some, especially the southern Italians, who may have already harbored suspicions about the northern origins of the priest. [31] If Giovannoni wished to present himself as a struggling missionary sympathetic to the workingman, the reality did not always match the image.

The role of ethnicity also complicates any understanding of Giovannoni. From all appearances, Giovannoni attempted to balance two divergent goals: promoting the "Americanization" of the Italian community in Utah, while simultaneously seeking to reinforce a self-conscious ethnic resiliency. In his activity with fraternal groups—particularly the Knights of Columbus and the Italian Americanization Club—Giovannoni appeared to be encouraging his fellow immigrants to adopt American customs and norms; yet he also proudly proclaimed membership in the openly ethnic Stella D'America lodge. Likewise, Giovannoni supported the establishment of a state Columbus Day celebration to honor an

Italian hero; yet, the holiday was intended to proclaim Italians' fundamentally "American" character more than to assert any ethnic uniqueness.

Here Giovannoni must be considered in the context of an evolving Catholic Church attempting to reconcile American and ethnic identity. Facing the massive movements of peoples throughout the late nineteenth and early twentieth centuries, the Catholic Church, rooted in Roman soil, always thought itself as much an *emigrant* as an *immigrant* institution, and Giovannoni himself reflects this double identity. Catholics in Italy who witnessed the exodus of their countrymen to America thought of ethnic parishes as Italian "colonies," not as American neighborhoods. Ethnic identity thus remained paramount to clerical prestige. Using the Scalabrini Order of priests in Chicago as an example, one historian claimed that "the Scalabrinians and the American church conspired to cultivate an identity grounded in Italian Catholic ethnic nationalism," an alliance that reflected the growing relationship between the Catholic Church and the Italian State. Just as Italian laborers rode the currents of the international industrial economy, so too did ethnic clergy exist in an international religious order. Italian American priests of Giovannoni's generation faced a great deal of pressure to encourage a defiant ethnic pride, particularly in the late 1920s after Benito Mussolini's government reconciled the historic conflict between the Italian State and the Catholic Church.[32]

Giovannoni himself certainly maintained contact with representatives of the Italian State, such as Fortunato Anselmo in Salt Lake City. In late 1928, Giovannoni met with the Italian consul stationed in Denver. The consul proceeded to write Giovannoni's bishop, John Mitty, asking for the bishop's assistance in establishing, of all things, Italian language courses for the immigrants under Giovannoni's pastoral care. The role of the Catholic Church in supporting ethnic nationalism seemed clear enough to the consul: "I consider the Catholic Clergy the best possible auxiliaries in my work to preserve the best racial assets of the Italian race, which can prove a valuable basis even for their Americanization." The close connection between Catholic clergy and the Italian "race" in the consul's letter seems striking, but so too does the seemingly self-defeating process of creating "Americans" by stressing their "Italian-ness." In fact, as the consul astutely realized, many migrating Italians did not develop a self-conscious identity as Italians until they settled in a foreign land. The consul stated his position even more clearly. "During my stay in Carbon County I studied how I could better exert myself in order to bring the co-nationals closer to that Church as to a foyer of morality *and national* co-operation."[33] Giovannoni clearly maintained an awareness of his specific role as an *Italian* priest, as a representative of both the "American" Church and Italian nationalism. And, if even an American institution-builder like Giovannoni felt the tug of ethnic loyalties, one can imagine that the lay Italians of Carbon County crafted their religion in even more emphatically ethnic tones.

Italian immigrants—the vast majority of them peasants from southern Italy—had troubled and perplexed the American Catholic Church almost from the moment they arrived en masse on American shores. As early as 1884, at the Third Plenary Council of Baltimore, American bishops bemoaned what they considered the woeful spiritual status of these immigrant outsiders. The council claimed that, "Italians suffered a spiritual destitution greater than that of all other immigrant groups." Indeed, it went so far as to declare that Italians exceeded all other Catholic immigrants in "crass and supine ignorance of the faith." [34] Much of the "Italian Problem" did in fact stem from Italian religious traditions, but the bishops of the Third Plenary Council were wrong to assume that Italian immigrants suffered a crushing spiritual poverty. The problem, rather, rested in the struggle of a largely Irish American Catholic hierarchy to control and discipline culturally dissimilar laity. Power, not faith, glimmered as the real prize at stake.

Italian Catholicism focused on cults and rituals primarily attending to saints or to the Madonna; or, put another way, it stressed the personal, familial, and experiential over the institutional. This Italian folk religion, so radically at odds with the standard practice of the American Catholic Church, survived the voyage to America's streets. Historian Rudolph Vecoli has described the Italian religious tradition as "a fusion of Christian and pre-Christian elements, of animism, polytheism, and sorcery with the sacraments of the Church." [35] Italians' religious tradition put little stock in the organized church, but found greatest succor in outdoor rituals and family celebrations. Journalist Jacob Riis observed one such Italian ritual, the *festa* in Italian Harlem. In occasionally grandiloquent language, Riis described the procession of women throwing themselves at the feet of the Virgin, of men mumbling prayers, of the procession of a banner of the Virgin bedecked in banknotes, as well as the accompanying gambling and socializing that so outraged clerics and other Catholic groups. He shrewdly understood what American bishops refused to accept: "The religious fervor of our Italians is not to be pent up within brick walls, and sunshine and flowers belong naturally to it. 'Religious' perhaps hardly describes it, yet in its outward garb it is nearly always that." [36]

How is one to understand a ritual like the festa? Recently, scholars have reevaluated religious history, stressing the role of religion in the common activities of ordinary people over the institutionally driven narratives typical in most accounts of religious history. This approach has been termed a study of "lived religion." Historians who employ this model emphasize the personal experience of religion and hence highlight those typically left out of religious histories. In this new approach, "'religion' cannot be neatly separated from the other practices of everyday life." Rather, like social history "from the bottom up," lived religion is the "study of how particular people, in particular places and times, live in, with, through, and against the religious idioms available to them in culture—*all* the idioms," not just their "own."[37]

Approaching religion as a set of experiences, rather than an institutional membership, clearly increases our understanding of Carbon County's Italian Catholics. Not only does this concept emphasize the vitality of religious cultures beyond church walls, but it also helps account for the persistence of religious traditions in a region where the growth of an institutional church was often insufficient. Given the remote location of the coal camps, as well as Italians' unsavory reputation within the larger church, one may expect to find a heavy coat of spiritual apathy covering the coal camps of eastern Utah. Yet such an assumption denies the immigrants the opportunity to draw upon other religious traditions to supplement their own, ignores lay initiative in church building, and misunderstands the nature of Italian religiosity.

The bonds of family for Utah's Italians, a characteristic that defined so much of Italian immigrant life, did not erode in the face of transnational migration, but actually sustained immigrant life. Indeed, an emphasis on family epitomized Italian settlement throughout the United States. Italian immigrants in Buffalo, New York, for example, "chose the familistic strategy of migration rather than any cooperative or class effort as their means to achieve or maintain security." These immigrants were decidedly "family-oriented."[38] In St. Louis, where many Italians were (like Utah's immigrants) veterans of coal mining, a similar pattern held: "Working conditions may have been bad, wages may have been abominable, but as long as family honor could be preserved, immigrants endured."[39] Beyond simple economic or even emotional ties, the Italian family should be understood broadly as the defining organizing principle of Italian life and the locus of Italian religion. Father Louis Giambastiani, in 1912, recognized the true nature of the interaction between family life and religious life: "the Italian home and family . . . *is* the religion of Italian Americans."[40]

Understood within the lived experience of family, Italian religion becomes less dependent on institutional forces and more broadly applicable in other realms of life. For many Italians, the most important trinity in Catholic thought was not the Father, Son, and Holy Ghost, but the Holy Family consisting of three members: Mother Mary, Father Joseph, and Child Jesus. Using the Holy Family as a prototype, *all* earthly families were infused with a "sacred quality."[41] Women typically expressed their religiosity by church attendance and personal relation-

ships with saints or the Madonna. For Italian men, work *outside* the home defined their responsibilities *to* the home, an obligation that symbolized men's commitment to the sacred nature of their own families.

The values of both men and women were deeply rooted in their family roles.
Moreover, because the family acted as the anchor of religious life, the sexes carried distinct religious frames of mind into their separate secular spheres. Family
roles created gender roles, and, as a result, also created gendered religious experiences. Given the emphasis on the family in defining roles, the familial function
and responsibilities of husbands, wives, mothers, fathers, and children differed
sharply. For Italian men, a secure masculinity rested on performance as an economic "provider" and in the appearance of ultimate authority on family issues.
Status as "father" or "head of household"—one who commanded respect and de-
rived the fruits of unpaid domestic labor—was an elemental aspect and benefit
of masculinity.[42] While entailing certain social privileges, the duties of manhood
could also prove stressful, particularly for the married sojourner. A photograph
taken in the mining camp of Castle Gate, Utah, in 1913 shows coal miner Frank
Mangone handing his paycheck over to his wife, Teresa. Both pairs of eyes fix
squarely on the money. The photograph was sent to Teresa's parents in Italy,
demonstrating Frank's fulfillment of manly duties, and, in the process, illustrating the expectations Frank strove to meet.[43] Perhaps the stress associated with
these expectations is what the miner Vito Bonacci had in mind when he told
an interviewer, "The family, that's all they do is make you go crazy."[44] The family provided the bonds of community, but by its very centrality could also breed
stress and conflict.

Appearances of male familial authority were not wholly unfounded, particularly for southern Italians. In Italy, before unification, wives typically depended
on their husband's permission before being allowed to buy or sell property,
and the legal authority of the father lasted until death.[45] The image of a male-
dominated society persisted in the minds of at least some Utahns. Clara Ruggeri,
a Catholic convert born into a family of lapsed Mormons in the heavily Irish
Catholic mining town of Park City, offers a revealing perspective. Clara married
the southern-Italian Catholic James Ruggeri. Before the marriage, friends and
relatives cautioned her about the autocratic nature of Italian men and Catholic
married life. One of her male friends, who eventually became a doctor, told her,
"you're not marrying a man, you're marrying a family. You know in the Italian
families why the woman does all the work. She's just a servant in the house."
Another man, who "didn't think people should have big families," told her "you'll
be pregnant all your life." A woman from Park City tried to steer Clara toward
Mormon marital choices. She opposed the marriage "because he [James] was a

Catholic." Finally, her uncle "had this idea that all Italian men were padrones, is that the word, bosses, you know."[46]

Appearances, however, could be deceiving. In many cases, wives and mothers exercised internal familial control. While the father occupied a "'pedestal of priority' . . . the real power, including control over the family purse strings, was in the wife's hands."[47] The Italian writer Luigi Barzizi cleverly captured the situation: "Men run the country but women run men."[48] Such was the conclusion of many Italians in Carbon County. Clara Ruggeri, for example, describing her husband's Italian parents, opined that, "if there was a boss in the Ruggeri family, I would be inclined to think it was Mrs. Ruggeri. You know many of these Italian provinces are matriarchal. The women are really the boss."[49] Mary Angotti Palomi, discussing her own Italian parents, agreed with Ruggeri's assessment: "My mother was the boss. My dad let her do anything. He never argued."[50]

Italian women also understood their role as the spiritual leader of the family. For Mary Juliano, the religious devotion she received was transmitted through matrilineal channels. "Mama and my grandma talked about Jesus," she said. Mary attended church with her grandmother, and remembered, "Mama used to tell me the story about Jesus's birth. . . . Grandma too."[51] Mary Angotti Palomi also remembered learning religion from her mother. "My mother taught us, taught me the rosaries. Taught me all about our Blessed Mother, the Lord, and all the stories that come with the church."[52] In Mary Palomi's reminiscence, stories regarding the "Blessed Mother" sprung to mind even before stories of "the Lord."

Italian women thus nurtured religion within the circle of the family, but they were not indifferent to the absence of an institutional church. Indeed, Italian women were deeply involved with the creation of an institutional Catholic religious life in Carbon County. In this, they were much like the laity in other rural and western locations. As one historian has observed, "one could not miss the vital role of the laity" in laying the groundwork for the Catholic Church's growth in isolated locales.[53] Laywomen in Carbon County organized the Saint Anthony Altar Society in 1910. Stanley Litizzette commended the Altar Society for its activism in establishing St. Anthony's Church in Helper, and attributed the "growth and prosperity of the Church" to "the superiority of their women."[54] After 1917 and the arrival of Alfredo Giovannoni, mass continued to be primarily a female affair, especially in the coal camps. In Castle Gate, according to Tony Priano, Giovannoni performed mass "all the time at Mrs. Tabone's house. He used to come every Sunday." Priano did not attribute female dominance of religious life completely to male apathy; rather sheepishly, he reported to an interviewer, "The men were tired. They worked hard. When Sunday morning come, you want to sleep a little bit."[55] Two and a half decades after the makeshift church in the coal camp bowed to formal parish life, Marian Bonacci Lupo remembered, with some bemusement, the men still loitering on the edges on the church: "[Giovannoni] was really out-spoken. . . . I remember a lot of times especially at funerals. The women went in and the men had to go out and they'd be talking out there and he'd holler at them from the altar. . . . He'd tell them it's a disgrace. They should stay quiet while they're out there. But you get a talking and you don't know how loud you're talking."[56] Even though women clearly took an active role in fostering religion, we should not automatically accept the assumptions of many Catholic prelates that Italian men were irreligious. Clara Ruggeri, for example, while admitting that her southern Italian husband was "not an active Catholic," nevertheless asserted a balanced gender division within the church. "When I would go to mass with my children," Ruggeri told an interviewer, "I think there was probably as many men there as women. We had quite an active Catholic group."[57]

In addition to expressing their religious attachments at church, Italian men in Utah also integrated religion into their social lives. The Knights of Columbus, a Catholic, male, fraternal organization, found a receptive home in Carbon County after Alfredo Giovannoni established a lodge in the 1920s.[58] Social gatherings and family celebrations, usually centered on traditional foodways, also tied both men and women into the religious patchwork. Food possessed a special significance because of its filial connection: As a symbol of its importance in the Italians' worldview, the family as an entity demanded high-quality food. Italians in Utah planted elaborate gardens, herded goats for milk and cheese, raised pigs to produce sausage, and utilized specific foods for specific social occasions. Food bound people together, a fact that sometimes expressed itself in class-based movements. According to Edna Romano, immigrants survived mining strikes "[b]y helping each other! Those that had the farms and cows and the milk helped the others. . . . They had huge gardens . . . and all kinds of animals." Folk life kept Italians' ethno-religious identity alive in tangible ways, and contributed irreplaceably "to the fundamental economic and social stability of Italian immigrants in the industrial, desert landscape of east central Utah."[59]

Even in their involvement with the labor movement, Italian men remained consistent with a "lived" approach to religion. Supporting a family was, after all, often regarded as a more sacred (and masculine) task than attending church; as such, Italian men could be said to fulfill their religious obligations through their work. Vito Bonacci recalled this attitude in the minds of many of his fellow miners: "I used to hear the guys say, well, the mine is just like going to church."[60]

Italians miners in Carbon County were not radical, but they did doggedly advance the conservative unionism of the United Mine Workers of America

(UMWA), striking in 1903, 1922, and 1933. Although dedicated unionists, Italian men did not view the labor movement as a tool of social revolution, but rather as a method of preserving a community defined by ethno-religious values. Rooted in the centrality of familial responsibilities, Italian men sought to ensure the continuation of a work culture that allowed them to fulfill their duties as fathers and husbands. Far from being simply a means of subsistence, labor was actually "an integral part of an individual's responsibility" to the all-important family.[61] Whereas radicalism could potentially disrupt an environment conducive to ethnic preservation, conservative unionism allowed workers to protect their health and economic livelihoods and, in effect, protect their families. Both the mine and the church represented obligations in service to the family—and, presumably, to God.[62]

Religion thus deeply colored the Italian community in Carbon County, sometimes below the surface, sometimes only emerging through family celebrations, but never abandoned. However, just as the Italian expression of Catholicism was unique among immigrant groups, so too Italian Catholicism on the Mormon frontier displayed regional peculiarities. Catholics adapted to their unusual situation in typical frontier fashion. Boundaries of religious peoplehood existed, but often they were membranes more than walls. Three Utah Italian Catholics—Clara Rugerri, Mary Juliano, and Joseph Bonacci—all demonstrate this principle in different ways.

Clara Ruggeri approached Catholicism as an outsider, but experiencing childhood in a largely Irish mining town produced in Clara a mind open to religious and cultural pluralism: "[Y]ou must remember there was no Mormon church in Park City when I was a girl. The Catholics predominated. We were used to Catholics. All of our friends, all of our companions, and playmates through grade school and high school were Catholics. I knew much more about Catholicism than I did about Mormonism. . . . There were mixed marriages in our family as long as I could ever remember."[63] After Clara married James Ruggeri, the couple moved to Carbon County. While there, her religious identity continued to be somewhat amorphous, only gradually taking shape. "I was not a Catholic," Clara told an interviewer, "but I worked in the Catholic Church organization and was a member of the Altar Society." Despite the fact that her ostensibly Catholic husband did not attend mass, Clara "was the one who did really." Only later in life did Clara make any firm commitment. "I was not baptized Catholic until after my whole family had been baptized, my two children had been baptized Catholic. . . . We had been married by a priest and so I just took some Catholic instruction."[64]

Mary Juliano's experience was in some ways the opposite of Clara Ruggeri's. Where Clara was a Mormon who drifted into Catholicism, Mary was a dedicated

Catholic who nevertheless expressed the frontier tendency to savor any available religious flavor.

> Mama and my grandma talked about Jesus. . . . Now in Hiawatha, I used to hear the Mormons singing in their church of [?] in the Sunday school, "Rock of Ages" . . . understand, Jesus loves me. But, anyway, then I'd sing those songs. I loved them because they were about Jesus. And then I'd go to Mormon Sunday School just to sing with them. . . . I've been through all the churches. I go to the Greek church for funerals, I go to the Mormon church, the Methodist church. Jesus is one, don't you see? And wherever they mention his name, I will go. I'm Catholic, yes. But if there's no Catholic church, I'll go where they talk about Jesus.[65]

On one occasion, her religious elasticity irritated a fellow Catholic. After letting a proselytizing Jehovah's Witness into her house, "someone got after to me—'What's the matter with you, you let everybody in.' 'They're human beings,'" Mary responded, "The Jesus that created me created them." Mary Juliano's piety seemed beyond doubt. She never abandoned her identity as either "Catholic" or "Italian." Yet, in a frontier community of many faiths, she was perfectly willing to express her religious devotion with any available congregation.

However visible Italian women were within the church, the religious environment in Carbon County was nonetheless fertile enough to produce men like Joseph Bonacci. The son of Vito Bonacci, Joseph was educated at the Catholic school in Price and, after completing high school, entered the seminary with the intent of joining the priesthood. Joseph described both his mother and his father as loyal Catholics, and said of himself, "I was very, very active in church. . . . I think I have a deep Catholic faith." In pursuing the priesthood, Joseph knew that he represented not just himself, but the larger Catholic world of eastern Utah, especially the Italian-dominated town of Helper. "They thought . . . this is really going to be a great honor to have a priest from Helper. They always had a great deal of respect for . . . the clergy." After much prayer and contemplation, Joseph finally decided against becoming ordained. "I worried a lot about mom and dad were [sic] very, very proud of the fact that I was going to be a priest. And for a Catholic family and they're really devout Catholics that would have been a great honor to their family. . . . And I knew that it was going to be a shock to them . . . but I still felt really comfortable calling them and telling them on the phone that I was coming home." Joseph returned to Carbon County, where he became a prominent Catholic layman, a teacher at the Catholic school, and eventually married a Catholic woman who arrived in Utah through the Extension Society.[66]

Joseph Bonacci, a man nearly devoted to the priesthood, was more aware than most of the potency of religious boundaries. And, by his own admission, the fragility of Catholicism in a Mormon-dominated cultural zone caused him to hold to his own religion with a greater intensity. "I was always concerned about that," Joseph told an interviewer. "I felt that I had to be a witness and felt that it was necessary." But even for those, like Joseph, who created a separation between themselves and religious "outsiders," amity and not animosity characterized their experiences with those of different faiths. "I never did have much difficulty with the LDS people," Joseph concluded.[67]

Stanley Litizzette captured this atmosphere of cultural coexistence better than most. He described Carbon County's religious temperament to an interviewer:

> [T]he Mormons that are here and have lived here are a type of Mormon which I don't think exist anyplace else in Utah. They're so much more liberal and Christianlike; that is, they don't hate us, they genuinely like us and we like them. That is to me the unique quality about Carbon County. . . . [L]et me put it this way, a real solid Mormon church official [never] quite trusts a born and bred Mormon bishop here in Carbon County. Contrariwise, we get very close to our Mormons here. I don't think the Catholic church ever quite trusts a Carbon County priest who breaks bread and gets along with them.[68]

Religion always remained an important element in the lives of Carbon County's residents, whether Catholic, Protestant, Greek Orthodox, or Mormon. But through Litizzette, we catch a glimpse of the flexibility and adaptability of religious identity. Enclaves in many other locations—both urban and rural, ethnic and Mormon—may have defined "religious peoplehood" strictly; Carbon County's Italians likewise preserved ethno-religious boundaries, but they also endeavored to nourish the pluralism of their social environment.

The chronicles of Clara Ruggeri, Mary Juliano, and Joseph Bonacci illustrate some of the varieties of lived experience typical of Italian Catholics on Utah's industrial frontier. As with most residents of western or rural locales, Italians constructed a community that respected their ethnic traditions while remaining open to the differences of their neighbors. The many different forums for this "lived religion" suggests that religion is malleable rather than static; that the laity define religious history as much as, and possibly more than, the clergy; that family and community, not just churches, demonstrate the marks of religious devotion; that gender produces distinct experiences for men and women; that ethnicity defines religious practice more than denomination; and that religious imagery, beliefs, and obligations may inform peoples' work lives in previously unexpected ways.

Notes

1. Alfredo Giovannoni, undated typed manuscript (TMs), Price Parish Records, Archive of the Diocese of Salt Lake City, Salt Lake City, Utah (hereafter, ADSL).

2. Alfred Giovannoni to Bishop Joseph Glass, undated typed letter, Papers of Alfredo Giovannoni, ADSL.

3. Alfredo Giovannoni, undated TMs, Price Parish Records, ADSL.

4. The vast majority of literature on immigrant religion has focused on urban communities. See, for example, Randall M. Miller and Thomas D. Marzik, eds., *Immigrants and Religion in Urban America* (Philadelphia: Temple University Press, 1977); Robert A. Orsi, ed., *Gods of the City: Religion and the American Urban Landscape* (Bloomington: Indiana University Press, 1999); Lowell W. Livezey, ed., *Public Religion and Urban Transformation: Faith in the City* (New York: New York University Press, 2000). For a general synthesis of immigrant historiography, see John E. Bodnar, *The Transplanted: A History of Immigrants in Urban America* (Bloomington: Indiana University Press, 1985).

5. On Italian-American Catholicism, see Rudolph J. Vecoli, "Prelates and Peasants: Italian Immigrants and the Catholic Church," *Journal of Social History* 2 (Spring 1969): 217–68; Silvano M. Tomasi, *Piety and Power: The Role of the Italian Parishes in the New York Metropolitan Area, 1880–1930* (Staten Island, NY: Center for Migration Studies, 1975); Robert A. Orsi, *The Madonna of 115th Street: Faith and Community in Italian Harlem, 1880–1950* (New Haven, Conn.: Yale University Press, 1985; repr. 2002). Other studies of Italian immigrant communities that highlight religion include Virginia Yans-McLaughlin, *Family and Community: Italian Immigrants in Buffalo, 1880–1930* (Urbana: University of Illinois Press, 1982); Gary Ross Mormino, *Immigrants on the Hill: Italian-Americans in St. Louis, 1882–1982* (Urbana: University of Illinois Press, 1986); Stefano Luconi, *From Paesani to White Ethnics: The Italian Experience in Philadelphia* (Albany: State University of New York Press, 2001).

6. Timothy L. Smith, "Religion and Ethnicity in America," *American Historical Review* 83 (December 1978): 1155–85, quote on 1161.

7. Ferenc Morton Szasz, *Religion in the Modern American West* (Tucson: University of Arizona Press, 2000), 33.

8. Carol L. Jensen, "Deserts, Diversity, and Self-Determination: A History of the Catholic Parish in the Intermountain West," in *The American Catholic Parish: A History From 1850 to the Present, vol. 2*, ed. Jay P. Dolan, 139–269 (New York: Paulist Press, 1987).

9. Donna R. Gabaccia, "Worker Internationalism and Italian Labor Migration, 1870–1914," *International Labor and Working-Class History* 45 (Spring 1994): 64.

10. David Montgomery, *The Fall of the House of Labor: The Workplace, The State, and American Labor Activism, 1865–1925* (New York: Cambridge University Press, 1987), 71–81.

11. Humbert S. Nelli, *From Immigrants to Ethnics: The Italian Americans* (New York: Oxford University Press, 1983), 41.

12. Mary Angotti Palomi, interview by Leslie Kelen, September 19, 1987, Interviews with Italian Americans in Utah, MS 516, Special Collections, Marriott Library, University of Utah (hereafter, Mary Palomi interview).

13. Filomena Fazzio Bonacci, interview by Leslie Kelen, September 18, 1987, Interviews with Italian Americans in Utah, MS 516, Special Collections, Marriott Library, University of Utah (hereafter, Filomena Bonacci interview).

14. Ibid.

15. Tony Priano, interview by Allan Kent Powell and Philip Notarianni, April 16, 1976, (hereafter, Tony Priano interview); Utah State Historical Society, Salt Lake City, Utah (hereafter, USHS).

16. Vito Bonacci, interview by Leslie Kelen, September 18, 1987, Interviews with Italian Americans in Utah, MS 516, Special Collections, Marriott Library, University of Utah (hereafter, Vito Bonacci interview).

17. Tabulation of census data from the collection, "Peoples of Utah," MSS B 239, Box 2, Folder 15, USHS.

18. Szasz, *Religion in the Modern American West,* 4.

19. Father Dennis Kiely to the Society for the Propagation of the Faith, in *The Frontiers and Catholic Identities,* ed. Anne M. Butler, Michael E. Engh, S.J., and Thomas W. Spalding, C.F.X., 79–85 (Maryknoll, NY: Orbis Books, 1999), quote on 80–81.

20. Stanley Litizzette, "Biographical Sketch of Caterina Pessetto Bottino," TMs, (n.d.), MSS A 2319, USHS.

21. E. B. Lebvina to Bishop Joseph Glass, May 15, 1919 and Lebvina to Glass, July 27, 1917, Price Parish Records, ADSL.

22. Francis C. Kelly, *The Story of Extension* (Chicago: Extension Press, 1922), 97.

23. Salt Lake City *Intermountain Catholic,* April 13, 1918.

24. The photo is reproduced in Butler, Engh, and Spalding, eds., *The Frontiers and Catholic Identities,* 99.

25. "Report of 1922 Missionary Trip," TMs, St. Anthony's Parish File, ADSL.

26. Bernice Maher Mooney, "The Americanization of an Immigrant, the Rev. Msgr. Alfredo F. Giovannoni," *Utah Historical Quarterly* 60 (1992): 168–86, quote on 170.

27. Donald G. Watt, *A History of Carbon County* (Salt Lake City: Utah State Historical Society Press, 1997), 238.

28. Alfredo Giovannoni to Bishop Joseph Glass, undated typed letter, Papers of Alfredo Giovannoni, ADSL.

29. Clara Ruggeri, interview by Allen Kent Powell and Philip Notarianni, August 27, 1975, MSS A 2787, USHS (hereafter, Clara Ruggeri interview); Marion Bonacci Lupo, interview by Allan Kent Powell and Philip Notarianni, August 6, 1975, MSS A 4048, USHS (hereafter, Marion Bonacci Lupo interview); *The Sun* (Price, Utah), December 19, 1929 and Gov. George H. Dern to Alfredo Giovannoni, November 22, 1929, Papers of Alfredo Giovannoni, ADSL.

30. Watt, *A History of Carbon County,* 240.

31. Mooney, "The Americanization of an Immigrant," 178.

32. Peter R. D'Agostino, "The Scalabrini Fathers, the Italian Emigrant Church, and Ethnic Nationalism in America," *Religion and American Culture* 7 (1997): 121–59, quote on 133–34.

33. Il Console Di S. M. Il Re D'Italia to Bishop J. J. Mitty, October 6, 1928, Papers of Alfredo Giovannoni, ADSL.

34. Bishop Thomas A. Becker, "American Bishops and Pastoral Care of Italians, 1884," in *Keeping Faith: European and Asian Catholic Immigrants,* ed. Jeffrey M. Burns, Ellen Skerrett, and Joseph M. White, 163–64 (Maryknoll, NY: Orbis Books, 2000).

35. Vecoli, "Prelates and Peasants." Although somewhat dated, Vecoli's article remains one of the best overviews and descriptions of the "Italian Problem."

36. Jacob Riis, "Feast Days in Little Italy" (1899), in Burns, Skerrett, and White, eds., *Keeping Faith: European and Asian Catholic Immigrants,* 167–73; quotes on 168, 169–70.

37. Robert Orsi, "Everyday Miracles: The Study of Lived Religion," in *Lived Religion in America: Toward a History of Practice,* ed. David D. Hall, 3–20 (Princeton, N.J.: Princeton University Press, 1997), quotes on 6, 7.

38. Yans-McLaughlin, *Family and Community,* 34.

39. Mormino, *Immigrants on the Hill,* 105–106.

40. Quoted in Orsi, *The Madonna of 115th Street,* 77.

41. Colleen McDannell, "Catholic Domesticity, 1860–1960," in *Religion and American Culture: A Reader,* ed. David G. Hackett (New York: Routledge, 1995), 305.

42. Gunther Peck, *Reinventing Free Labor: Padrones and Immigrant Workers in the North American West, 1880–1930* (New York: Cambridge University Press, 2000), 117, 129.

43. The photograph and description are provided in Watt, *History of Carbon County,* 164.

44. Vito Bonacci interview.

45. Marzio Barbagli and David Kertzer, "An Introduction to the History of Italian Family Life," *Journal of Family History* 15 (1990): 371.

46. Clara Ruggeri interview.

47. Nelli, *From Immigrants to Ethnics,* 133.

48. Quoted in Yans-McLaughlin, *Family and Community,* 85.

49. Clara Ruggeri interview.

50. Mary Palomi interview.

51. Mary Juliano, interview by Leslie Kelen, May 2, 1987, MS 516, Interviews with Italian Americans in Utah, Special Collections, Marriot Library, University of Utah (hereafter, Mary Juliano interview).

52. Mary Palomi interview.

53. Anne M. Butler, "Western Spaces, Catholic Places," *U.S. Catholic Historian* 18 (Fall 2000): 29.

54. Stanley V. Litizzette, *A Catholic History of North Carbon County* (Helper, Utah: Pecauh Printing, 1974), 6. Copy in Merrill Library, Special Collections, Utah State University, Logan, Utah.

55. Tony Priano interview.

56. Marian Bonacci Lupo interview.

57. Clara Ruggeri interview.

58. For a further description, see Philip F. Notarianni, "Italian Fraternal Organizations in Utah, 1987–1937," *Utah Historical Quarterly* 43 (Spring 1975): 172–78.

59. Steve Siporin, "Folklife and Survival: The Italian-Americans of Carbon County, Utah," in *Old Ties, New Attachments: Italian-American Folklife in the West,* ed. David A. Taylor and John Alexander Williams, 81–93 (Washington, D.C.: Library of Congress, 1992), Edna Romano quote on 90, author's quote on 82.

60. Vito Bonacci interview.

61. Orsi, *The Madonna of 115th Street,* 197.

62. On the labor movement in Carbon County, see Allan Kent Powell, *The Next Time We Strike: Labor in Utah's Coal Fields, 1900–1933* (Logan: Utah State University Press, 1985). For another study that makes a similar argument for a different Catholic ethnic group, see David M. Emmons, *The Butte Irish: Class and Ethnicity in an American Mining Town, 1875–1925* (Urbana: University of Illinois Press, 1989). For a further discussion of religion and labor for Carbon County's miners, see Matthew Pehl, "Visions of Two Gods: Religion, Class, and the Italian Community of Carbon County, Utah, 1900–1930" (masters thesis, Utah State University, 2003).

63. Clara Ruggeri interview.

64. Ibid.

65. Mary Juliano interview.

66. Joseph S. Bonacci, Interview by Leslie G. Kelen, September 18, 1987, Interviews with Italian Americans in Utah, MS 516, Special Collections, Marriott Library, University of Utah.

67. Ibid.

68. Stanley Litizzette, interview by Allan Kent Powell, n.d., MSS A 2781, USHS.

"For Both Cross and Flag"
Catholic Action in Northern California during the 1930s

William Issel

The separation of church and state has been a central principle of American life since the Bill of Rights became part of the Constitution in 1791. However, concern about the interconnection of politics and religion predated the Constitution by more than a century, and today Americans continue to debate the extent to which religious faith should guide public policy. This chapter seeks to recover a forgotten segment of this aspect of American cultural history by focusing on one area of the West. It relates the story of the origins, development, and consequences of a campaign in northern California when the men and women activists of Catholic Action worked to infuse everyday life and public policy with Catholic Christian principles. During the 1930s and beyond, they worked to neutralize those tendencies in American life that Walter Lippman, in his 1929 work *A Preface to Morals* famously identified as "the Acids of Modernity."

On May 12, 1935, Sylvester M. Andriano gave the commencement address at St. Mary's College in Moraga, a community located east of San Francisco. A 1911 graduate of St. Mary's, Andriano spoke on "Catholic Education and the Lapse of Catholic Action." Six days later, Archbishop John J. Mitty thanked the San Francisco attorney and added that he was "delighted beyond measure" with the talk. A lay activist for years, Andriano founded and presided over the Young Men's Institute Forum and the Laymen's Retreat Movement. In 1922, the Italian-born attorney (he became a naturalized citizen in 1914) founded the Dante Council of the Knights of Columbus (K of C) affiliated with the Italian national parish operated by Salesian priests in the city's North Beach neighborhood. In 1937, Mitty appointed Andriano director of the Holy Name Society, and in January 1938 the Archbishop asked Andriano to head a new Catholic Action men's organization. James L. Hagerty, a philosophy professor at St. Mary's College, was named executive secretary of the new group.[1]

Hagerty edited the *Moraga Quarterly*, a journal of literary and social criticism that addressed Catholic readers throughout northern California. In 1939, the *Quarterly* published a recent speech by a young San Franciscan, a speech devoted to "the preparation for entrance into the field of labor relations" and titled "The Catholic College Graduate and Labor." The author was John F. (Jack) Henning, a recent St. Mary's College graduate who later became the head of the California State Federation of Labor as well as Undersecretary of Labor in the Kennedy and Johnson administrations. Henning argued that, "The army of the Church is today engaged in a stern struggle" and "the need of the Catholic Church for an articulate laity in Labor is too gigantic to question." He stressed that Catholics in labor relations needed to fight both "American Way" individualism and the "painted panaceas" of "the land of Communism or the land of Fascism." Henning praised "those who act only as the voice of the membership, the voice of the rank and file, who administer their offices upon the direct rule of the majority of the membership." He also urged Catholics in the labor movement to avoid red baiting: "question the motives of those leaders who brand every militant surge of rank and file activity the result of 'red agitation.'" Catholic workers should endorse genuinely democratic unionism and become involved with the "Association of Catholic Trade Unionists, the Catholic Worker movement, and other similar enterprises which sponsor Catholic labor schools."[2]

During the 1930s, Sylvester Andriano, James Hagerty, Jack Henning, and numerous Catholic men and women campaigned for Catholic Action. In concert with their Archbishop Mitty, they saw themselves engaged in a struggle against secularism, materialism, fascism, and communism. The activists combined zeal to revitalize their personal faith with a determination to be politically influential. The California activists took their charge from Pope Pius XI's calls for revitalization of the Church's mission as outlined in series of encyclical letters from 1922 to 1937 (*Ubi Arcano Dei Consilio* [1922], *Quas Primas* [1925], *Non Abbiamo Bisogno* and *Quadragesimo Anno* [1931], and *Divini Redemptoris* [1937]). Their campaign was a northern California expression of an important but neglected cultural dynamic of the New Deal era.

The Catholic Action campaigns have been ignored in general histories of the period from the Great Depression to the Cold War. Even historians of the American Catholic experience have failed to appreciate the significance of the grassroots campaigns for Catholic Action. The secondary literature on Catholicism in the United States pays scant attention to this initiative, which took place at the very moment that Catholics abandoned their "immigrant church" mentality and moved into to the mainstream of American public life. Sometimes, Catholic Action work complemented the work of liberals in the New Deal and post–New Deal period; this was particularly the case with Catholic social welfare and labor relations efforts, although tensions over the balance of local, state, and federal control of welfare existed. Sometimes the principles of Catholic activists clashed with the priorities of other, secular and liberal, supporters of Franklin D. Roosevelt's liberal Democratic coalition. This was the case with their opposition to communists in the labor movement, their condemnation of the Loyalist side in the Spanish Civil War, and their opposition to birth control.[3]

This examination of the complex intersections of religion and politics focuses on the grassroots and examines the Catholic Action campaign in the Archdiocese of San Francisco. During the period the Archdiocese contained 171 parishes, some six hundred priests, and over four hundred thousand Catholics living in thirteen Bay Area counties from Santa Clara in the south to Mendocino in the north. Four interrelated projects comprised the agenda of the northern California Catholic Action campaign. This chapter touches briefly on each in the interest of suggesting the broad outlines of this Church and lay endeavor: 1) revitalization of religious practice; 2) social welfare reform; 3) the Catholic labor movement; and 4) public policy lobbying efforts by the Church and by lay Catholic organizations.

I.

The Catholic Action campaign began on May 7, 1932, with a speech by Coadjutor Archbishop John J. Mitty at a reception for the Archdiocesan Council of the National Council of Catholic Women (NCCW). Five weeks earlier, Mitty had arrived from Salt Lake City to take up his new responsibilities under Archbishop Edward J. Hanna (Mitty succeeded Hanna when he retired in March 1935). During his first weeks in San Francisco, Mitty corresponded with John J. Burke, the general secretary of the National Catholic Welfare Conference (NCWC), about the need to intensify the Church's efforts to mobilize laymen and laywomen in legislative lobbying. Burke shared with Mitty his pleasure at having the complete text of the papal encyclical *Quadragesimo Anno* published in *The Congressional Record* for the first time. He urged Mitty to take pains to convince Bay Area men and women to write to their congressmen and senators opposing legislation such as the Sheppard-Towner Maternity Bill. That bill and others, according to Burke, "assumes for the Federal Government an authority and an administration which our Federal Constitution never contemplated, and its gross paternalism [is] particularly injurious in that it moves farther away from the individual citizen that civic responsibility which rests upon him and of which he should be actively conscious." Burke also urged Mitty to encourage Catholics' opposition to a

Senate bill, still in subcommittee, that, given its origins in the lobbying of "Mrs. Sanger," would "promote the propaganda of birth control."[4]

In the May 7 speech that initiated his Catholic Action campaign, Mitty told the NCCW women in his audience that he wanted "greater effort and activity on your part" to monitor and shape the work of "our State Legislature and our National Congress." "You have to take an active part [to] prevent over central-ization and too much bureaucracy [and] bills [that] totally ignore fundamental Christian and American principles." Then Mitty moved beyond political action and called for a broad campaign on several fronts. "Catholic Action" the Arch-bishop reminded his audience, "has been preached to us in season and out of season" and it was time to move beyond rhetoric to practice. "Our aim [in this campaign] is to bring the ideals and principles of Christ into every phase of hu-man life, into our own individual life, into family, social economic, professional, political and national life. We are striving to advance the interests of Christ, to bring the spirit of Christ into our homes, our reception halls, our workshops, our offices, our legislative assemblies. We have a duty to make a contribution of Christian ideals and principles to the nation." The "purpose and object" of lay organizations, Mitty stressed, "is not political. Neither as a Church nor an organization are we interested in any political aim or any political party." How-ever, "We cannot live as if we were not part of the country" and we must "work unceasingly for both Church and country, for both Cross and Flag."[5]

In his position as Coadjutor Archbishop, Mitty continued to boost the ex-pansion and activism of the NCCW. By the end of 1934, with the support of Archbishop Hanna, who served as chairman of the Administrative Committee of the NCWC, all thirteen counties of the Archdiocese had established chapters. The work proved slow and difficult, as suggested by a Mrs. W. H. Culigan in a let-ter to the Archbishop in March 1933. We have "a hopeless case here in Santa Clara," she claimed, because of "too much foreign element and too few women of the stamp needed to get together a suitable quorum for organization." In San Francisco, where the campaign proved most successful, the Archdiocese spon-sored the first regional conference of the NCCW in February 1933, highlighted by a "mass meeting" at the War Memorial Opera House in the Civic Center. In May 1933, the Industrial Problems Committee of the Archdiocesan NCCW cosponsored, in conjunction with the Social Action Department of the NCWC, an Industrial Problems conference in the city. By February 1935 an estimated 4,652 women belonged to twenty-one of the forty-five parish women's organiza-tions affiliated with the NCCW. Another 6,679 women held membership cards in the thirty-three nonparochial NCCW affiliates (the largest groups were the

Loyola Guild, the alumnae of Sacred Heart Convents, and the Ladies Auxiliary of the Apostleship of the Sea). Despite the apparent success of the campaign, the group's secretary, Christine Regan O'Toole, urged the Archbishop to continue his appeal for participation during his annual address to the local NCCW "because so many are present, who are indifferent to the work of the Council."[6]

II.

Catholic Action during the last three years of Archbishop Hanna's service (1932–34) and during Archbishop Mitty's tenure (1935–60) developed through the efforts of women like Christine Regan O'Toole and men like Jack Henning and Sylvester M. Andriano. They built the infrastructure of their lay organizations in a process that included cooperation with the Chancery office and deference to the hierarchy's authority. However, the initiatives of the Archdiocese and the work of O'Toole, Andriano, and others did not take place in a vacuum, because like other residents of San Francisco and the Bay Area they found themselves forced to meet the challenges posed by the Pacific Coast maritime strike from May through July of 1934. Catholic Action in the labor field took shape as activists sought to implement the policies of Pius XI in competition with communist and other leftist activists involved in the dramatic struggle over power on the waterfront. On June 9, at the end of the first month of the strike by longshoremen and sailors, the official Archdiocesan newspaper presented the Church's point of view in a front-page editorial on "The Maritime Strikes." "The rights of the ship-owners over their ships do not give them the right to impoverish the whole community; nor do the rights of the striking workers include the right to pursue their aims regardless of the consequences to the third party in the dispute, namely the people who are not directly involved, but whom depend upon cargoes for their livelihoods and sustenance." The *Monitor* urged, "all Catholics, who are employers, or who are in any way directly connected [with management] to read and know the contents of the encyclicals . . . that treat of the problems of capital and labor . . . and to acquaint their associates and acquaintances with the contents of these encyclicals and to give them copies of them." According to the editorialist, should Catholic San Franciscans fail in this duty "then those Catholics will be held to answer."[7]

In addition to prescribing the moral responsibility of all San Franciscans to involve themselves personally in helping to settle labor conflicts according to Catholic principles, the editorial alerted Catholics to the particular danger posed by extremism:

Shipowners have a perfect right to refuse to deliver the management of their business to a soviet. Longshoremen have a perfect right to organize in a union

Sylvester Andriano, Jack Henning, and Archbishop Mitty continued their working relationship beyond the 1930s. When the archbishop celebrated the Golden Anniversary of his ordination and his thirty years as bishop and archbishop (1926, Salt Lake City; 1935, San Francisco) at a banquet in the Sheraton Palace Hotel on October 25, 1956, Andriano sat on Mitty's right and gave the keynote address, and Henning, seated on Mitty's left, served as toastmaster. Photo permission of San Francisco History Center, San Francisco Public Library.

and to bargain collectively for wages and hours that will enable them to support their families in frugal comfort, to educate their children, and to lay something by for sickness and old age. But these rights are obscured because of the laissez faire extremists on the one hand and the communist fanatics on the other. The public has had enough of both. . . . We regret that hate motivates both of these groups. The Communists hate injustice more than they love justice. The ruthless "individualists" among employers do not consider justice at all, but hate all who check their lust for power and money.

San Franciscans needed to organize a Catholic counterforce:

If Christian workers would stem the tide of Communism, they must bring to the workers' cause as devoted an energy and as strict a discipline as members of the Communist Party manifest. Communism is a religion—a materialistic religion [and] appeals to many workers because the apostles of Communism work with a zeal worthy of a better cause. They can be challenged and checked only by men, who for the love of God study the Catholic teaching as thoroughly as Communists study the Communist theory; who devote as much energy to the propagation of the principles contained in the encyclicals on labor as the Communists do in spreading the doctrine of Marx; who labor as industriously to apply Catholic principles as the Communists work to apply the principles of Lenin.

During the worst violence of the waterfront strike, from July 3 to July 5, Archbishop Hanna invited economist Sam Kagel and unionist E. B. O'Grady to Archdiocese headquarters and personally urged them to do what they could to stop the bloodshed. On July 13, with the city in the throes of a general strike, Hanna addressed San Franciscans in a speech broadcast over radio stations KGO, KPO, and KFRC. Returning to the themes enunciated in his newspaper's June 9 editorial, the Archbishop explicitly endorsed both labor unions and collective bargaining, and condemned employer exploitation that ignored "the human character of the worker." Then, in a blunt rejection of the Communist Party slogan "class against class," Hanna criticized unionists who premised their activities on the necessity of "conflict between class and class," and warned leftist unionists that, "rights must be religiously respected *wherever* they are found." Both sides in the waterfront strike, Hanna insisted, should move quickly to accept the results of arbitration, keeping in mind the "underlying principles which have ever been the teaching of Christianity during 2,000 years."[8]

The parties involved in the waterfront strike settled the dispute during the next two weeks. Catholic activists who were close to the Archbishop played key roles. Michael J. Casey, a long-time president of the local teamster's union and confidant of Archbishop Hanna, opposed the General Strike of July 16 to 19. He failed to stop it, but he did convince the five teamster delegates to the Labor Council's General Strike Committee to vote against the citywide shutdown. Casey's influence helped shape the divided vote on the General Strike: 315 yes, 245 abstain, and 15 no. Another Catholic activist, lawyer Francis J. Neylan, used his influence to assemble the recalcitrant shippers at his home in suburban Woodside. He served them a "cold water lunch," and he argued that continuing to hold to a union-busting position and refusing to compromise would cause long-term harm to the city's economy and business prospects. Neylan convinced them to move to the center and endorse a moderate settlement. Finally, the National Longshoremen's Board, on which Archbishop Hanna served, added its influence on the side of compromise. The strike settlement realigned the relationship between organized labor and business in the direction called for by Catholic leaders. Business leaders agreed to arbitration. They expressed a public commitment to respect the rights of labor and to treat workers with dignity. They also pledged themselves, in the words of the Chamber of Commerce president, "to see that those isolated instances in which labor has been exploited shall be corrected."[9]

Working closely with the Church and local government, moderates from business and labor constructed the settlement and brought the strike to an end. These leaders, and the city press, particularly the *Monitor,* immediately set to work representing the settlement as a victory for business unionism, with its emphasis on putting pork chops on the table, and a defeat for radical unionism, with its call for proletarian revolution in the streets. The city's voters expressed their moderate character in many ways, perhaps none more dramatically than by reestablishing the right to peaceful picketing by unions while at the same time consistently choosing moderate businessmen over leftist reformers for mayors and supervisors. Tension persisted in the city's public life. Business leaders' rhetorical affirmation of labor's rights clashed with their practical desire to limit union power, but the Catholic principles that had shaped the outcome of the Great Strike became increasingly a part of San Francisco's public culture in the decades to come.[10]

III.

When Archbishop Mitty took office in March 1935, he followed up on the waterfront strike settlement by encouraging additional lay activism on the political and cultural fronts. Support for patriotism and opposition to communism constituted an important element of this effort. On March 22, the Archbishop encouraged local participation in the "proposed mobilization plan of the Knights of Columbus." The San Francisco efforts paralleled the national "Mobilization for Catholic Action" drafted by William P. Larkin and distributed by the K of C Supreme Council in New Haven, Connecticut. Demonstrating the executive abilities that would be a hallmark of his entire tenure, the new Archbishop, through Rt. Rev. Monsignor Richard Collins, State Chaplin, fostered "A Plan for the Knights of Columbus in California."[11] Drafted by State Deputy William T. Sweigert of San Francisco, the seven-page Plan outlined an ambitious program: "**The present loose association of councils must be replaced by something more sensible and more conducive to progress and action.**" San Francisco Knight Edward Molkenbuhr, chairman of the Department of Parish Cooperation and Catholic Activities, explained that the purpose of "the mobilization of Catholic man-power" was "to effectually [sic] combat the destructive forces and the 'isms' [sic] that are becoming so rampant, and which are undermining Christianity and the welfare of nations." Pleased that "the Knights of Columbus have had bestowed upon them the appellation, 'Standard Bearers of Catholic Action,'" Molkenbuhr urged "every member of our Order to enlist under this banner, and zealously work in its interest."[12]

Molkenbuhr and his colleagues, along with numerous lay volunteers, worked closely with the Archbishop to limit the influence of the Communist Party during the next several years. Archbishop Mitty also made common cause with the American Legion, of which he had served as director of the California department of the organization in 1935, as well as with several local business leaders affiliated with the Industrial Association of San Francisco. On January 5, 1936, at the golden jubilee dinner of the St. Vincent de Paul Society, the Archbishop spoke out against "a new philosophy abroad in the world today, the philosophy of the Totalitarian State." Under the bold headline "Communism, a Monstrous Evil," he published his speech alongside a reprinting of Pope Leo XIII's encyclical *Quod Apostolici Muneris* in the official newspaper on Washington's Birthday. In June, in a speech that brought the Regional Catholic Conference on Industrial Problems to a close, the Archbishop argued that "we cannot put religion in one compartment and industry in another, and social amusements in another, and political and legislative in another. Religion is worthless unless it has its message for human beings in every phase of human life [and] before we can attempt a satisfactory solution of the problems of industry . . . we need a renewal of the Christian spirit in our own hearts and our own souls."[13]

The chief target of anti-Communist effort in the Bay Area was Harry Bridges, the Australian-born head of the new International Longshoremen's and Warehousemen's Union (ILWU). The Archbishop, Jack Henning, and the other leading Catholic labor activists opposed the Communist Party's agenda in the ILWU, but they refused to endorse the campaigns to deport Bridges. Henning and Mike Casey (until his death in May 1937) maintained cordial relations with Bridges. The records of the American Communist Party (CP) and related Comintern files on the American party, recently opened to historians in Moscow, indicate that Bridges was, in fact, a member of the Central Committee of the American CP. However, the new evidence does not support the claim that the Party controlled Bridges or that Moscow gold financed the ILWU's work.[14]

To his credit, the Archbishop refused to encourage the personal vilification and character assassination of Bridges practiced by the most aggressive of the local superpatriots. Mitty also decided, after an investigation that yielded ambiguous information about the personal history of the organizers, not to affiliate the Church with an American League against Communism that appeared in the city in 1936. However, he did assist in the organization of a "United Front" against "Radical and Communistic Activities," which had been organized by the American Legion, the K of C, the Ancient Order of Hibernians, and the Young Men's Institute. In addition, Mitty received detailed reports of the activities of several Communist Party activists in San Francisco from private investigators hired by Hugh Gallagher, chairman of the Pacific American Ship-owners Association. When Communist Party front organizations successfully attracted hundreds to public meetings in 1936 and 1937, the Archdiocese responded with programs that drew thousands to Kezar Stadium and the Civic Auditorium. At the Kezar Stadium event, Mitty forthrightly condemned "appeals to class warfare" and the "philosophy that at once blasphemes Christ and aims to destroy our Government." [15]

Then, in 1938, Jack Henning, John F. Maguire, and Laura Smith organized a San Francisco chapter of the Association of Catholic Trade Unionists (ACTU). [16] The new organization, its membership restricted to Catholics, ratified a constitution that declared its purpose in language that Henning used in his St. Mary's College speech: "To foster and spread . . . sound trade unionism built on Christian principles." The ACTU program drew upon Catholic labor teachings and stressed both the rights and the duties of workers. The rights included job security; an income high enough to allow a family to live a decent life; collective bargaining through independent, democratic unions; a decent share in employer profits; and the right to strike and picket for a just cause, a just price, and decent hours and working conditions. Duties included performing an honest day's work, joining a union, striking only for a just cause, refraining from violence, respecting property rights, living up to agreements freely made, enforcing honesty and democracy in the union, and cooperating with employers in establishing industry councils and producer cooperatives. In San Francisco and elsewhere, the ACTU sponsored educational programs designed to increase the number and influence of Catholic unionists as organizers, officers, and negotiators. Later, in 1948, the local chapter amended the constitution to add clauses requiring "strict honesty within the union and a square deal for everybody regardless of race, color, or creed" and prohibiting membership to anyone "who is a member of any subversive organization." [17]

Archbishop Mitty gave the ACTU his "wholehearted approval," and he gave his blessing to Rev. Hugh A. Donohoe's request to serve as its chaplain, the only ACTU office that was not an elective position. Initially, the Archbishop instructed Donohoe to steer the ACTU away from "political activities and from possible difficulties between various labor organizations." However, as Mitty became convinced of the ACTU's commitment to the spread of unionism based on Christian principles, he quickly recognized the organization's potential to counter the influence of communism within the local labor movement, and gave it his unreserved full support. The ACTU received public praise as an excellent example of the type of Catholic worker societies called for by Pius XI in *Quadragesimo Anno*. Business leaders received assurance that the new organization had

Members of the ACTU posing on the steps of St. Mary's Cathedral after a Labor Day Mass, ca. 1950, with Auxiliary Bishop Hugh A. Donohoe, first chaplain of the organization front row center. Photo from the author's collection.

the endorsement of the Archdiocese. Catholic workers received encouragement to join the organization.[18]

John F. Maguire served as president of the ACTU during its active years from 1939 to the mid-1950s. Like Hugh Donohoe and John Shelley of the American Federation of Labor County Council, Maguire was a graduate of St. Paul's grammar school in San Francisco's heavily Catholic Mission District. By 1944, ACTU membership within the Archdiocese had swelled to the point where a second chapter was established in Oakland. The Oakland chaplain was Father Bernard Cronin, a graduate of the archdiocesan Social Action School for Priests.[19] After twenty-five years of operation, some 750 applications had been distributed and six hundred union members joined and paid dues, though monthly meetings and communion breakfasts typically attracted fewer than two dozen activists. By the time Laura Smith, a retail clerk's union member who had been a founding member, closed the checking account in 1963, the group had been largely inactive for five years.[20]

During its first decade, San Francisco ACTU members self-consciously drew upon principles of Catholic Action to make a difference in the San Francisco labor movement, particularly on the waterfront. The longshoremen's unions dominated the organization, with the 274 members from the ILWU divided as follows: 191 from Local 10, and sixteen from Local 6. Another sixty-seven belonged to Warehouse Union Local 34. Fifty teamsters from Local 85 belonged to the ACTU, as did forty retail clerks from Local 1100. The building trades unions, which also enrolled large numbers of Catholic members, were poorly represented, perhaps due to the fact that the Communist Party had not targeted the trades in the way it had the maritime unions. The most dramatic evidence of the ACTU's work occurred in Local 10 of the ILWU, where ACTU members made a concerted effort to compete with left-wing candidates for local offices. Harry Bridges, international president of the ILWU, scoffed at charges that he operated a communist dictatorship and boasted of his union's democratic procedures. Bridges had a point. In 1943, James Stanley Kearney, who joined the ACTU in early 1940, ran against Communist Party member Archie Brown in the election for Local vice president. Kearney won the election. Then, during the subsequent twenty-seven years, Kearney won elections for nine one-year terms as the president of Local Ten. This record is more impressive than it may appear at first glance, because the union bylaws required incumbents to stand down after each term to keep a president from succeeding himself. When Kearney died suddenly in 1970 he was still serving as president, and the entire waterfront shut down in honor of his memory. It is not surprising that Paul Pinsky, the director of the Research Department of the ILWU, sent an informant to ACTU meetings who took notes on the proceedings. Kearney's Catholic Action leadership style, like that of George Bradley, another Local 10 officer and ACTU activist, has been ignored in previous accounts of the ILWU. When Catholic activists have been acknowledged, the pejorative phrase "right-wing faction" is often used.[21] As a consequence of such biased interpretations, the importance of Catholic Action in the work of the San Francisco ACTU activists has been forgotten, their religious principles and motives ignored; when mentioned at all, they have been vilified as misguided anti-Communists.[22]

IV.

The efforts of Jack Henning and his colleagues to bring Catholic Action into the labor movement by means of the ACTU were matched on another front by the work of Sylvester Andriano and James L. Hagerty. They pursued the Catholic Action agenda through the medium of a new organization called The Catholic Men of San Francisco. Andriano graduated from St. Mary's College in 1911, Hagerty in 1919. Andriano immersed himself in his San Francisco law practice, in the public affairs of city government, and in the North Beach Italian American community. His civic appointments were noteworthy: Mayor James Rolph appointed Andriano to the Board of Supervisors, and Angelo Rossi, mayor from 1931 to 1943, appointed his friend and personal attorney Andriano to the Police Commission. When Mayor Rossi assembled a Citizen's Committee of twenty-five during the "July Days" of the 1934 strike, he appointed Andriano one of the members. Andriano later recalled being the sole pro-union voice in an otherwise hostile business and professional group; he vigorously and successfully argued that the mayor should not request a martial law proclamation from Governor Merriam. In contrast to Andriano's active public life, Hagerty, a bachelor, pursued a more contemplative career devoted to his students and to the cause of Catholic Action. He began teaching at his alma mater immediately after receiving his baccalaureate degree, earned an M.A. in 1921, and commenced a career as a philosophy professor at St. Mary's that continued until his death in 1957. Hagerty edited the *Moraga Quarterly* from its first issue in 1930 through the years of World War II.[23]

Two years before Hagerty received his bachelor's degree, Andriano and a partner established an Italian Catholic Union in North Beach and the group began publication of a weekly newspaper, *L'Unione;* the Archdiocese assumed responsibility for the weekly in 1927. Andriano maintained a residence in the Italian town where he was born, Castelnuovo Don Bosco. In 1931, during a summer trip to Italy, he "became really interested in Catholic Action and upon my return to San Francisco undertook the study of it in earnest." In 1935 Andriano spoke at the Archbishop's request on Catholic Action to the graduating class at St. Mary's, and in the following year the Archbishop asked him to address the combined Catholic high school graduation ceremony at the city's Dreamland Auditorium. Andriano's high school commencement address came four weeks after the nationwide radio broadcast of Baltimore's Auxiliary Bishop John M. McNamara's speech at the annual University of Notre Dame reunion in Washington, D.C. McNamara renewed the call for laymen and laywomen to "share in [the mission of the hierarchy] . . . to promote the good of human society throughout the world and to combat the evils which make for its destruction." By this time, Hagerty and Andriano had formed a Catholic Action prayer and study group, and they asked Archbishop Mitty to approve and endorse plans for a more extensive program of study and action. While impressed with their zeal—Mitty observed that "Mr. Andriano has probably read everything that has been published on the subject and has the Catholic ideal of it"—the Archbishop proceeded cautiously. Mitty dispatched Rev. Thomas N. O'Kane of St. Joseph's

College to meet with Andriano and Hagerty and their colleagues "so that the group would keep within the reservation."[24]

By the autumn of 1937, Andriano and Hagerty had met with the pastors of each of the sixty parishes in San Francisco to solicit support for a citywide Catholic Action lay organization, and presented the Archbishop with a draft "Plan for Catholic Action." In the introduction to the "Plan," the authors defined the problem and outlined a solution: "Despite flowery statements perhaps Catholicity is not making much progress. Perhaps barely holding its own. Perhaps really losing. Not only in numbers but also in fervor and fidelity. Birth Control, Practical cessation of immigration, the American materialistic environment, atheistic anti-clericalism. The old self-sacrificing, self-denying Catholicity would seem to be rapidly dying out. A fervent few . . . an overwhelming majority of normal Catholics. Communistic propaganda may have made far more inroads than it appears. AND NOW THE SUGGESTED REMEDY. The best defense is an attack. *Systematic, co-ordinated, directed, expository, Nationwide evangelization.* Under direction and control of the Apostolic Delegate and Bishops."

The plan of action called for a *"constant, patient, consistent Crusade."* This included a diocesan "truth crusade," diocesan mission bands of priests who are "young, zealous, enthusiastic Americans," and an adaptation of Mormon and various other missionary methods for laymen and laywomen. It also involved an education strategy, such as pamphlets and lectures and Catholic shelves in public libraries. The goal: "Arousing the zeal of pastors for this work by propaganda, assistance, suggestions, and contact."[25]

On December 22, 1936, the Archbishop invited several dozen men from throughout the city for a meeting in the basement of St. Mary's Cathedral to discuss "uniting the parishes of San Francisco in a definite program of Catholic Action." In addition to representatives from the largest parishes, the invitation list included high-ranking officers from the more important municipal government departments and executives from the city's largest and most prestigious business firms. Most of the men who attended this first meeting on February 12, 1937 continued to gather every other week during that year for focused discussions on how to move from the theory of Catholic Action to the practice. Then, on the Feast of the Epiphany, January 6, 1938, between two hundred and 250 men gathered in the Cathedral basement and formally inaugurated The Catholic Men of San Francisco. James L. Hagerty announced that, "Confirmation is the Sacrament of Catholic Action, making men soldiers" and suggested that the assembled volunteers should regard themselves as part of the "priesthood of the layman." The Rt. Rev. Monsignor Charles A. Ramm stressed that "personal sanctification [is] necessary in order that the Holy Ghost might find them fit to be the instruments of the work; second, the necessity of remembering that this 'participation in the apostolate' meant the saving of souls to compose the Mystical Body of Christ."[26]

Mitty appointed Sylvester Andriano and James Hagerty to the positions of president and executive secretary of the new organization, and in March, Andriano traveled to Rome to secure official Vatican approval of the Catholic Action initiative in San Francisco. Pope Pius XI gave the group his blessing, and Cardinal Giuseppe Pizzardo, the chief assistant for Catholic Action in Italy, and Monsignor Luigi Civardi, author of the official *Manual of Catholic Action* (1935), assured the San Franciscan that his plan was a sound one. On October 29, 1938, the eve of the Feast of Christ the King, Archbishop Mitty announced that, "I like to sum [Catholic Action] up in one phrase: That what the Holy Father wants you to do is to vitalize your religion, make it something really vital in your lives." The Archbishop criticized the notion that,

> Religion is not supposed to come out of that [certain limited] compartment and overflow into our being. We have a feeling of inferiority about religion, due to an historic situation where we were out-numbered. But there is no necessity for it today. Human life has been practically denuded of Christian principles. What the pope wants is to vitalize them. That is the meaning of Catholic Action—no more, no less . . . in doing that we not only make a contribution to the progress of the Church, but we are making a substantial contribution to the welfare of our own land, a contribution to America which it badly needs; we are making a contribution to human civilization, until we bring about a right balance between material and spiritual things, which are going topsy-turvy.[27]

From 1938 until the beginning of 1942, when World War II sidetracked their work, Andriano and Hagerty gradually built up the numbers and expanded the activities of the organization at the citywide and parish level. The Archdiocesan Council operated as a Bay Area lay interest group, working with the K of C and Ancient Order of Hibernians. They successfully lobbied for local ordinances prohibiting sexually explicit magazines in sidewalk news kiosks and magazine racks, and they boycotted movies that sympathized with the Spanish Republic or included licentious behavior on the screen. Parish Councils, charged with organizing Catholic Action Circles in each of the city's sixty parishes, pursued a three-part agenda of devotional revitalization involving individual sanctification, sanctification of the home, and sanctification of society. The program included participation in parish holy hour devotions; regular celebration of annual feast days; daily blessing of homes, grace before meals, family communion, and renewal of marriage vows; parish Sunday mass crusades aimed at increasing regular attendance and limiting latecomers and those leaving early; use of the missal; and active participation in rosaries, benedictions, and stations of the cross. By mid-1941, according to an official report, 90 percent of the parishes in the Archdiocese, 160 parishes, had established Catholic Action Circles involving 1,500 men and three hundred women. Catholic Action schools for parish priests and parochial school teachers operated in San Francisco, Alameda, San Mateo, and Santa Clara counties. The Archdiocese published a local manual for Catholic Action work, as well as the booklet "Catholic Action and the Priest," by Rev. John J. Hunt, the group's chaplain. The Archdiocesan Council published a monthly newsletter and operated a Speakers Bureau that dispatched lecturers to meetings and radio programs in all the Bay Area counties. St. Patrick's Seminary in Menlo Park added a required Catholic Action course to its curriculum and Bay Area Catholic high schools established student Catholic Action Circles.

Attorneys in the organization established a separate Catholic lawyer's guild called the St. Thomas More Society. The lawyers organized a Spanish Relief Committee and raised funds for reconstruction of battle-scarred communities. In 1937, the Committee published *Democracy! Which Brand, Stalin's or Jefferson's.* The author was Umberto Olivieri, a professor at the Jesuit-run Santa Clara University. Sylvester Andriano wrote the preface, arguing that "the Red Government of Spain, far from being the champion of democracy, is a regime of tyranny, persecution and barbarism and the only hope for the triumph of order and justice and of true democracy lies with the Nationalists." One leading attorney in San Francisco, John Francis Neylan—who, like Andriano, had close personal ties with Archbishop Mitty—lashed out at the New Deal with particular fury. He did so on the grounds that it violated morally acceptable relations between the central government and American citizens. Neylan served as general counsel to William Randolph Hearst's business empire from 1925 to 1935, and did so with considerable intensity. In a lengthy address to the San Francisco Bond Club on April 28, 1938, titled "The Politician—the Enemy of Mankind," he excoriated "mad schemes and ambitions which are fundamentally responsible for the amazing conditions existing in this country today." Neylan especially castigated "the multitudinous schemes of spending public money" by "the coterie that has controlled patronage, appropriations and relief expenditures." [28]

V.

Archbishop Mitty's Catholic Action campaign encompassed legislative activism in addition to building a Catholic labor movement and encouraging laymen and laywomen to revitalize their personal faith and become political activists dedicated to infusing public life with Catholic principles. During his first year in office, the Archbishop delegated legislative work to Monsignor James Cantwell, a member of the Archdiocesan staff. Cantwell worked with pastors of northern California parishes to develop a database that could be used during political campaigns. The priests responded with information on the socioeconomic background, religious affiliation (and sometimes local gossip), and voting records of members of the California State Assembly and Senate in counties within and beyond the Archdiocesan boundaries. From 1935 to 1939, Andrew R. Johnson, a San Francisco realtor and insurance broker, monitored the legislature's activities and lobbied in Sacramento on behalf of the interests of the Archdiocese. Attorney Andrew Burke, a member of the law office of Garret W. McEnerney, the counsel for the Archdiocese, worked with Johnson in Sacramento. They were thus no strangers to taking stands on politics. In the late 1930s, for example, Burke and McEnerney played key roles in the national campaign to deny Franklin D. Roosevelt a third term because, like numerous Catholic critics across the country, they regarded FDR's attempts to "pack" the Supreme Court a sure sign of his dictatorial propensities. During the first four years of Mitty's tenure, Burke and Johnson kept Mitty apprised of the introduction of numerous bills and solicited his advice on how to proceed during the legislative process. In 1935, for instance, Mitty opposed a bill that never passed but would have created a State Department of Eugenics with responsibility for forced sterilization of prison and mental hospital inmates. During the second half of the decade, the Archbishop attempted unsuccessfully to convince bishops in the other dioceses to cooperate with him in coordinating legislative work on behalf of the Church in California. He attempted to improve the efficiency of the Church's organized lobbying activities, and he tried to eliminate duplication of effort between diocesan legislative representatives and lobbyists from the Knights of Columbus. Although a variety of measures met defeat due to lobbying directed by the Archbishop, notably a law to empower the State Board of Education and State Superintendent of Schools to approve private school curricula, Mitty's attempts to improve organized Catholic legislative work at the state level seem to have been only partially successful.[29]

If the success of Archbishop Mitty's efforts to improve the effectiveness of legislative lobbying at the statewide level yielded ambiguous results, the outcome of Catholic Action–oriented political work in San Francisco was more positive. In 1937 and 1938, Mayor Rossi signed into law a spate of antismut and antiprostitution ordinances; these were passed by the city Board of Supervisors after being introduced by board members close to Sylvester Andriano. Although primarily symbolic (and often not enforced in years to come), they did signify that the city respected Catholic principles. In 1939, Catholic Action won another victory. The Catholic Men of San Francisco convinced the administration of the upcoming Golden Gate International Exposition to cancel an exhibit in the Hall of Science sponsored by the Birth Control Federation of America. Margaret Sanger happened to be speaking to the League of Women Voters of San Francisco the same week that the Exposition announced the cancellation of the birth control exhibit. Sanger expressed her disappointment to a reporter for the *People's World,* the local Communist Party newspaper: "Wherever I go I meet the same opposition—and I must say that it is most insidious and effective." [30]

Conclusion

This study of the Catholic Action campaign in northern California is meant to contribute to a growing scholarship based on detailed empirical research in local sources about the ways that Americans motivated by religious beliefs sought to influence public life during the period from the Great Depression to the Cold War. The historical literature about this era, while rich in many ways, has tended to neglect Catholic activism as a source of public policy innovation. When Catholic political action does make an appearance in the literature, it typically figures either as an aspect of "American Conservatism" or appears in biographies of unrepresentative persons such as the demagogue Father Coughlin or the inspirational Dorothy Day. However, the evidence from San Francisco, and recent work based on the cases of Pittsburgh, Pennsylvania; St. Paul, Minnesota; and Providence, Rhode Island provide an alternative approach. In his book *A Catholic New Deal,* Kenneth Heineman demonstrated the powerful influence of the Catholic Church and Catholic laymen and laywomen in shaping the New Deal in the Steel City. The St. Paul and Providence cases are illuminated in Mary Wingerd's *Claiming the City: Politics, Faith, and the Power of Place in St. Paul* and Evelyn Savidge Sterne's *Ballots and Bibles: Ethnic Politics and the Catholic Church in Providence.* They provide striking evidence of the influence of the Catholic faith in St. Paul's and Providence's cultural and social history from the late nineteenth century to the New Deal era. The evidence from northern California, Pittsburgh, St. Paul, and Providence is powerful, extensive, and suggestive. Additional research into Catholic Action campaigns at the grassroots may well result in assigning greater importance to the role that religion played in American culture during this important period in the twentieth century, especially the complex intersection of religion and politics. [31]

A vignette from the biography of one of the city's most influential political figures in the post–World War II years, Joseph L. Alioto, illustrates the post-1930s importance of Catholic Action. Eighteen months after Sylvester Andriano's 1935 commencement address at St. Mary's College, a St. Mary's student from North Beach named Joseph L. Alioto delivered a prize-winning speech in San Francisco.

Catholic Action work in San Francisco parishes continued after World War II and stimulated devotional practices that involved thousands of the city's Catholics. In this July 21, 1947, photograph, residents of the city's Sunset District marched in procession during the annual Novena to St. Anne. Photo permission of San Francisco History Center, San Francisco Public Library.

A future mayor of San Francisco, Alioto graduated in 1937 and then earned a law degree at the Catholic University of America in Washington, D.C. Alioto's philosophy professor James L. Hagerty published his student's 1936 speech. Alioto's title was "The Catholic Internationale," and he used his talk to warn his audience at the St. Ignatius Council of the Young Men's Institute that "Communism has attained the position of a universal power [and] stands today as a cancer in the world's social organism." Given its international scope and its appeal as a "counterfeit religion," Alioto claimed that only a true religion "that is likewise international" would be able "to cut away this cancerous growth." He concluded that "[t]here is only one power in the world which answers that description: the Roman Catholic Church. The battle lines . . . are clearly marked: It is to be the Catholic Internationale arrayed against the Communist Internationale; Rome against Moscow; Christ against Anti-Christ." Six years later, Alioto spoke on "The American Catholic Tradition" at the First Regional Catholic Congress. Archbishop Mitty organized the event in connection with the wartime Bishop's Committee to Unite the Catholic Youth of America. In subsequent years after World War II, as a member of the city's Board of Education and Redevelopment

Agency, Alioto drew upon principles of Catholic Action in his public policy activities. In 1967, voters elected Alioto to the mayor's office, where he continued to draw inspiration for public policy from Catholic principles. Veterans of the Catholic Action campaign of the 1930s would have appreciated the combination of magnanimity and Machiavellianism evident in the new mayor's appointment of several Old Reds, including Harry Bridges, to important San Francisco city commissions.[32]

Notes

1.   John J. Mitty to Sylvester Andriano, May 18, 1935, Correspondence files, 1935, Folder A, Chancery Archives of the Archdiocese of San Francisco (hereafter, CAASF); *Monitor*, May 11, 1935; Sylvester Andriano to James L. Hagerty, March 10, 1935, Box 237, James L. Hagerty Collection, St. Mary's College Archives.

2.   Jack Henning, "The Catholic College Graduate and Labor," *Moraga Quarterly* 3 (Spring 1939): 165–70.

3.   On Catholic Action in the local labor movement, see William Issel and James Collins, "The Catholic Church and Organized Labor in San Francisco, 1932–1958," *Records of the American Catholic Historical Society of Philadelphia* 109 (Spring and Summer 1999): 81–112. A revised and expanded version of that article, William Issel, "A Stern Struggle: Catholic Activism and San Francisco Labor," appears in *American Labor and the Cold War: Grassroots Politics and Postwar Political Culture*, ed. Robert Cherny, William Issel, and Kieran Taylor (New Brunswick, N.J.: Rutgers University Press, 2004). For another study that includes evidence of the influence of Catholic social thought in the city's public life, see William Issel, "Business Power and Political Culture in San Francisco, 1900–1940," *Journal of Urban History* 16 (November 1989): 52–77. On Catholic Action more generally, see Joseph P. Chinnici and Angelyn Dries, eds., *Prayer and Practice in the American Catholic Community* (Maryknoll, N.Y.: Orbis Books, 2000), 115–79; Joseph P. Chinnici, O.F.M., *Living Stones: The History and Structure of Catholic Spiritual Life in the United States*, 2nd ed. (Maryknoll, N.Y.: Orbis Books, 1996), 166–213; Jeffrey M. Burns, *Disturbing the Peace: A History of the Christian Family Movement, 1949–1974* (Notre Dame, Ind.: University of Notre Dame Press, 1999), 13–18. See also Dennis Michael Robb, "Specialized Catholic Action in the United States, 1936–1949: Ideology, Leadership, and Organization" (Ph.D. diss., University of Minnesota, 1972); Jay P. Dolan, *In Search of An American Catholicism: A History of Religion and Culture in Tension* (New York: Oxford University Press, 2002), 154–55, 157, 160, 177–78, 186–87; and John T. McGreevy, *Catholicism and American Freedom: A History* (New York: W.W. Norton, 2003), chaps 5 and 6. Monsignor Francis J. Weber, Archivist of the Archdiocese of Los Angeles, chronicles some forty projects in *Examples of Catholic Action in the Archdiocese of Los Angeles* (Mission Hills, Calif.: Saint Francis Historical Society, 2003).

4. John J. Burke to John J. Mitty, February 5, 1932; May 6, 1932; May 23, 1932, Correspondence files, 1932, NCWC Folder 1, CAASF.

5. Sermon by Coadjutor Archbishop John J. Mitty to the Council of Catholic Women, May 7, 1932, Mitty Sermon Collection, CAASF.

6. [Mrs.] W. H. Culigan to Dear Archbishop, March 29, 1933; Announcement of the First Regional Conference of the NCCW, both in Correspondence files, 1933, NCWC Folder 2, CAASF; Christine Regan O'Toole to Most Reverend John J. Mitty, February 15, 1935; "Catholic Action," n.d., four-page report by the Archdiocesan Council, both in Correspondence files, 1938–39, NCCW/NCCM Folder 2, CAASF.

7. *Monitor*, June 9, 1934. Quotations in the next paragraphs are from this front-page editorial.

8. *San Francisco News*, July 14, 1934. Sam Kagel, interview by author, June 15, 1998. Hanna, having been involved in a variety of labor arbitration roles during the 1920s (at a time when many leftist unionists spelled arbitration "arbetraytion"), was then serving on President Franklin Roosevelt's National Longshoremen's Board. Kagel and O'Grady served on the Joint Maritime Strike Committee. See David F. Selvin, *A Terrible Anger: The 1934 Waterfront and General Strikes in San Francisco* (Detroit: Wayne State University Press, 1996), 100, 159.

9. John W. Mailliard, quoted in *San Francisco News*, July 23, 1934; Kagel interview; Neylan letters, John F. Neylan Collection, Bancroft Library, University of California at Berkeley (BL); Selvin, *Terrible Anger*, 169.

10. For a detailed analysis of these developments see William Issel, "New Deal and World War II Origins of San Francisco's Postwar Political Culture," in *The Way We Really Were: The Golden State in the Second Great War*, ed. Roger W. Lotchin, 68–92 (Urbana: University of Illinois Press, 2000), and William Issel, "Liberalism and Urban Policy in San Francisco from the 1930s to the 1960s," *Western Historical Quarterly* 22 (November 1991): 431–50.

11. Jeffrey M. Burns, "Mitty, John Joseph," in *The Encyclopedia of American Catholic History*, ed. Michael Glazier and Thomas J. Shelley, 967–68 (Collegeville, Minn.: Liturgical Press, 1997); "Life Summary of Archbishop Mitty," *Monitor*, August 31, 1935, 2.

12. William T. Doyle to John J. Mitty, March 22, 1935; "A Plan for the Knights of Columbus of California"; "Plan for Council Participation, Knights of Columbus, Mobilization for Catholic Action," all in Correspondence files, Knights of Columbus Folder, 1933–36, CAASF (boldface in original); Edward Molkenbuhr, "Catholic Action in Our Order," *Knights of Columbus Historical Review* (1936): 35.

13. "Address at St. Vincent de Paul Golden Jubilee Dinner," January 5, 1936, Mitty Sermons, CAASF; *Monitor*, February 22, 1936; "Closing Address, Regional Catholic Conference on Industrial Problems," *Monitor*, June 9, 1936.

14. Robert W. Cherny, "Harry Bridges and the Communist Party: New Evidence, Old Questions; Old Evidence, New Questions," paper delivered at the annual meeting of the Organization of American Historians, April 4, 1998, copy in author's possession. See also Harvey Klehr, John Earl Haynes, and Fridrikh Igorevich Firsov, *The Secret World of American Communism* (New Haven, Conn.: Yale University Press, 1995), 104.

15. Author's interview with Jack Henning, October 7, 1998, San Francisco. Joseph S. Connelly to Rev. Dr. Thomas A. Connolly, August 31, 1936; Ret. Rev. Thomas A. Connolly to Joseph S. Connelly, September 2, 1936; Hugh Gallagher to Most Reverend John J. Mitty, June 5, 1936, August 3, 1936, November 2, 1936; "9th Convention of Communist Party in America," handwritten notes, September 1936; "Special Memorandum in re: Harry Bridges," October 25, 1936; "San Francisco Mailing List of the American Friends of the Soviet Union," n.d.; John J. Mitty to My dear Jim, November 13, 1936, marked "confidential"; John J. Mitty to Rev. Bryan J. McEntegart, April 14, 1937, all in Correspondence files, 1936, Communism 1936–37 Folder, CAASF. *San Francisco Chronicle,* October 25, 1936; *San Francisco News,* April 29, 1937.

16. Henning interview. Laura Smith to Msgr. Connolly, enclosing a copy of a mimeographed pamphlet, "It's Our City Too," September 26, 1938, Labor file, 1934–1939, CAASF; Gus Gaynor, Brotherhood of Railway Clerks, press release dated October 18, 1938 in Labor file, 1934–1939, CAASF.

17. "ACTU Preamble, Constitution, Pledge" and "Proposed Changes . . . San Francisco Chapter 6," mimeo, July 8, 1948, Labor Management School Records/ACTU, Archives of the University of San Francisco (hereafter, ACTU Records).

18. *Monitor,* September 9, 1939; May 10, 1941; August 28, 1943; November 18, 1944; April 26, 1947; March 5, 1948. John J. Mitty to Hugh Gallagher of Matson Navigation Co., March 20, 1941, Labor file, 1939–1943, CAASF.

19. *Monitor,* January 15, 1944.

20. Data on the ACTU is from the organization's membership and dues ledgers, checking account statements, attendance lists at meetings, and correspondence in the ACTU Records. At the point of its greatest activity, the organization had 599 dues paying members; I have been able to identify the union affiliations of all but sixty-four members.

21. Data on Kearney's and Bradley's electoral successes in Local 10 is from the subject card files and from various issues of the union's newspaper *The Dispatcher* in the ILWU's Anne Rand Library. Handwritten notes taken at ACTU meetings are in the Paul Pinsky Collection, Northern California Labor Archives and Research Center, San Francisco. That the leftist officers of the ILWU's International organization took the ACTU considerably more seriously than have subsequent historians is evident from the research director's careful monitoring of its activities during the late 1940s. See Howard Kimeldorf,

Reds or Rackets?: The Making of Radical and Conservative Unions on the Waterfront (Berkeley: University of California Press, 1988), 138, 150.

22. Kearney's Catholicism is ignored altogether by historian Howard Kimeldorf, as are the dozens of ILWU members who paid dues to the ACTU as well as to the ILWU. Kearney does merit a mention as a popular officer of Local 10 and one of many Catholic officers in various CIO unions in Vincent Silverman's recent book. Silverman, however, does not take the religious character of the ACTU seriously, characterizing it wholly negatively as an anti-Communist outfit. He is dismissive toward Kearney's Catholicism and the work of the ACTU in San Francisco on the basis of oral history testimony by a single informant. To his credit, Silverman is forthright about his point of view: "I grew up almost instinctively hating such nefarious figures as Walter Reuther, James Carey, and Joe Curran." Vincent Silverman, *Imagining Internationalism in American and British Labor, 1939–49* (Urbana: University of Illinois Press, 2000), xi, 130, 242.

23. *St. Mary's Collegian*, September 13, 1957; Sylvester Andriano to James L. Hagerty, March 10, 1943, Hagerty Collection, St. Mary's Archives; e-mail letter from Rose Marie Cleese (Angelo Rossi's granddaughter) to Bill Issel, January 24, 2002.

24. Cleese to Issel, January 24, 2002; "Bishop McNamara Defines Catholic Action in Address at Notre Dame U. Reunion," *Monitor*, May 2, 1936; John J. Mitty to Sylvester Andriano, March 4, 1936, Correspondence files, 1936–37, Folder A; John J. Mitty to Rev. Thomas N. O'Kane, October 7, 1936, letter marked Confidential, Correspondence files, Catholic Action 1936–1940 Folder, CAASF.

25. "Plan for Catholic Action," Correspondence Files, Catholic Action 1936–1940 folder, CAASF; Andriano to Hagerty, March 10, 1943, Hagerty Collection, St. Mary's Archives (emphasis in the original).

26. John J. Mitty to various addressees, December 22, 1936, Correspondence files, Catholic Action Folder, 1936–1940, CAASF; uncorrected draft "Catholic Action Group" marked "News item: *The Monitor*," and attached typewritten notes of January 6, 1938 meeting in Catholic Action Folder 1936–1940, CAASF.

27. John J. Mitty, "Address on Catholic Action," October 29, 1938, Mitty Sermons and Addresses, CAASF; Sylvester Andriano to Most Reverend and dear Archbishop, May 19, 1938, Correspondence files, Catholic Action 1936–1940 Folder, CAASF; Mgr. Luigi Civardi, *A Manual of Catholic Action* (1936; New York: Sheed and Ward, 1943).

28. James L. Hagerty to Most Reverend John J. Mitty, March 28, 1938; Catholic Men of the Archdiocese of San Francisco, "Summary of State of Organization Following Spring Series of District Meetings, 1941," both in Correspondence files, Catholic Men Folder 1, 1938–1941, CAASF; John J. Hunt, *Catholic Action and the Priest* (San Francisco: Archdiocese of San Francisco, 1938); John J. O'Connor, "Emphasis on Action," *St. Anthony Messenger* (February 1942); Sylvester Andriano to James L. Hagerty, March 10, 1943, Hagerty Collection, St. Mary's Archives; Umberto Olivieri, *Democracy! Which*

Brand, Stalin's or Jefferson's? (San Francisco: The Spanish Relief Committee of San Francisco, 1937); John Francis Neylan, "The Politician—Enemy of Mankind," address delivered at the San Francisco Bond Club Luncheon, April 12, 1938, privately printed, copy in the Neylan Collection, BL.

29. The archival evidence regarding this subject is limited and further research needs to be done before a more definite conclusion can be offered about Mitty's degree of success in influencing state legislation and improving the efficiency of the Church's statewide lobbying efforts. The following letters provide evidence of the complexity of the issues: John J. Mitty to Most Reverend Robert Armstrong, D.D., March 18, 1939; John J. Mitty to Most Reverend John J. Cantwell, D.D., January 6, 1937; John J. Mitty to Hon. Culbert L. Olson (governor of California), November 27, 1939, all in Correspondence Files, Legislature 1935–1939 Folder 2, CAASF. See also Msgr. James Cantwell to various pastors and letters from pastors to Cantwell, various dates in 1935, in Correspondence files, 1935–1939, Legislature Folder, 1935–39, Folders 1 and 2, CAASF; Andrew Burke to Most Reverend John J. Mitty, March 26, 1935, CAASF. See also Christine Rosen, *Preaching Eugenics: Religious Leaders and the American Eugenics Movement* (New York: Oxford University Press, 2004), 139–64.

30. Sue Barry, "News and Views," *People's World*, May 22, 1939; Anthony B. Diepenbrock to Board of Directors, Golden Gate International Exposition, March 4, 1939, Correspondence Files, Golden Gate Exposition Folder 1, 1939–1940, CAASF.

31. Two groundbreaking studies present the case for reorienting American intellectual history during this period in such a direction. See Christopher Shannon, *A World Made Safe for Differences: Cold War Intellectuals and the Politics of Identity* (Lanham, Md.: Rowman and Littlefield, 2001) and Eugene McCarraher, *Christian Critics: Religion and the Impasse in Modern American Social Thought* (Ithaca, N.Y.: Cornell University Press, 2000). See also Mary Lethert Wingerd, *Claiming the City: Politics, Faith, and the Power of Place in St. Paul* (Ithaca, N.Y.: Cornell University Press, 2001); Evelyn Savidge Sterne, *Ballots and Bibles: Ethnic Politics and the Catholic Church in Providence* (Ithaca, N.Y.: Cornell University Press, 2004); and Kenneth J. Heineman, *A Catholic New Deal: Religion and Reform in Depression Pittsburgh* (University Park: Pennsylvania State University Press, 1999).

32. Joseph L. Alioto, "The Catholic Internationale," *Moraga Quarterly* 7 (Winter 1936): 68–72; *Monitor*, March 21, 1942. For more on Joseph L. Alioto, see William Issel, "Joseph L. Alioto," *Scribner Encyclopedia of American Lives* (New York: Charles Scribner's Sons, 2002), 5: 10–11; and William Issel, "'The Catholic Internationale': Mayor Joseph L. Alioto's Urban Liberalism and San Francisco Catholicism," *U.S. Catholic Historian* 22 (Spring 2004): 99–120.

Into One Parish Life
National Parishes and Catholic Racial Politics at Midcentury

Gina Marie Pitti

I n November 1950, a committee of seven Spanish-speaking Catholics in San José, California, dispatched a petition to their Archbishop, John J. Mitty of San Francisco. Signed by almost 2,500 Mexican and Mexican American residents, the document asked Mitty to establish a Mexican national parish in their neighborhood. The petition read in part:

> For years it has been the longing of many of the Spanish-speaking families in this city and other surrounding communities, (in its great majority Mexicans), who are permanent residents and some of whom own their homes, to have, like they have in other cities, a church of their own where they can worship God according to their traditions and customs.[1]

This petition represented an important community protest against the institutional marginalization of Mexican Americans within the Catholic Church. The wartime and post–World War II years have been called the "Golden Age" of Northern California Catholicism, when the Archdiocese of San Francisco launched numerous church-building projects to serve the rapidly growing Catholic population. However, few churches could be found in most Mexican American neighborhoods during the 1940s.[2] Patterns of residential settlement and segregation had long relegated Mexicans to the poorer outskirts of developing cities like San José, leaving them marginalized in both a civic and ecclesiastical sense. For instance, the closest Catholic church to the primary Mexican American barrio in San José was Five Wounds, located more than two miles away—a prohibitive distance for the many residents who did not own cars. Furthermore, as a national parish serving Portuguese Americans, its devotions, church services, and activities were conducted primarily for the benefit of that ethnic community.[3]

In petitioning Mitty for a "church of their own," the Mexican parishioners of San José sought the same treatment that the Catholic Church had long sanctioned for other immigrants and ethnic minorities in the region. By the end of World War II, the Archdiocese of San Francisco had at least eighteen national parishes. Stretching from San José to San Francisco to Oakland, these churches served primarily German, Italian, French, and Portuguese immigrants.[4] At the national level, such ethnic-specific parishes had long been the Catholic Church's solution to a diverse immigrant population. As early as 1788, national parishes had emerged in the Northeast to help European immigrants adjust to, and integrate into, American Catholic life.[5] By the early twentieth century, they were a fixture of urban Catholic life. Given the long history of establishing churches for a single ethnic group, there was good reason for Mexican American Catholics to expect that the Archbishop would approve their request for such a parish. Instead, their petition was swiftly denied.

On the surface, this failed petition appears to be nothing more than a footnote in the history of Mexican American Catholicism. The entire episode lasted a scant two months and ended in rebuff. Why, then, does this story matter? Chicano historians and other scholars have often cited these events as evidence of the Church's lack of true interest in Mexican Catholics.[6] Certainly, this incident offers insight into the institutional relationship between the Catholic Church and Mexican Americans, but only if it is read against a backdrop of developments in both the Catholic Church and the Mexican American community in northern California during the mid-twentieth century.

This story unfolds against the new social, economic, and political changes wrought by World War II. The war refashioned the West as a region and transformed the lives of residents there, as federal military contracts and wartime production demands altered the region's demographic profile. These wartime changes energized the Catholic Church in California. In Northern California, the population of the Archdiocese of San Francisco—which comprised some of California's most important metropolitan as well as economic centers, including San Francisco and Oakland—tripled between 1935 and 1961. Dozens of new Catholic schools and parishes, high rates of Mass attendance, a full seminary, and Church influence in the civic sphere all indicated that Catholicism was thriving in the immediate postwar years.[7]

Meanwhile, the war had transformed the state's Mexican American communities as well. In addition to stimulating European American and African American migrations, the state's labor needs lured Mexican immigrants and Mexican Americans to both rural and urban areas. Although Los Angeles remained the

Southwest's largest Mexican American city, Northern California was becoming an increasingly important site of Mexican settlement, drawing newcomers from Mexico, southern California, Texas, and other southwestern states. These new arrivals to northern California settled in *colonias* (communities) in San José, Decoto, Gilroy, Mountain View, Stockton, and Modesto.[8]

Mexican labor migrations were processes that accelerated and took on a greater national importance as part of the transformation of the American West. More than changing demography characterized the region in this era, however. California witnessed a new confrontational ethno-racial politics, symbolized most famously by the 1943 Zoot Suit Riots. These high-profile attacks on Mexican American youth by military servicemen in Los Angeles dramatized the hostility and discrimination that Mexican-origin residents faced daily. Such incidents galvanized Mexican American politics in the 1940s. Juxtaposing this and other incidents of racial violence against wartime rhetoric about unity and democracy on the home front, ethnic Mexican activists in the 1940s fought for inclusion into the institutions that had historically excluded them.

These incidents also prodded California civic and religious leaders to allot greater consideration to their Mexican and Mexican American constituents. Indeed, across the country, the wartime era invigorated the Catholic Church's interest in this population, its fastest growing minority. Along with his fellow prelates in San Antonio, Texas, and Yakima, Washington, Archbishop John Mitty put his San Francisco Archdiocese at the forefront of innovative missionary efforts. Mitty pioneered new approaches to the challenge of Mexican American ministry, including one of the Catholic Church's first coordinated pastoral programs for Spanish-speaking farmworkers.[9]

The local priests involved in these new missionary programs were deeply concerned with civil rights, race relations, and inequality. So too, of course, were the ethnic Mexican activists who organized to challenge continuing inequalities within the Church. As a result of this shared preoccupation with social justice issues, a dynamic relationship developed between priests and the laity. Marked by both conflict and collaboration, this ongoing interaction made the Catholic Church a vital public space in working-class immigrant Mexican communities.

The relationship between parishioners and clergy illuminates the larger significance of this story. All too often, Chicano history has left religion unexamined or characterized it primarily in terms of its devotional and cultural importance to Mexican Americans. Religious history, meanwhile, has downplayed the presence—and even more, the activism—of Mexicans and Mexican Americans, treating them most typically as missionary subjects. However, in the late 1940s and early 1950s, religion would prove central to the expression of Mexican American protest. The era's campaigns for social justice were not, of course, simply the products of Anglo Catholic progressivism. Rather, ethnic Mexicans—recent immigrants and longtime residents, U.S. citizens and Mexican nationals alike—were essential players.

As the national church episode illustrates, the early postwar parish was one place where both Mexican Americans and their pastors addressed issues of discrimination, parity, and inclusion. The dramatically different arguments embedded in the national church petition and the Archdiocese's response suggest that this incident should be understood primarily as an ideological clash over the best approach to enacting racial justice. Although both the laity and clergy acknowledged the reality of anti-Mexican discrimination, they defined different avenues and priorities for addressing it. Most fundamentally, then, this episode illuminates the racial and ethnic politics that marked both the Church and Mexican American communities in the West at midcentury. These politics in turn emerged out of Mexican American community organizing efforts and Catholic engagement with new intellectual, theological, and political currents of the day.

Ethnic Mexican Activism

The 1950 petition to Archbishop Mitty represents an early example of social activism and community organizing by Mexicans in the postwar period. In 1950, San José had a year-round population of perhaps fifteen thousand ethnic Mexicans. Initially, local residents simply sought more consistent ministry than the infrequent parish mission or Spanish-language devotions that priests at two churches, Five Wounds and Holy Family, were able to offer. Such limited outreach meant that many Mexican Catholics rarely attended their local parish, a fact that caused great consternation to both Church officials and Latino coreligionists. Church leaders frequently blamed an innate Latin American casualness toward the sacramental obligation, but parishioners themselves pointed to institutional neglect: too few churches in Mexican neighborhoods, a shortage of Spanish-speaking clergy, and a weak commitment to the needs of the Mexican American population. As one immigrant, Juanita Álvarez, reflected several decades later, "I felt that they put Latinos to the side."[10] Álvarez's complaint gave voice to her and her compatriots' sense that their native church treated them more like visitors than full members of the parish.

Some Mexican and Mexican American Catholics challenged their exclusion and neglect by "voting with their feet," attending Protestant services or no church at all. In the early 1950s, one San José woman told sociologist Margaret Clark that "lots of times they [her neighbors] just didn't go to church. Then the Protestants started coming around and inviting the people to go to their churches. Plenty of times they tried to get me to go, and if the fathers hadn't come about that time, we would all be *Protestantes* now!" [11]

Her allusion to the belated arrival of Catholic personnel in the neighborhood referred to recent campaigns by local residents. By the 1940s, a group of Mexican and Mexican American Catholics—mostly women—had concluded that, "the need for a special church on the Eastside [of San José] was obvious." [12] After several years of independently arranging neighborhood devotions, catechism, social welfare services, and children's recreation in their neighborhoods, lay leaders like Leta Elizondo, Macaria de la O, Clare Guidotte, and Naomi and Mercedes Berryessa now hoped to organize a more formal Catholic presence in East San José.

In the late summer of 1949, these women asked Archbishop Mitty to assign a pastor to their neighborhood. Mitty, already formalizing a plan to establish a traveling "mission band" of Spanish-speaking priests, refused the request. Although rebuffed, the activists did not abandon their goal of instituting formal Catholic religious services in East San José. By the end of 1949, they had persuaded a local Jesuit to celebrate a monthly Mass in a building that they had rented from a neighborhood burial aid society. [13]

But these activists soon set their sights higher, on the establishment of a church specifically for the Spanish-speaking population. They aimed for a church where they—not Italian, Portuguese, or Irish Americans—could hold the central share of parish life. Only this commitment of institutional resources, they suggested, would overcome their second-class status in the Church. By November 1950, a committee of four women and three men had collected 2,469 signatures on their petition and dispatched it to the Archdiocese headquarters in San Francisco.

In many ways, this story echoed the larger historical pattern by which ethnic communities mobilized for Catholic services. As Jay Dolan has observed, European immigrants typically organized groups to find a location for a church, then petitioned the local bishop for a priest of their own ethnicity, and eventually won permission for a national parish. [14] Evidently the Mexican parishioners of San José hoped to proceed along the same lines. Indeed, the San José request was not the first attempt to establish a "Mexican church" in Northern California; it followed five years after a similar proposal from parishioners in the East Bay town of Richmond.

The rhetorical strategy of the two petitions reflected the social and political consciousness of ordinary Mexican Catholic residents of Northern California. Drafted in November 1945, just after the end of World War II, the Richmond petition invoked wartime ideals of democracy, fairness, and faith in the underlying principles that governed the United States. The petitioners began by emphasizing their religious credentials, informing Mitty that they were faithful Catholics who belonged to an organized apostolic society. Even as they assured Mitty of their Catholic loyalties, they also claimed a broader social identity; their assurance that "we are able . . . [to] give to [you] many other signatures" indicated that they represented and had the support of a community that was bigger than their parish group.

However, the boundaries of this community were not necessarily defined by ethnicity or national origin. Although their Spanish surnames and request for a Capilla de Guadalupe (Guadalupe Chapel) made their ethnic background evident, the signers never once referred to themselves as Mexicans. Rather, they asserted themselves as Americans and situated their request as a fundamental civil right, declaring, "we hold our petition, in the beautiful principal of our Constitution which gives to every citizen the right of freedom of speech, freedom of religion and other rights." The petitioners further invoked a liberal faith in the power of the state by having their petition officially notarized and a copy sent to the governor of California. Such a move signaled that the request for a chapel was a civic matter and not just a religious one.[15]

The women and men who drafted the San José petition infused their appeal with a different tone, hoping to sway archdiocesan officials by drawing on familiar premises that had long justified Catholic outreach to Mexican and other immigrants. The four-page document invoked priests' longstanding concerns about the quality of Mexican faith and argued that a national parish would recuperate the community's religious dedication. The petitioners referred to the Church's preoccupation with marriage outside the Church, low rates of Mass attendance, sexual immorality, religious ignorance, superstitious practices like consulting "diviners and spiritists [sic]," and apathy, arguing that these trends were the inevitable consequences of institutional neglect. The most powerful of these arguments appealed to enduring Catholic fears of apostasy, claiming that the Church's invisibility in Spanish-speaking neighborhoods fostered Protestant conversion campaigns and threatened to divert Mexicans permanently into the Protestant fold.[16]

The committee counted on the threat of left-wing radicalism resonating equally strongly with Catholic officials. The petition raised the possibility that "communists [who] are working so hard among these people in our country" would gain a foothold among the disheartened Mexican population. Not only did this statement invoke Cold War fears of immigrant and minority radicalism, it also subtly reinforced Catholic officials' belief that the Church was the primary bulwark against socialism. These allusions were certainly timely, as news stories about "Red" agents crossing the U.S.-Mexico border stirred fears of communist influence in Latin America. More immediately, recent local labor struggles appeared to highlight the threat of radicalism in San José. Four years earlier, in 1946, a struggle between rival unions had erupted in the nearby Santa Clara Valley canneries. California growers and cannery owners had joined in red-baiting the more militant union, and they had enlisted the Church to sway the largely Catholic workforce. The day before the union vote, Catholic priests in San José had dutifully pressed workers to vote against the "subversive" local.[17] Four years later, Mexican residents of San José—some of whom no doubt were among those cannery workers—strategically brandished the same concern about radicalism as leverage in their petition for a Mexican national parish.

In addition to appealing to concerns about communism, Protestant proselytism, and flagging faith, the San José committee argued that Mexicans' presence in the body politic entitled them to certain treatment. Like the Richmond activists, San José petitioners claimed that living in the United States conferred a set of mutual rights and responsibilities on residents, regardless of citizenship status or formal political allegiance. Whereas the 1945 petition deliberately cast the call for a church as a privilege granted by the American Constitution, the San José signers wove together claims based on labor, residency, and community. They argued that their hard work, especially in farm labor, ought to win them the same religious privileges that other Catholics enjoyed. The petition referred to the many residents who "labor on their knees, accompanied by their young children, in the wet fields in cold winter and under the scorching sun in summer, picking vegetables and fruits for our tables—whose ancestors helped with their gold, prayers, and sacrifices the great Missionaries from Spain."[18]

This history, the petition implied, gave workers a claim on the region's wealth that they had helped create through many lifetimes' worth of unrecognized, poorly compensated service. However, the document assured Archbishop Mitty that workers' poverty would not prevent them from raising the necessary funds for the proposed parish, urging him to "consider that . . . Catholics of this race are generous to their Church even when very poor."[19] In this way, petitioners openly dismissed the common charge that Mexicans failed to support their local parish; on the contrary, they declared, they sustained it.

Moreover, the petitioners argued that their longevity in the region justified the call for a parish church of their own. In addition to noting the centuries-old presence of Mexicans in Northern California, the document reminded Mitty that many current residents had lived in San José long enough to own their own homes. The testimony of homeownership no doubt was intended to persuade the Archbishop that the investment of capital and a priest would be repaid with long-term church attendance in the area. But homeownership and history also asserted to Catholic officials that Mexicans were no "birds of passage" who aspired to return to their native land.[20] Rather, they were markers of permanent residency in the United States, substantiating the declaration that Mexicans were ready for, and entitled to, a full parish life of their own.

Recently, scholars like William Flores, Renato Rosaldo, and others have identified these kind of appeals for proper treatment as cultural citizenship claims, meaning that they assert that community membership can take other forms besides legal citizenship per se.[21] Whether formally U.S. citizens or not under the law, Mexican Catholic activists insisted that they belonged in the parish and were entitled to full rights of membership and inclusion therein. These claims to cultural citizenship compose a common theme of parish activism in the mid-twentieth century. A decade later, in a similar campaign for Catholic services at St. Peter's parish in San Francisco, Isaura Michell de Rodríguez justified her compatriots' demands on the grounds that their dedication and sacrifice to their adopted country warranted a return. A resident of the city since 1943, she recalled, "I worked for the soldiers in the war, for the injured soldiers; and in general I worked six days out of the week for the soldiers who were in the war, and here there were no religious services."[22] That civic sacrifice, she maintained, gave her and her neighbors a claim on parish resources. Likewise, the San José petitioners testified that they asked for no favors, but only that for which they were entitled in exchange for their demonstrations of loyalty and labor.

While the San José committee appealed to American values and entitlements, its most controversial arguments had little to do with Americanism. Leta Elizondo and her colleagues maintained that, as immigrants, they were heirs to a different religious and linguistic heritage than European American Catholics. The petition maintained that the Mexican American community's unique cultural and religious needs, along with its daily encounter with discrimination, prevented Mexican Catholics from attaining full membership in existing Catholic parishes. The Catholic Church's traditional reliance on accommodating ethnic distinctiveness in order to evangelize immigrants had taught Spanish-speaking residents that the Church would be sympathetic to this argument.

However, the 1950 petition went beyond the assertion of ethnic difference, raising the issue of race, and especially the persistence of racial boundaries. The committee declared that they sought a "church of their own" in order to

> receive the sacrament of matrimony through a Priest of their own race who
> understands their psychology and customs and who can also read to them in
> Spanish those parts of the liturgy that may be recited in the vernacular and,

finally, where they can feel at ease in a church of their own, without fear of humiliations due to racial discrimination which unfortunately still exists even among some Catholics.[23]

Mexican American activists in San José and Richmond thus marshaled a wide array of arguments for a national church, but none of these campaigns persuaded the clergy that the Archdiocese should establish a new national church for Mexican Catholics. Except for a few pastors, like the Gilroy priest who insisted that, "the Mexican people are most welcome in the parish church," local priests did not dispute the underlying problem of Catholic discrimination and neglect. Indeed, some readily acknowledged the Church's complicity in fostering poor intercultural relations. At one archdiocesan conference in 1949, for instance, a Spanish-surnamed priest declared that it was Church officials, not just the laity, whose hostility was the "big obstacle to Mexican work—[the priests] despise them."[24]

But while sympathetic to the social isolation and unequal treatment that ethnic Mexicans faced in predominantly European American churches, priests resisted the call for a separate Mexican parish. In the political, ecclesiastical, and social climate of the early postwar years, they deemed such a church indefensible, citing reasons that ranged from the difficulty of administering such a church to its simple inappropriateness in the modern era. But the most frequent charge was that a national parish violated the Church's social justice goals. Asked his opinion on the issue, San José priest Donald McDonnell pronounced succinctly that, "The aim of work among the Spanish-speaking people in San Jose is INTEGRATION into the parish not SEGREGATION into a national parish."[25]

To priests like McDonnell, integration was the only acceptable social goal in their work with Mexican Americans. But what did integration mean? Catholic officials defined it variously in racial, cultural, community, and institutional terms. Here they were influenced by broader social currents and newly popular theological principles that suggested that separate institutional spaces contradicted both civic and parish ideals. The clergy's arguments against a Mexican parish reflected two overlapping conclusions: the Church must continue to emphasize the Americanization of immigrants, and Catholic parishes must adopt a strong stance in support of racial justice. Both of these goals helped to determine the contours of Church ministry to Mexicans and Mexican Americans in the post–World War II era. Increasingly, prelates like Mitty concluded that separate institutional spaces, even ones proposed by Spanish-speaking parishioners, contradicted both civic fairness and Catholic universalism.

Catholic Racial Progressivism

Catholic officials quickly honed in on the question of race as the very heart of the 1950 national church debate. Mexican American activists themselves had defined race as a central theme in their experience of living in Northern California during the early postwar years. Their petition emphasized not just ethnicity—their unique traditions and customs—but a more fundamental and enduring difference that separated them from other immigrant Catholics: membership in a specific racial group that was marked by a unique "psychology." With this claim, the signers suggested that their distinctiveness from European American Catholics was permanent and that this difference gave them a need for their own church as well as a "priest of their own race," not just a Spanish-speaking one.

Given the larger thrust of Mexican American politics at midcentury, this was perhaps a peculiar claim to pursue. Racial categories had long been a Mexican American political issue; for several decades, activists had fought any racial designation—whether bestowed by federal edict or popular sentiment—as nonwhite. Many in the community still believed that claiming whiteness was the only path to social equality and mobility. But the national church petition's argument that racial difference engendered certain entitlements did not necessarily require the nearly 2,500 signers to believe themselves to be members of a separate race. The question was less racial difference than racial status. Mexican Catholics' testimony about the "humiliations" they suffered in their parishes was meant to show how pervasive was white Americans' belief in Mexican racial inferiority. The petition suggested that the daily experience of racism demonstrated that Mexicans operated from a different position in the American racial hierarchy than most other Catholics. Treated poorly and apparently unwanted in European American churches, they laid claim to the right to their own protected space in which to worship.[26]

As religious historians have recently pointed out, churches are bellwethers of politics, reflecting larger debates in the public and political arena while also shaping the institutional options for responding to those debates.[27] By the late 1940s and early 1950s, Catholic leaders were actively engaged in the racial politics of the era. Interracial violence on the wartime home front had recently helped to transform the agenda of American liberalism in the 1940s, spurring the rise of a new philosophy of racial liberalism that was moderate, reformist, and focused on overcoming segregation and discrimination. John McGreevy has demonstrated that the relationship between Catholicism and American liberalism had been strained since the nineteenth century, but now Church intellectuals drew on a tradition of Catholic social teachings to lend support to new civil rights struggles.[28] In so doing, they articulated a new Catholic racial progressivism. Its origins lay in the interwar years, when what Jay Dolan has termed a "public Catholicism" emerged out of "New Deal participatory ideology and socially progressive papal encyclicals."[29] These provided the moral and intellectual rationale for Catholics to pursue social justice and social activism with vigor. By the 1950s, the Catholic Church had become a player in American reform movements, lending support to the growing call for civil rights and integration.

In Northern California, Catholic progressives linked the debate about national churches to a larger conversation about race relations in the United States. As supporters of civil rights, Archbishop Mitty's younger priests regarded arguments about permanent racial difference with dismay. If the goal of racial liberalism was to overturn segregated facilities and discriminatory statutes, then certainly progressive priests who subscribed to this viewpoint could not countenance any measure that endorsed or perpetuated separate institutions. Pastors insisted that the Church must advance race relations by tirelessly promoting racial integration. "Racial discrimination is not overcome by such segregation, even though it be voluntary," Father McDonnell explained.[30] Accordingly, he said, Archbishop Mitty must oppose the establishment of any more national parishes.

By the 1950s, many American Catholic leaders had reached the same verdict. After almost a quarter century of Catholic intellectuals advocating interracial ideals, racial integration had become a near-official Catholic position. To racial progressives declaring that, "racial prejudice must go," national parishes increasingly seemed to be an explicit challenge to civil rights goals. Catholic racial liberals now viewed national parishes as a symbol of prejudice and an "unfortunate aspect of American Catholic history."[31]

These responses signaled not only the Church's endorsement of American racial liberal principles but also a determination to define them in specifically Catholic terms. Church intellectuals claimed antiracist struggles as their own by harnessing them to the theological principle known as the Mystical Body of Christ. Grounded in the Pauline books of the New Testament and emphasizing the concept of human solidarity from the social encyclicals of popes Leo XIII and Pius XI, this theology taught that the Catholic Church was Christ's Mystical Body on earth. Through membership in the Church and the sharing of the Eucharist, all disciples of Christ were equal, regardless of race, nationality, or any other secular distinction. To Catholic racial liberals, the Mystical Body of Christ offered the ideal for community life.[32]

After its endorsement by Pope Pius XII in 1943, the theology of the Mystical Body of Christ propelled interracial ideals forward; its universalist emphasis on the "transcendent bonds . . . between all members of the Church" brooked no racial distinctions or discrimination.[33] During the 1940s and 1950s, San Antonio's Archbishop Robert Lucey relentlessly promoted the Mystical Body as a "challenge and a promise" that bound true Christians to the cause of social justice in the Southwest. Lucey called on his fellow Catholics to fight racism because

> The Catholic way of life is above all this. We hold no one in contempt because of his ancestors or the color of his skin. We recognize clearly that man is made to the image of God. . . . When Catholics indulge in the dubious luxury of hating their neighbor, they squander their inheritance as sons of God.
>
> Race discrimination must go. In this new era, the voice of humanity cries out against it. The conscience of the Church condemns it. The commandment of love will tolerate it no longer.[34]

The Mystical Body principle offered a hefty moral validation to priests who hoped to reform race relations in their parishes. During this era, race resentments and the corresponding absence of parish harmony alarmed many clergy. Not only did the Mystical Body doctrine seem to demand that churches be free of the sin of segregation, it also promised to make parish life itself the instrument of interracial harmony. It was the actual Church liturgy, Archbishop Lucey contended, that would bring people together across racial, ethnic, cultural, and class lines, making them aware that "[t]here are no minorities in the Mystical Body of Christ." Calling for Catholics to join together in "the unity of love," Lucey repeatedly reminded his audiences that "[t]he people of a parish or a community perform a social as well as a religious function by worshiping God together with their neighbors."[35]

The Texas Archbishop's ideas influenced pastors' understanding of urban race relations in the Southwest. In Stockton, California, for example, Father Edward J. Noonan testified to the Church's role in bringing harmony to the racially and culturally diverse neighborhood. Whatever their relationship outside the church building, Mexicans, Filipinos, and Italians coexisted peacefully at St. Mary's, he insisted, because "[r]egardless of how they spell their name, they have one thing in common. They're good to the Church. They really support their parish."[36]

A handful of pastors went further, proposing fledgling interracial projects to bring together Catholics of different ethnicities. At San José's Holy Family Church, for example, Father Louis Kern attempted to resolve ethnic tensions by establishing "a program of [i]ntegration of the Italian and Mexican parishioners by mutual cooperation between the two groups." And in the East Bay, Father John García suggested to Mitty that "[s]omething might be done to start an interracial group, where for example white, colored, Mexican and so on would meet socially and spiritually—much might be done in this way."[37]

Such projects—although only sporadic efforts until the early 1960s—testified to the growing momentum of American civil rights movements and the increasing influence of the theology of the Mystical Body. In response to Mexican lay activists' continued calls for a national church throughout the 1950s, a report from Father McDonnell asked rhetorically, "Why not establish a National Parish for the Mexican people?" His answer—"The Church should be Catholic, that is[,] for everyone"—reflected these two larger ideological currents, neatly reiterating the doctrine of the Mystical Body of Christ as it reaffirmed that parish minorities must be integrated into existing churches.[38]

Priests in the San Francisco Archdiocese maintained that the majority of Mexicans themselves felt this way. It is likely that there was, indeed, a lack of consensus among Mexican American Catholics about whether a "separate church" constituted a segregated one. Although the 1950 petition was signed by nearly one-sixth of the city's Mexican population, the ethnic Mexican community was divided along class, citizenship, generational, and political lines. Some residents may well have decried separate churches as a step backward. Certainly priests claimed this to be the case. One report from a parish in Gilroy, located thirty miles southeast of San José, alleged that the laity, too, viewed national parishes as a form of segregation, declaring, "The Latins do not wish to form a separate church but to be incorporated as an integral part of the *Catholic* Church." Only recent immigrants and older parishioners desired a national church, the report maintained; the remainder of residents "wish to be integrated with the Church as Catholics, not segregated." Accordingly, the parish declined to build a separate chapel for Mexicans. Instead, although the priest would eventually agree to institute a Spanish Mass for immigrants, the report emphasized that the church would focus on incorporating and Americanizing the second generation, since any other strategy "would only prolong the problem of total integration down into the third generation."[39]

This explanation highlights that more than simply an emerging liberal consensus against racial segregation influenced Church officials' decision not to establish new national parishes for Mexicans. The focus on the second and third generations demonstrates the Church's revived interest in Americanizing immigrant loyalties. This agenda would prove to play an equally determinative role in the Archdiocese's denial of the national church petitions.

The Catholic Church and Americanization

As early as the 1920s, prelates had begun to doubt the wisdom of establishing national parishes. The question of Americanization infused these discussions, as leaders like George Cardinal Mundelein of Chicago criticized national churches on the grounds that they reinforced the popular image of Catholicism as a foreign religion, thus intensifying anti-Catholic nativism and hindering assimilation.[40] Some critics believed that national parishes and other vestiges of immigrant religiosity threatened the already tenuous relationship between Catholicism and American society. The postwar era only intensified this concern. As the social and political climate heightened anxieties about un-American values and institutions, Catholic progressives again voiced their longstanding concern that many Americans perceived Catholicism as incompatible with cherished ideals of democracy, freedom, and liberty. Such sentiments would continue to fuel anti-Catholicism in the United States well into the mid-1950s, when fears of communism would finally trump anxieties about Catholic authoritarianism.[41]

Concerned about the public face of Catholicism, then, Catholic intellectuals called on the Church to assert its Americanism unequivocally. Reasoning that the Church's integration into the U.S. mainstream required the Americanization of the Catholic faithful themselves, commentators like John Cogley of *Commonweal* sharply criticized the insularity and archaic practices they associated with "the inadequacies of immigrant Catholicism."[42] As much as antidiscrimination principles, then, such anxieties over demonstrating the Americanness of Catholicism help to explain why national parishes were falling out of favor by the late 1940s.

Catholic bishops called for assimilating newcomers into American parish life as quickly as possible. More so than about most other ethnic groups, however, Catholic officials harbored deep reservations about what they viewed as the persistent "foreignness" of Mexican immigrants. Although some priests insisted that Mexicans were simply the latest newcomers to the Archdiocese, arguing that "these people are very much in the same position of the Catholic Irish and Italian immigrants of an earlier generation who have now become integrated into American society," others flatly disagreed, citing the different histories and experiences of immigration.[43] Twenty-five years earlier, European migrations had been abruptly cut off by the passage of restrictive immigration laws that were not applied to Latin America. As a result of the continuing migration flow across the border, Mexicans' cultural loyalties, unlike those of other immigrants, had been continually reinvigorated.

By the early 1950s, Mexican immigration—specifically undocumented immigration—was beginning to take center stage as a national policy issue. This political debate inevitably affected Church officials' perspective. While they rarely commented on the issue of legal migration or residence, many priests cited low naturalization rates and transnational ties as evidence that Mexicans were unwilling or unable to adjust to the United States. One California priest observed that immigrants "remain tied to Mexico legally, or at least in their social environment and economic status," which made him frankly question whether Mexican nationals could truly be Americanized. They were, he judged, an "impediment."[44]

In this context, the petition for a Mexican national parish appeared dangerously close to a repudiation of Catholic Americanization goals. To Northern California priests, such a church promised to conserve not only Latin American religious traditions but also a foreign identity. Cautioning even against an over-reliance on visiting Latin American clergy, Father Ralph Duggan warned Archbishop Mitty that "Priests of their own national groups, *while necessary at this stage of the work,* tend too much to conserve a foreign culture and mentality and thus prevent the real solution of the problem which is that of integration into American life and thought."[45] Even worse, Duggan feared that such priests—and certainly a Mexican church—might promote loyalties beyond the American border, a resonant concern in this Cold War era.

In any case, Duggan and his colleagues dared not take steps that might promote the permanent estrangement of Spanish-speaking Catholics from the American mainstream. Instead, the Church continued to seek a course of ministry that welcomed Mexican immigrants without yielding to their apparent desire for community separatism. A 1961 Catholic conference panel title—"Catholicism, Three Kinds: Latin, American, and?"—captured this attempt to negotiate between the twin goals of cultural sensitivity and assimilation.[46] In short, the Church endorsed pluralism, a religious *"e pluribus unum"* that situated Mexican Americans firmly—and permanently—within American parish life.

Conclusion

In the end, this story illustrates several themes that resonate far beyond the fields of either Chicano or religious history. Perhaps most evidently, Church officials' responses to the national parish petitions testify to the nature and limits of Catholic racial liberalism in the postwar period. In the end, Catholic leaders defined their primary argument against establishing a "Mexican parish"—the call for integration—in terms of both race and nationality, as concerns about racial subordination proved inseparable from fears of foreignness.

Here, Catholic preoccupations mirrored the politics of the Southwest, where race relations have been historically and inexorably linked to concerns about immigration, noncitizens, and the proximity of a porous border. Catholic anxieties about Mexicans' foreignness, although defined in terms of culture rather than citizenship, were neither politically insignificant nor politically neutral in the Cold War era—particularly in light of the landmark 1954 Immigration and Naturalization Service (INS) deportation campaign, Operation "Wetback," that loomed on the horizon. The inseparability of race and foreignness helps to explain why the Church was a formidable but inconsistent ally of Mexican American civil rights efforts in the 1950s. Few Catholic officials spoke out against the 1954 deportations of more than a million Mexicans from the United States, but priests were vociferous critics of the labor and human rights abuses that characterized the Bracero Program. Ultimately their protests would help bring an end to that program in 1964.

In addition to illustrating the contours and implications of Catholic politics in the early postwar period, the national church story points to the dialectical nature of identity and social reform. Rejecting the suggestion that either race or nationality made perpetual outsiders of Mexican and Mexican American Catholics, priests defined them primarily as an ethnic group. This reinforced the clergy's sense that their mandate was to foster Mexicans' cultural and institutional incorporation, helping them achieve what one Catholic agency called "a full, complete participation in the American way of life and the Catholic Church."[47] Here priests averred that they took their cue from the rising generation. Mexican American young people, Father Thomas McCullough said, "use English and want to be known as Americans of 'Spanish' descent." In other words, he claimed, the second generation identified only as members of an American ethnic group, rather than a foreign or racial one.[48]

But Mexican Americans' self-understanding was always more complex than Church officials comprehended. Men and women defined themselves variously in terms of ethnicity and race, nationality and culture, religious faith and parish membership, and neighborhood residence and citizenship status. The national church petitions revealed the broad range of social categories to which Mexicans belonged and from which they made claims to certain treatment. On a broader level, then, the petitions and the priests' responses serve as a reminder that social reform efforts are essentially dialectical, forged in dialogues and contestations between participants who may well have competing agendas, strategies, and identities.

This incident also demonstrates the salience of culture, race, and religion as rallying points in mid-twentieth-century politics. At issue was the question of how the Church as an institution could best help Mexicans achieve equality and defeat discrimination. Catholic intellectuals and racial progressives upheld liberal ideals of incorporation, reciprocity, and the ability of human reason to overcome prejudice. Ethnic Mexicans were more skeptical. To them, a national church promised to serve as a community institution, offering strength and solidarity against the often-hostile surrounding municipality.

The themes in this episode foreshadowed some of the political, cultural, and institutional conflicts of the 1960s. In the early postwar period, the dynamic collaboration between priests and laity gave progressive clergy like Donald McDonnell an influential role in Mexican American politics and community activity. But the national church debate revealed a division between lay and official visions of the parish church as a community institution, rather than simply a religious one. This divide likely strained the dynamic relationship between pastors and parishioners. As the 1950s unfolded, Mexican American activists increasingly turned outside the Church to further their civil rights goals, drawing more on Mexican cultural traditions and American political tactics than on Catholic teachings.

As Mexican American civil rights efforts intensified in the late 1960s, the new breed of activist was rarely inclined to see the Church as a key ally in social justice struggles. The emerging Chicano Movement's more aggressive politics emphasized overturning Mexican Americans' second-class status and promoting cultural pride. Young Chicanos now demonstrated their emphatic rejection of earlier groups of Mexican Americans who had participated too much in mainstream, Anglo-dominated religious and political organizations.[49] Their suspicion of "outsider" institutions and an insistence on self-determination called into question the place of the Church in the Mexican-origin community and heightened resentments toward the priesthood.

As a result of changing ethnic and institutional politics, the late 1960s witnessed some vivid controversies that pitted Chicano activists against Church officials. The Chicano activists of that decade who engaged the Church head-on likely had little sense that liberal clergy had chosen to affirm a principle of integration over segregation two decades before. Nonetheless, by the 1970s, that decision still reverberated, albeit in a different tone, as activists now remembered the denial of a national church and other such decisions as evidence that the Catholic hierarchy had kept ethnic Mexicans in a subordinate, powerless position. These were surely legacies of 1940s racial politics that neither Catholic progressives nor ethnic Mexican activists could have forecast when they debated what it meant to bring Latino Catholics "into one parish life."

Notes

For their assistance, I thank especially Michael Friedman, Steve Pitti, Shana Bernstein, and Steve Avella. I dedicate this paper to my family.

1. Petition for a National Parish, November 16, 1950, Archives of the Archdiocese of San Francisco (hereafter, AASF), Box A67.1, file "General."

2. Jeffrey Burns, *San Francisco: A History of the Archdiocese of San Francisco*, vol. 3, *1945–2000, A Journey of Hope* (Strasbourg, France: Editions du Signe, 2002), 2–4.

3. This chapter is part of a larger project on Mexican Americans, ethnic identity, and Catholicism in Northern California after World War II. See Gina Marie Pitti, "To 'Hear about God In Spanish': Ethnicity, Church, and Community Activism in the San Francisco Archdiocese's Mexican American Colonias, 1942–1965" (Ph.D. diss., Stanford University, 2003).

4. Jeffrey Burns, *San Francisco: A History of the Archdiocese of San Francisco*, vol. 2, *1885–1945, Glory, Ruin, and Resurrection* (Strasbourg, France: Editions du Signe, 2000), 26; Josephine Kellogg, "The Spanish Mission Band, 1948–1961" (master's thesis, Graduate Theological Union, 1974); Jeffrey Burns, "The Mexican Catholic Community in California," in *Mexican Americans and the Catholic Church, 1900–1965*, ed. Jay P. Dolan and Gilberto M. Hinojosa (Notre Dame, Ind.: University of Notre Dame Press, 1994), 134, 167.

5. Timothy Matovina, "The National Parish and Americanization," *U.S. Catholic Historian* 17 (Winter 1999): 46, 57; Roberto R. Treviño, "From Pariahs to Participants: Ethno-Catholicism in Mexican American Houston, 1911–1972" (draft of book manuscript in author's possession), 156; Jay P. Dolan, *In Search of an American Catholicism: A History of Religion and Culture in Tension* (New York: Oxford University Press, 2002), 60–61, 133–34, 138–42.

6. See, for instance, Salvador Álvarez, "The Roots of Mestizo Catholicism in California," in *Fronteras: A History of the Latin American Church in the USA since 1513*, ed. Moisés Sandoval, 239–54 (San Antonio: Mexican American Cultural Center, 1983), 241; Antonio R. Soto, "Dimensions of Religiosity in the Mexican American Community of the New Almaden Quicksilver Minds," paper presented at the Conference on Religion and Society in the American West, St. Mary's College, Moraga, California, June 15–16, 1984), 11–13, in Anthony Soto Papers, Box 1, Stanford University Archives, (hereafter, Soto Papers); and Allan Figueroa Deck, S.J., "At the Crossroads: North American and Hispanic," in *We Are a People! Initiatives in Hispanic American Theology*, ed. Roberto S. Goizueta, 12–14 (Minneapolis: Fortress Press, 1992).

7. On changes in the American West, see, for instance, Gerald D. Nash, *The American West Transformed: The Impact of the Second World War* (Lincoln: University of Nebraska Press, 1990); Glenna Matthews, "'The Los Angeles of the North': San José's Transition from Fruit Capital to High-Tech Metropolis," *Journal of Urban History* (May 1999); and Shana Bernstein, "Building Bridges at Home in a Time of Global Conflict: Interracial Cooperation and the Fight for Civil Rights in Los Angeles, 1933–1954"

(Ph.D. diss., Stanford University, 2003). On the San Francisco Archdiocese, see Jeffrey M. Burns, *San Francisco: A History of the Archdiocese of San Francisco*, vol. 3, *1945–2000, A Journey of Hope.* For general surveys of American Catholic history, see Jay P. Dolan, *The American Catholic Experience: A History from Colonial Times to the Present* (Garden City, N.Y.: Doubleday, 1985) and Philip Gleason, *Keeping the Faith: American Catholicism Past and Present* (Notre Dame, Ind.: University of Notre Dame Press, 1987).

8. Mexican labor migrations were driven in part by the federally negotiated, binational Emergency Farm Labor Program (commonly known as the Bracero Program), which arranged the employment of thousands of Mexican nationals every year. On World War II and Mexican Americans, see Albert Camarillo, *Chicanos in California: A History of Mexican Americans in California* (San Francisco: Boyd and Fraser, 1984); Stephen J. Pitti, *The Devil in Silicon Valley: Northern California, Race, and Mexican Americans* (Princeton, N.J.: Princeton University Press, 2003); and David G. Gutiérrez, *Walls and Mirrors: Mexican Americans, Mexican Immigrants, and the Politics of Ethnicity* (Berkeley: University of California Press, 1995).

9. See Burns, "The Mexican Catholic Community in California"; Pitti, "To Hear about God in Spanish."

10. Translation mine. Interview, Jeffrey Burns with Juanita Álvarez, July 10, 1989; transcript in St. Peter's Parish Papers, AASF, Folder 84.6.

11. "Paula," quoted in Margaret Clark, *Health in the Mexican-American Culture: A Community Study* (1959; Berkeley: University of California Press, 1970), 99, 110.

12. Anthony R. Soto, "History of Our Lady of Guadalupe Parish" (unpublished manuscript, n.d.), 2–3, in Soto Papers, Box 1.

13. Mrs. Robert Elizondo to Rt. Rev. Hugh A. Donohoe, September 16, 1949, in AASF, Box A67.1, file "General"; Clare Guidotte to Rev. Donald McDonnell, June 30, 1950, in Rev. Donald McDonnell Papers, AASF, Box 2, file "Missionary Apostolate Reports, 1948–1962" (hereafter, McDonnell Papers); Rev. Donald McDonnell to Most Rev. Hugh A. Donohoe, August 16, 1949 and Report, "Priest's Conference on Minority Groups," August 26, 1949, both in AASF, Box A67, untitled folder. See also Anthony R. Soto, "History of Our Lady of Guadalupe Parish," 2; Clark, *Health in the Mexican-American Culture*, 99.

14. Dolan, *In Search of an American Catholicism*, 79–82.

15. Petition to Most Rev. John J. Mitty, November 27, 1945, AASF, Box "Spanish Speaking," file "Mexicans." Historian Shana Bernstein calls this strategy an "American approach," in which civil rights activists in the early Cold War–period made use of the language of Americanism and democracy to fight discrimination, racism, and inequality. See Shana Bernstein, "Cold Warriors of a Different Stripe: Interracial Civil Rights in Early Cold War Los Angeles" (unpublished paper in author's possession, 2004), 31–32, 36.

16. Petition for a National Parish, November 16, 1950, AASF, Box A67.1, file "General." On Catholic suspicions of Mexicans' faith, see Burns, "The Mexican Catholic Community in California" and Dolan, *In Search of an American Catholicism*, 142–43.

17. Petition for a National Parish, November 16, 1950, AASF, Box A67.1, file "General"; Vicki Ruiz, *Cannery Women, Cannery Lives: Mexican Women, Unionization, and the California Food Processing Industry, 1930–1950* (Albuquerque: University of New Mexico Press, 1987), 111–12.

18. Petition for a National Parish, November 16, 1950, AASF, Box A67.1, file "General."

19. Ibid.

20. On stereotypes of Mexicans, see Mark Reisler, *By the Sweat of Their Brow: Mexican Immigrant Labor in the United States, 1900–1940* (Westport, Conn.: Greenwood Press, 1976).

21. Renato Rosaldo, "Cultural Citizenship, Inequality, and Multiculturalism," in *Latino Cultural Citizenship: Claiming Identity, Space, and Rights*, ed. William V. Flores and Rina Benmayor (Boston: Beacon Press, 1997).

22. Translation mine. Jeffrey Burns, interview with Isaura Michell de Rodríguez, July 17, 1989, AASF, St. Peter's Parish Papers, Folder 84.11.

23. Petition for a National Parish, November 16, 1950, AASF, Box A67.1, file "General."

24. Report, "Conference of Priests and Lay-Workers on the Spanish-Speaking Peoples of the Archdiocese of San Francisco," November 6, 1949; Remarks of Father Muez [first name unknown], handwritten notes attached to Report, "Priest's [*sic*] Conference on Spanish-Speaking People," March 10, 1949, both in AASF, Box A67, untitled folder.

25. Emphasis in original. Rev. Donald McDonnell to Most Rev. John J. Mitty, January 2, [1951], AASF, Box A67.1, file "General."

26. For more on Mexicans' racial status in California, see Tomás Almaguer, *Racial Fault Lines: The Historical Origins of White Supremacy in California* (Berkeley: University of California Press, 1994); Pitti, *The Devil in Silicon Valley*; and Gutiérrez, *Walls and Mirrors*.

27. See particularly David L. Chappell, *A Stone of Hope: Prophetic Religion and the Death of Jim Crow* (Chapel Hill: University of North Carolina Press, 2004), esp. 8, 102.

28. Historian Mark Brilliant defines racial liberalism as a "robust, if not radical, set of ideas . . . [including] a New Deal–inspired faith in the helping hand of government; a focus on racial discrimination and the inequities it bred; an emphasis on 'non-discrimination' and 'equal opportunity' legislation and litigation . . . to redress racial inequality; and a social science scholarship-informed belief in race as a social construct rather than a scientific fact." John McGreevy notes that Catholics strove to "march . . . in step with the liberal vanguard" on the subject of civil rights in order to prove that the Church was

not inimical to American values. Defending human and civil rights in Catholic terms allowed Catholic leaders to demonstrate their own Americanness. Mark R. Brilliant, *Color Lines: Civil Rights Struggles on America's "Racial Frontier," 1945–1975* (Oxford University Press, forthcoming), 12–16, esp. 13 (ms. pp.). See also John McGreevy, *Catholicism and American Freedom: A History* (New York: W. W. Norton, 2003), 170, 192–211; Chappell, *A Stone of Hope*, 37–43. On the politics of racial liberalism, see Ruth Feldstein, *Motherhood in Black and White: Race and Sex in American Liberalism, 1930–1965* (Ithaca N.Y.: Cornell University Press, 2000).

29. Dolan, *In Search of an American Catholicism*, 148–52.

30. Rev. Donald McDonnell to Most Rev. John J. Mitty, January 2, [1951], AASF, Box A67.1, file "General."

31. Clarence M. Zens, "Racial Prejudice Must Go, Educators Assert At NCEA Convention," *The Monitor* (San Francisco), April 21, 1950, 1; John T. McGreevy, *Parish Boundaries: The Catholic Encounter with Race in the Twentieth-Century Urban North* (Chicago: University of Chicago Press, 1996), 82; David W. Southern, *John LaFarge and the Limits of Catholic Interracialism, 1911–1963* (Baton Rouge: Louisiana State University Press, 1996); Jay P. Dolan, "The Catholic Encounter with Race," *Reviews in American History* 25, no. 2 (1997): 282–87.

32. See McGreevy, *Parish Boundaries*, 43–44, 52, 70; Dolan, *In Search of an American Catholicism*, 152.

33. McGreevy, *Parish Boundaries*, 44.

34. *Bishops' Committee for the Spanish Speaking Newsletter*, no. 39, December 1958, in Robert E. Lucey Papers, University of Notre Dame Archives, Box 16, Folder 3.

35. "Prelate Urges Training for Latin Americans," *The Monitor* (San Francisco), August 29, 1947, 13; "Prelate Raps Exploitation of Farm Labor," *The Monitor* (San Francisco), May 22, 1959, 1.

36. "Bless Stockton Church, Mission," *The Monitor* (San Francisco), November 21, 1958, 4.

37. "Report on Work in Santa Clara County Permanent Settlements," May 16, 1951, McDonnell Papers, AASF; Rev. John García, "Report for Archbishop," February 12, 1952, AASF, Box A67.1, file "General."

38. "Proposal to Make Our Lady of Guadalupe a Territorial Parish," n.d., AASF, Box A67.1, file "Guadalupe Center, San José."

39. Emphasis in original. Report, "Conference of Priests and Lay-Workers on the Spanish-Speaking Peoples of the Archdiocese of San Francisco," November 6, 1949, AASF, Box A67, untitled folder; "Proposal to Make Our Lady of Guadalupe a Territorial Parish," AASF; Charles E. Pillman et al., *St. Mary's Church, Gilroy, California* (Gilroy, Calif.: Dispatch Printing, 1965), 58.

40. Dolan, *In Search of An American Catholicism* 137–40; Matovina, "The National Church and Americanization."

41. Dolan, *In Search of an American Catholicism,* 165–66; McGreevy, *Catholicism and American Freedom,* 168–69.

42. "Come out of the Ghetto, Catholics Told," *The Monitor* (San Francisco), June 5, 1959, 3; Gleason, *Keeping the Faith,* 64.

43. "Women Hold Key to Catholic Culture, Speaker Tells NCCW Delegates," *The Monitor* (San Francisco), October 22, 1954, 11.

44. Rev. Alfred Boeddeker, O.F.M., "NOTES—Not a treatise or paper—on THE MEXICAN YOUTH PROBLEM AND ITS SOLUTION," n.d. [ca. 1955] in Rev. Ronald Burke Papers, AASF, Box 3, file "Catholic Council for the Spanish Speaking—Pastoral Care." On the emergence of undocumented migration as a political issue, see also Gutiér-rez, *Walls and Mirrors;* Juan Ramon Garcia, *Operation Wetback: The Mass Deportation of Mexican Undocumented Workers in 1954* (Westport, Conn.: Greenwood Press, 1980); and Manuel García y Griego, "The Importation of Mexican Contract Laborers to the United States, 1942–1964," in *Between Two Worlds: Mexican Immigrants in the United States,* ed. David G. Gutiérrez, 45–85 (Wilmington, Del.: SR Books, Inc., Jaguar Books on Latin America Number 15, 1996).

45. Rev. Ralph Duggan to Most Rev. John J. Mitty, August 26, 1949, AASF, Box A67.1, file "General."

46. [Rev. John A. Wagner], "Brief Outline of Conference," San Juan Bautista, California, April 3–7, 1961, in Rev. James L. Vizzard Papers, Stanford University Archives, Box 21, Folder 6.

47. Quoted in Burns, "The Mexican Catholic Community in California," 149.

48. "Report of the Priests' Conference on the Spanish Speaking, February 10, 1949," AASF Box A67.1, untitled folder.

49. On the Chicano Movement, see Gutiérrez, *Walls and Mirrors,* 183–87; Camarillo, *Chicanos in California,* 88–103; Pitti, *The Devil in Silicon Valley,* 178–88; and Ernesto Chávez, *"¡Mi Raza Primero!" (My People First!): Nationalism, Identity, and Insurgency in the Chicano Movement in Los Angeles, 1966–1978* (Berkeley: University of California Press, 2002).

Faith and Justice
The Catholic Church and the Chicano Movement in Houston, 1965–72

Roberto R. Treviño

On a typically balmy Houston night in September 1971, a group of young Chicano activists stormed out of a meeting with a priest at Resurrection Catholic Church. "May God protect us from guys like you," one of the frustrated activists yelled at the priest. Others who had come to the meeting likewise spewed their anger at the pastor as their parents watched "with glassy eyes of disbelief." The activists had come to talk to the priest about supporting a school boycott they had started against the Houston Independent School District; they wanted to use the parish hall for classrooms for the boycotting students. But the pastor refused. That week a Chicano newspaper screamed, "The Shepherd Refuses His Flock." It went on to claim that, "the majority of the Catholic Schools, in time of need, have refused to help the people that they should be serving."[1]

These scenes illustrate how the tumultuous years of the civil rights era rocked the Galveston-Houston Diocese. This chapter focuses on the relationship between Mexican Americans and the Catholic Church in Houston during the turmoil of the mid-1960s to early 1970s, the years that saw the climax of the Chicano quest for social and religious self-determination. The chapter examines three things: the challenges the Catholic Church faced from Houston's Chicano community; the nature of its responses to those challenges; and some of the results of the Church's involvement in the events of this period. I argue that the Church in Houston alternately resisted and embraced the cause for Mexican American equality and, while it was not at the forefront of social change, its cautious support helped to bring positive changes to the lives of Mexican Catholics in the Bayou City.

The Church Is Challenged
During the civil rights era, many people questioned American values and institutions. Religious institutions were no exception, as they often seemed to maintain

the status quo. Indeed, churches often came under fierce attack as disaffected groups challenged their own subordinate status in society.[2] Mexican Americans also questioned the role of religious institutions in their lives. Since most Mexican Americans were Catholic and made up a significant portion of the U.S. Church (about one-fourth of the membership), local and national leaders frequently looked to the institution for help in addressing pressing social issues. For instance, when labor organizer César Chávez emerged as a national symbol of the Chicano Movement in 1965, the institutional Church figured prominently in his struggle for economic justice for California farmworkers. Although many individual clergy and nuns actively supported his cause, Chávez challenged the Church hierarchy to throw its formidable influence and resources behind the striking agricultural workers. "We don't ask for more cathedrals," he stated, "We ask the Church to sacrifice with the people for social change, for justice."[3]

Calls for the Galveston-Houston Diocese to step up its social activism came from many quarters as hometown politicians, congressional representatives, local barrio activists, and other Chicanas and Chicanos increasingly prodded the institution. In 1965 Manuel Crespo, chair of the Houston chapter of the Political Association of Spanish-Speaking Organizations (PASSO), called on Church leaders to do more to encourage Mexican American interest and participation in politics. Clergy "could help Latin Americans very much by mixing more with them, talk[ing] to them and encourag[ing] them in their political obligations," Crespo urged. Similarly, Texas congressman Henry B. González urged a meeting of clergy in Houston to "redefine" their social action programs to be more relevant. Likewise, local activist William Gutiérrez called for Church officials to stop taking Mexican Catholics for granted, and urged priests to "become deeply involved and active in the plight of the Mexican American."[4]

Over time the voices of protest became increasingly strident. For example, Herman Gallegos denounced the institutional Church's failure toward Mexicans at a Houston conference in October 1969. As the executive director of the Southwest Council of La Raza, a coordinating organization of Mexican American advocacy groups, Gallegos charged that the Church was "too far removed" from Chicanos and Chicanas and that it was at least partly to blame for some of the social problems facing them. Gallegos offered a solution that demanded greater Church involvement, challenging the representatives of Catholic charities to help remedy some of these ills by creating housing, education, and economic development programs for Mexican Americans.[5]

Others used angrier language. Lalo Delgado, a Chicano academic and activist, told a gathering of lay and clerical officials in Houston that the Catholic Church was a racist institution, that "bishops, priests and Sisters have turned it into an ugly church." Yolanda Garza Birdwell, a Mexican American Youth Organization (MAYO) leader in Houston, similarly assailed the Church in a newspaper interview. "[W]hen the dogs in River Oaks [Houston's most affluent neighborhood] are eating more meat than a lot of her northside friends," the *Houston Chronicle* reported, "a woman has a right to fight back." "So it's a sin to stop having children?" Birdwell asked rhetorically. "Okay, mothers have more children and there's malnutrition and a great injustice is done. I have no doubt the Church is very responsible for this situation," Birdwell charged as she pointed the finger of blame for the poverty in Houston barrios.[6] Chicanas who attended the Conferencia de Mujeres por la Raza (National Chicana Conference), held in Houston May 28–30, 1971, echoed this anger. Many denounced the oppression of Mexican American women by men at home and in the Church, and a resolution defiantly "recognize[d] the Catholic Church as an oppressive institution." The conference went on record in support of abortion and resolved "to break away" from the Catholic Church.[7]

The Chicano press voiced virulent attacks on the Church during the late 1960s and early 1970s, publishing scathing editorials that condemned the failings of institutional Christianity. Chicano journalists accused Church personnel of hypocrisy and insensitivity toward Mexican American parishioners. For example, the editor of *Compass* likened Catholic clergy to "[p]arrots, who do not know or understand the seriousness of the doctrine being taught." In another editorial, the paper charged that clerics would rather dedicate themselves to building beautiful structures than to speak out against discrimination and economic injustice.[8]

Another community newspaper, *Papel Chicano*, aimed most of its ire at Protestants, but it also reminded readers that "the Catholic Church [was] unmindful of the needs of the Chicano." The paper criticized the institutional Church for neglecting social issues that affected both the spiritual and material welfare of its parishioners, claiming that priests did more harm than good and were "such cowards" that they were afraid to denounce bigotry, racism, and discrimination. Church officials who lacked the courage or ability "to relate Christian teachings to the community's everyday life and problems," the article continued, "should find other vocations where they will not do such damage to the parishioners' spiritual lives." The newspaper's denunciations not only revealed disillusion but also reflected the historical anticlericalism and self-sufficiency of Mexican Catholics, asserting that the people owed no allegiance to an institutional Church "that pretends to teach doctrines which are alien to the spirit of the Chicano," notions such as turning the other cheek and being long-suffering.[9]

An anonymous poem in one of Houston's Chicano newspapers reflected the disillusionment many felt with the Catholic Church:

I was hungry
and you formed a humanities club
and discussed my hunger.
Thank you.
I was imprisoned
and you crept off quietly
to your chapel in the cellar
and prayed for my release.
I was naked
and in your mind
you debated the morality of my appearance.
I was sick
and you knelt and thanked God for your health.
I was homeless
and you preached to me
of the spiritual shelter of the love of God.
I was lonely
and you left me alone
to pray for me.
You seem so holy;
so close to God.
But I'm still very hungry,
and lonely,
and cold.
So where have your prayers gone?
What have they done?
What does it profit a man
to page through his book of prayers
when the rest of the world
is crying for his help?[10]

During the 1960s and 1970s many Chicanas and Chicanos vented a palpable anger and estrangement they felt toward the Church. They lashed out at the institution's historical relationship with Mexicans—some seeing it as blatantly racist, others as paternalistic and insensitive at best—and they accused the

Church leadership of perpetuating their inequality. These Chicanos and Chicanas wanted more than just spiritual comfort from the institutional Church; they expected it to be their ally in social matters, not their oppressor through its inaction. Prayers without social action, many Mexican Catholics felt, left them "still very hungry, and lonely, and cold." For them the institution was out of step with their struggle for social change.[11]

Some parishioners expected their churches to work for social justice in the barrios. In the fall of 1970, parishioner Eduardo López sought his bishop's support on a divisive issue. López explained to Bishop John Morkovsky that the members of Our Lady of Sorrows Parish were polarized over whether "a church [should] bury its head in the sands of complacency or . . . try to aleviate [sic] the everyday problems of the community."[12] López described what he and other members thought their church should be and do:

> We feel that a church or a religion is not judged by the beautiful buildings in the parish or by the amount of money raised or the amount of money in the bank. We feel a church should be judged by the amount of faithful who participate in church activities. By the amount of faithful who are allowed to participate in its government. We feel that to preach of charity and brotherlly [sic] love is not sufficient . . . that it is imperative that we go out and actually put into practice those beautiful [C]hristian teachings; especially in the poverty level community in which we live.[13]

These parishioners urged their parish council to get involved in issues affecting their neighborhood. "We wanted to tell them how deeply we feel that our community has no recreational activities for our children, no parks, no boy scouts, no girl scouts, [and that] our teenagers have no place to go," the parishioner explained. "We told them of the drug addiction problem amoung [sic] our school children; the necessity of more and better police protection." The group pleaded with their parish council for permission to use church facilities for activities "that would not only deal with the spiritual but also the material needs of our community." But those who controlled the parish council and day-to-day church activities disagreed completely with the petitioners' vision of the church, asserting that it "is a spiritual body that must not get involved in the civic affairs of the community."[14] Although this particular attempt to involve a church in social issues was staved off for the time being, the efforts of López and like-minded parishioners at Our Lady of Sorrows sent a strong message to the diocesan leadership. Chicana and Chicano laypeople increasingly stepped forward and pressed the Catholic hierarchy in Houston to join their quest for social justice.

The Challenge Within: Activist Priests and Nuns

By the later 1960s, the Galveston-Houston Diocese also felt pressured from within its own ranks to support Chicano social causes. The most outspoken local cleric was Father Patricio Flores, who had long ministered to Mexican Catholics in and around Houston before he was selected to head the Bishop's Committee for the Spanish-Speaking in the Diocese in 1964.[15] Reverend Flores cautioned that there would be a mass exodus of Mexicans from the Church unless it showed more concern and sensitivity toward them. "We, as a big body [the institutional Church] are not doing enough," the priest admonished. His message was clear: Despite the fact that the great majority of Mexican Americans were Catholics, "the Church has not really been sympathetic or sensitive to us in our social, economic or educational struggle," Flores charged. On another occasion, the outspoken cleric decried that Mexican Americans "have been victims of . . . semi-slavery . . . lived in conditions sometimes worse than animals in the zoo and yet the Church keeps silent."[16]

In October 1969, Father Flores was among fifty or so Chicano priests who met in San Antonio to form an organization called Padres Asociados para Derechos Religiosos, Educativos y Sociales (Priests Associated for Religious, Educational and Social Rights, or PADRES). These Chicano clerics vowed to take "the cry of our people" to the hierarchy of the Church, and to involve it in

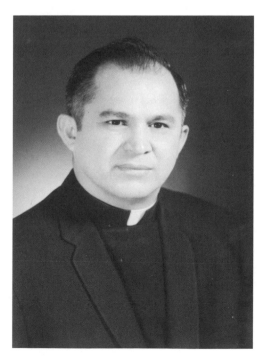

Father Patricio Flores, shown here prior to his ordination as the first Mexican American bishop, became a high profile civil rights leader in the Houston area in the 1960s. Courtesy *Texas Catholic Herald*.

el movimiento. The formation of PADRES owed much to the pressures exerted by the Mexican American laity. Their awareness of the Chicano Movement, the group's information officer told the press, was "one of the principal reasons the priests had come together."[17] Father Ralph Ruiz, the first national chairman of PADRES, explained that Mexican American Catholics resented the fact that "the Church is not Mexican American oriented." The cleric declared that PADRES would "have to make the Church cognizant of the fact that we exist and that we wish no longer to be ignored or taken for granted."[18]

A group of Chicana nuns soon joined the drive to gain the institution's attention and support. Two activist sisters, Gregoria Ortega and Gloria Gallardo, founded Las Hermanas (Sisters) in a conference held in Houston in April 1971. Gallardo and Ortega were elected president and vice president, respectively, of the new organization dedicated to promoting social change, cultural pride, and Chicana leadership.[19] Similar to PADRES (which Gallardo also helped establish in Houston), Las Hermanas declared that they sought "revolutionary" changes within and outside of the Church. Refusing to be constrained by the notion of separate sacred and secular spheres, Gallardo declared, "We agree that there should no longer be a dichotomy between religion and social aspects."[20] At the initial meeting of Las Hermanas the conference program tantalized the participants with such questions as: "Do Politics Turn You On?"; "How Do Sisters Promote Social Justice?"; and "What Is the Church's Role with La Raza?" At a national conference the sisters discussed how they might help raise the economic status of Mexicans and Mexican Americans in the United States and develop barrio leadership. In Houston they appeared on community center programs to publicize their message and were also active in barrio issues.[21]

Asserting that they would not be ignored, Las Hermanas aimed to bring the Mexican community's needs "more forcibly" to the attention of the Church hierarchy. If the hierarchy did not support Las Hermanas, a sister warned, it would "hear from us."[22] Clearly, these Chicana nuns had developed far beyond the "maternal feminism" that characterized precursors such as Sisters Benitia Vermeersch and Dolores Cárdenas in the early to mid-twentieth century. Sisters active in Las Hermanas understood themselves as political agents. In the early 1970s they understood, as other sisters more recently have recognized, that being "political" did not necessarily "mean being a registered member of the Democratic or Republican party . . . [or] running for public office." Rather, it meant "to grasp one's elemental kinship with a 'people' . . . to discern, however inchoately, that one is *of* the people, which is to say that little in one's life is ever wholly private and that one's most personal spaces have import for the public weal." Las Hermanas paved the way for today's activist sisters who understand that "to be political is to

Sisters Gloria Gallardo and Gregoria Ortega founded the outspoken Chicana nuns' organization Las Hermanas in Houston, an organization that pressed the Catholic Church to step up its advocacy for Mexican Americans. Courtesy *Texas Catholic Herald*.

incorporate into one's self-identification the fact of one's rootedness in a people and to make and act on choices that contribute to the welfare (good journeying) of that people."[23] They provided important inspiration in the Mexican Catholic pilgrimage in the Bayou City, and helped turn the tide. The Church clearly heard the rising chant of protest and the calls for support of the Chicano Movement both from within and outside its ranks, and began to respond.

The Institutional Rationale

Church involvement in the Chicano Movement in Houston took two forms. Institutionally, the Galveston-Houston Diocese played the role of supportive ally of *el movimiento*, albeit within cautiously prescribed limits. Significantly, however, the catalysts for social change were individual priests and nuns, many acting alone or through newly formed organizations like PADRES and Las Hermanas. Political activism by religious personnel dramatically departed from the traditional patterns of Church activities in Houston's Mexican American communities. While some individuals within the Church had long worked to improve the material lives of Mexican Americans, they had never led efforts to mobilize their parishioners on a large scale for social and political change. Nor had the diocesan leadership ever supported a movement for social change to the extent that it did in the 1960s and 1970s. The unfolding of *el movimiento* did not wait for the Church's blessing. Rather, Chicanas and Chicanos were in the vanguard of social change and the Church hierarchy followed with its support.

The institutional role the Church would play had begun to take shape in the early 1960s. During all the Masses conducted on Sunday, August 25, 1963, for instance, Houston Catholics heard an explanation of the Church's official position on "the race question." Pastors were instructed to read a three-page pastoral letter to their parishioners from the Bishops in the United States that eloquently declared that, "[d]iscrimination based on the accidental fact of race or color, and as such injurious to human rights, . . . cannot be reconciled with the truth that God has created all men with equal rights and equal dignity." The following year, the Galveston-Houston Diocese instituted "Social Justice Sunday," an annual "day of prayer focused on human rights and human dignity." In the ensuing years, Bishop John Morkovsky established committees and sponsored forums to address racial unrest and social inequality in Houston. Although these developments arose in response to the Black Freedom Struggle, the Church also recognized "the disabilities visited upon other racial and national groups."[24] The policy developed in the early 1960s in response to the black civil rights struggle thus had a direct bearing on the diocese's reaction to the Chicano Movement.

The declarations of the United States Conference of Catholic Bishops and the activities of Bishop Morkovsky in Houston outlined the stance of the institutional Church on social change. Although Church leaders eloquently denounced

As the leader of the Galveston-Houston Diocese, Bishop John Morkovsky was an important behind-the-scenes supporter of Chicano causes during the civil rights era. Courtesy *Texas Catholic Herald.*

social oppression, they left it to those outside the institution to actually initiate changes; the role of the Church was that of moral suasion in support of progressive change. "We should do our part," the U.S. Bishops stated, "to see that voting, jobs, housing, education and public facilities are freely available to every American." In the same spirit, Bishop Morkovsky declared that minority grievances in Houston were moral issues and "definitely concerned" the Church. But official Church policy made it very clear that "civic action" in defense of human rights was primarily the concern of the laity, and particularly, of course, the prime duty of civil authorities.[25]

In Houston, the Bishop's Interracial Committee promoted interracial justice by working with Catholic lay organizations in the city. The committee "[did] not feel that it should . . . react toward civic problems or enter into the field of community relations," because it recognized "that there were already existing organizations which were formed to react to interracial injustice in the community." The role of the Interracial Committee was, therefore, "to use every persuasive means available to bring about interracial justice." "Necessary persuasion" then demanded "action on the part of the committee and its lay working group." This approach meant that the Church's role was to facilitate problem-solving and social reform by providing forums, finding ways to air issues, and bringing together parties in conflict. Thus the U.S. Bishops suggested that Catholics work for social justice "through various lay organizations . . . as well as with civic groups of every type," and that the places to discuss social issues should be the parish and diocesan societies, political gatherings, and civic and neighborhood associations.[26] This policy of guidance and facilitation recalled the position Church personnel had taken in the past, when they encouraged the formation of parish-based mutual aid societies like the Ligas de Protección Mexicana and other self-help organizations. It was within this framework that the Catholic Church in Houston responded to *el movimiento*. In the meantime, individual sisters and priests seized opportunities to spearhead social causes themselves, beginning with the key events of 1966.

Individual Responses of Clergy and Nuns

The Chicano Movement in Texas was sparked by "La Marcha"—a dramatic protest march staged by striking farmworkers from the Río Grande Valley of South Texas to the state capital in Austin during the summer of 1966. The march originally aimed to publicize the strikers' demands by staging a pilgrimage from Río Grande City to nearby San Juan Shrine Church, a place of special religious significance for Mexican American Catholics. However, it quickly assumed a broader purpose with larger ramifications; it became instead the "Minimum

Led by (left to right) Rev. James Novarro, Father Antonio Gonzales, and labor organizer Eugene Nelson, striking Mexican American farm workers (and their donkey mascot "Huelga") marched to the state capital in Austin in the summer of 1966 to demand decent wages and working conditions. In the process, they spurred the nascent Chicano Movement in Texas. Courtesy Mexican-American Farm Workers Movement Collection, The University of Texas at Arlington Library, Arlington, Texas.

Wage March," a 490-mile trek to the capitol steps that marked a pivotal event for Mexican Americans in Texas. Father Antonio Gonzales, the assistant pastor of Houston's Immaculate Heart of Mary Church co-led the march, along with labor organizer Eugene Nelson, of the National Farm Workers Association, and Rev. James L. Novarro, the Mexican American pastor of Houston's Kashmere Baptist Temple.[27]

As the farmworkers' strike unfolded in Starr County in June 1966, Gonzales and Father Lawrence Peguero of Our Lady of St. John visited the area to assess the conditions surrounding the conflict. Father Gonzales reported that there was a dire shortage of basic necessities among farm laborers and that families were "going hungry."[28] The two priests collected food and clothing among their parishioners in Houston and delivered them to the strikers, and still more donations as the strike garnered support from Houston labor unions.[29] Supporters of the strike soon formed a Valley Workers Assistance Group in Houston and, with Father Gonzales as its chairman, the group held rallies at different parishes and coordinated the flow of support from Houston to the strikers.[30]

As both enthusiasm and the temperature soared on July 4, seventy-five farm-workers began the pilgrimage to San Juan Shrine, accompanied by Father Gonzales and some forty supporters from Houston. Four days later in San Juan, the strikers and other state leaders decided to march to the state capital to demand that a minimum wage law of $1.25 per hour be passed by the legislature. The purpose of the protest thus shifted from the demands of a fledgling farmworkers' union to the larger issue of economic justice for Mexican Americans. Gonzales agreed to remain with the farmworkers until Labor Day (when they planned to present their demands on the steps of the capitol), and thus he emerged as one of the leaders of the "march for justice."[31]

As the marchers inched their way toward the capital under the scorching Texas sun, tremendous demonstrations of support buoyed their spirits. Hundreds of Chicanos and Chicanas joined the caravan at different points and thousands attended the rallies in the larger cities along the way. But five days before reaching their destination, Gov. John Connally and an entourage of officials suddenly confronted the marchers on the highway. Father Gonzales and coleader Rev. James Novarro warmly greeted the governor, but were soon disappointed. Although he complimented the peaceful nature of the protest, the governor lectured the marchers on the possibility of violence if they continued. Furthermore, he bluntly told them he would not meet with them in Austin or call a special session of the legislature to consider a minimum wage bill. The governor's words stunned Father Gonzales like a slap to the face. "We feel that the lamentation and the sufferings of so many poor people in Texas were directed to the governor and . . . they were not heard," the dejected priest reported. Another marching cleric noted that Connally's demeanor was "a pat on the head, a great white father-type of thing" that angered the marchers. But the governor's rebuff backfired and only strengthened the protesters' resolve; the march continued.[32]

The demonstrators finally reached the state capitol in Austin on September 5, 1966 (Labor Day), where some ten thousand clamoring supporters greeted them. Drama and poignancy reigned that afternoon. A former farmworker himself, Father Gonzales visibly moved the crowd when he introduced his parents, migrant workers for forty years. His mother had borne eighteen children and his father suffered from cancer, the priest revealed, and yet they still depended on back-breaking migrant work for a living, earning wages that were a "disgrace" to Texas and the nation. Gonzales ended his talk by declaring a "Vigil for Justice." He would bless two farmworkers—who he called "two of the poorest of the poor"—and station them in front of the capitol where they would remain until the state legislature passed a minimum wage law. That afternoon, César Chávez and other labor political and religious leaders demanded social justice for Mexican Americans amid thunderous cheers that echoed the success of the "march in the sun." [33]

After the march, Father Gonzales and Reverend Novarro moved quickly to capitalize on their success. Gonzales met with Governor Connally three days after the rally and reported that the governor had agreed to cooperate. That same week, the Valley Workers Assistance Committee met at Immaculate Heart of Mary Church in Houston and announced the next stage of the struggle for fair wages. Stating that their work had "just begun," Gonzales and Novarro outlined an ambitious agenda. First of all, they planned to organize thirty-six secondary assistance committees to help impoverished workers in South Texas. In addition, the clerics aimed to organize Mexican and other workers in sixteen states throughout the Southwest and Midwest in the coming year. [34]

Despite the success and momentum of *la marcha*, however, its immediate goals were lost: the farmworkers' strike failed and in its next session the state legislature failed to pass a minimum wage law. However, in a more important sense the Minimum Wage March proved to be a pivotal historical moment. During and after the march Mexican Americans across the state showed an increased political awareness and a heightened ethnic consciousness that gave direction to their long-held resentments and energized the budding Chicano Movement in Texas. [35] Strike organizer Eugene Nelson neatly summed up the new mood when he observed, "The Tejanos no longer tip their hats to the *gabachos* (Anglos)." [36] Mexican deference to the white establishment crumbled in the aftermath of the march. Early in *el movimiento*, then, clerical leadership fueled the fire of Chicano resistance to subordination in Texas.

In addition to the role played in the Chicano Movement by Gonzales, another priest, Father Patricio Flores, earned a reputation as a leading social activist and advocate of Mexican Americans in Houston. Father Flores forcefully reminded his colleagues and the public, for example, not to let the plight of farmworkers be "swept under the rug." [37] Many of his fellow priests disapproved of Flores's support of César Chávez and the United Farm Workers' grape boycott, but the cleric stood firm. He encouraged the Houston grape boycott committee to meet at his parish, and attended rallies and meetings at which he eloquently defended the strikers who, he stated, worked under "inhumane conditions." [38]

As director of the Committee for the Spanish-Speaking in the Galveston-Houston Diocese, Flores demanded greater material support for programs for Mexican Americans. But many of Houston's Catholic churches refused to allow the use of their parish facilities to implement federal antipoverty programs. Even Flores's own committee, he complained, lacked sufficient staffing and cooperation from the diocese. [39] Flores particularly decried the lack of educational opportunities for Mexican Americans, and he tried to focus Church attention on it. Like other social reformers, Flores realized that low educational achievement locked Mexican Americans out of good jobs and in turn created other serious problems. In addition, educational underachievement precluded the development of a significant body of homegrown priests and sisters to serve their own people.[40] Himself a high school dropout, Flores understandably placed frequent and heavy emphasis on education as a key to social progress. Father Flores also worked for change through his involvement in PADRES, although his activities in this regard were not in Houston proper. PADRES was not established in Houston until about a year after its founding and after Flores's departure to the episcopacy in San Antonio.[41] Flores escalated his advocacy after his elevation to bishop and as PADRES national chairman in the early 1970s. The Houston PADRES, bereft of a powerful leader, never evolved into an activist organization comparable to its counterparts elsewhere in Texas and the Southwest.[42]

While priests like Gonzales and Flores agitated for Chicano rights, Chicana nuns also confronted the Catholic hierarchy and society with demands for change. Sister Gloria Gallardo, for example, went to Houston in early 1970 after being active in community organizing in her native San Antonio. Recruited by Father Flores to help in his work in Houston, Gallardo became a coordinator for the Bishop's Committee for the Spanish-Speaking in the Galveston-Houston Diocese and immediately took up various Chicano causes.[43] In autumn 1970, Houston public school officials subverted a court-ordered desegregation plan by integrating schools that were predominately black and Mexican American, leaving Anglo schools virtually unaffected. Outraged, community leaders formed the Mexican American Education Council (MAEC) headed by prominent lay activist Leonel Castillo. MAEC quickly organized a boycott and set up a number of *huelga* (strike) schools to tutor the boycotting students.[44] Sister Gallardo played an integral role in the lengthy campaign that followed. Reinterpreting the traditional role of a nun and her ascribed role as a passive Mexican American woman, she participated in protest rallies, spoke publicly for MAEC, and for a time served as its acting director.[45]

The activities of Father Gonzales, Las Hermanas, and PADRES were clearly a break from any social action undertaken in the past by Church personnel on behalf of Mexicans in Houston. Unlike the individual efforts of nuns and priests in the past, these religious activists mobilized Mexican Americans on a large scale for social change. Acting on their own initiative, they sought social justice by engaging in political protest and by using church facilities and religious forums to help propel the Chicano Movement. Individually and in concert, these religious men and women played an important part in moving the Catholic Church

A Chicano volunteer teacher conducts a class in a Houston church during the Chicano boycott of Houston public schools sponsored by the Mexican American Education Council. Courtesy Houston Metropolitan Research Center, Houston Public Library.

toward its role as an ally of *el movimiento*. Thus pressured, the Galveston-Houston Diocese responded with institutional programs that complemented the individual actions of socially conscious religious personnel.

Institutional Actions

One of the ways the Galveston-Houston Diocese responded to the Chicano Movement was by continuing its charitable works among Mexican parishioners. During the 1960s and 1970s, the diocese expanded some of its long-standing social services to barrio residents, particularly health services of various kinds. For example, one of the oldest Catholic charitable institutions in Houston was the San José Clinic. Founded in 1924 as the "Mexican Clinic," San José began specifically to stem the alarming mortality rates among Mexican children in El Segundo Barrio during the 1920s, and since then had provided free medical services to the poor. In 1970, the diocese significantly expanded the clinic's services, doubling the size of the facility and adding new medical and social services. Appropriately, newly appointed Bishop Patricio Flores presided over the dedication ceremonies.[46] The diocese also sponsored many ad hoc projects at predominantly Mexican American parishes, including nutrition programs, tutoring and cultural enrichment activities, and summer recreation programs. Coordinated with public agencies and community groups, these efforts channeled more money to "less fortunate" parishes through Bishop Morkovsky's personal initiatives and a greater emphasis on the Christian obligation of charity.[47]

Some of these efforts were ecumenical and cross-ethnic. In the post–Vatican II years, the Galveston-Houston Diocese joined with various white, brown, and black Protestant groups to attack poverty in Houston barrios. One such initiative was the Latin American Community (LAC) Project, sponsored originally by the United Church of Christ and Houston Metropolitan Ministries, but soon designated a project of Volunteers in Service to America (VISTA). The LAC Project aimed to empower the "hard core poor" of Houston's East End, a predominantly Mexican American section of the city. Between 1965 and 1972, LAC tried to organize residents "to attack the root causes of deprivation, alienation and discrimination." Its operations included educational and employment services, coordination of emergency relief and recreational services, as well as non-partisan political activities. LAC's programs involved parish people and facilities in the targeted ship channel area, including some from Our Lady of Guadalupe, Immaculate Heart, Blessed Sacrament, and St. Alphonsus.[48] These parishes and others provided volunteer workers, trustees, and material and moral support for LAC projects.[49]

By far the most ambitious ecumenical and interethnic venture was the building of Oxford Place, a $2.7 million interfaith housing project cosponsored with the Episcopal Church. The apartment complex in Houston's North Side offered government-subsidized rent and a number of social services for its residents (the majority of whom were Mexican Americans and blacks), including English lessons, basic education, and child care. The diocese also helped to sponsor the Centro de la Raza community center, which had aims and activities similar to the LAC Project.[50]

Projects like Oxford Place and some of the social services provided by the diocese were in keeping with established practices, yet different in an important respect. Church-sponsored social services had a long history, but the idea of developing self-help in the barrios was more recent. Hence, a project director insisted that a literacy program for Mexican Americans was "not looked upon as a handout, but rather as one that will train them to develop leadership within their own community."[51] Similarly, the LAC Project claimed it was vastly different from "traditional welfare agencies" in that it aimed to "help people break their dependency on 'charity,' paternalism and on the welfare system."[52] The Church's support for self-help projects meshed with its policy of indirectly nurturing social change rather than leading frontal assaults on social problems. As evidenced by the religious and ethnic diversity of the Oxford Place staff led by Baptist Rev.

Lupe Maciel, it also reflected a shift from competition to more cooperation with local Protestants and other ethnic communities.

The Texas farmworkers' strike of 1966 also illustrated the Church's policy of indirectly supporting social change. When Father Antonio Gonzales became a coleader of the Minimum Wage March in July 1966, the Galveston-Houston Diocese explicitly gave him its blessing. "I am happy to have you take leave of absence from Immaculate Heart of Mary until Labor Day," wrote Bishop Morkovsky to Gonzales, "to represent myself and this diocese in the efforts for just wages for the working man in the Valley Marchers' project." The prelate even authorized the priest to use the parish car and credit card in pursuing these activities. Gonzales's religious order, the Oblates, also approved his participation, thanking Bishop Morkovsky for his support of "the cause of the underdog."[53]

Soon after the beginning of the strikers' march, the Galveston-Houston Diocese and four other Texas dioceses publicly supported the farmworkers' right to unionize. Bishop Morkovsky gave his "blessing to the efforts of those who are directly concerned with the problems of justice and the dignity of man."[54] Less publicly, Anglo diocesan officials carried on behind-the-scenes activities to support the Chicano Movement. For example, the diocese gave some direct financial and material support to the farmworkers' cause. Bishop Morkovsky donated money to help with Eugene Nelson's living expenses while he was in Houston in early 1966 organizing a grape boycott to support striking California farmworkers. Father John McCarthy and other Houston priests also helped, guaranteeing Nelson a small monthly income during his organizing efforts among the Río Grande farmworkers. Father McCarthy also headed the diocesan Community Relations Council (CRC). Under his leadership, the CRC brought together the handful of religious and labor leaders in Houston, San Antonio, and Amarillo to form the Valley Workers Assistance Committee, which channeled money and supplies to the strikers in South Texas. McCarthy gave important support to the farmworkers' cause, but purposely kept a low profile because, as he explained, "I was always very sensitive about being an Anglo cleric who did not even speak Spanish."[55]

These actions by Catholic officials in Houston revealed their stance on social issues. Bishop Morkovsky was careful to emphasize the intermediary role of the Church. The first step toward settling the Río Grande Valley strike, Morkovsky explained, was "the voicing of problems by the people involved and an appraisal of the problems by mutual trust and communication."[56] On the one hand, such wording reflected the hierarchy's belief that both labor and management had the right to organize to protect their interests, a position which had encyclical precedent. On the other hand, this position also expressed the diocesan leadership's desire to facilitate, rather than directly lead, efforts for social change. The diocese consistently reflected this position in the ensuing years. As the farmworkers' strike wore on in the Río Grande Valley, the Community Relations Council under Father Emile Farge continued to send aid to the strikers from Houston parishes.[57] On another front, Bishop Morkovsky joined other Houston clerics who voiced support of the California farmworkers' grape strike. Again, Houston's highest Catholic cleric reiterated that Church teachings and papal encyclicals emphasized the right of workers to organize collectively.[58] The limits of this policy became quite clear, however, when Father Gonzales overstepped the boundary set by the hierarchy for political activism among its clergy.

The Limits of Church Support

Gonzales continued to be active in political circles in Houston after the Minimum Wage March. In an address to a PASSO convention in August 1967, however, he incurred the wrath of the political establishment when he called for more Chicano militancy. "PASSO doesn't throw bricks and cause riots," the priest reportedly declared, "but some Negroes have caused some riots, and I compliment them because they stirred up the cities." Gonzales did not condone violence and in "complimenting" those involved in rioting he meant that he understood the reasons why it happened. In calling for Chicanos and blacks to form a powerful political coalition, Father Gonzales evidently assumed that this alliance would help validate both groups' causes. With these assumptions, Gonzales also apparently believed his superiors would support his work toward this goal.[59]

But he was mistaken. Democrats and Republicans alike quickly attacked Gonzales in the press. Within a day of the press accounts, Bishop Morkovsky mildly reprimanded the activist-priest and explained the Church's position. The bishop stated that he did not intend to curb efforts to promote "Christian principles of justice and charity," but that it was "to the disadvantage of justice and charity for the Church or its leaders to engage in political controversy." The priest's role was to teach lay people Christian principles, the Bishop explained, and "it is up to the lay people to put these in practice in the political arena."[60] The prelate also rebuked Gonzales for attacking politicians "by name." The local press had reported that Gonzales had "swapped verbal blows" with the former Texas attorney general (who had been in the entourage that tried to dissuade the farmworkers' march on the capital).[61] "Whether they needed this criticism of yours or not," the bishop lectured Gonzales, "it was not fitting nor is it going to help the promotion of Christian principles for the Church or its representatives to take up this kind of attack."[62]

Bishop Morkovsky offered a contemporary example to explain his reasoning.

In Morkovsky's opinion, the Rev. Martin Luther King Jr. had "lost some of his effectiveness by publicly expressing himself against the government policies in Viet Nam." "His cause for peace may certainly be right," Morkovsky argued, "but possibly it was a mistake in leadership on his part to publicly adopt one side of a concrete application of principles in which there are sincere Christians on both sides." The bishop reiterated that Gonzales could be most effective by giving his people "spiritual guidance" and "in this way help to develop leadership among them." After this incident, Father Gonzales was ordered to clear his public appearances beforehand with his superior and the bishop's office.[63]

Gonzales's predicament illustrated that the Galveston-Houston Diocese would pursue social justice within clearly defined limits and protocol. The diocese supported the Chicano Movement by allowing and even encouraging some activism among its clergy, such as Father Gonzales's involvement in the Minimum Wage March. It also took a public stand on certain principles, such as the right of workers to organize and strike, and it even gave some financial and material support to the striking farmworkers. But Father Gonzales's remarks at the PASSO convention went beyond what the Church leadership in Houston saw as its proper role in social issues and, consequently, the priest's activities were reined in. After his controversial speech, Gonzales was reassigned to a rural outpost in East Texas, "to help him settle down to the regular parochial duties." In February 1968, the priest's superior wrote to Bishop Morkovsky that Gonzales now recognized "his limitations in the social action field and in the jungle world of politics."[64]

The Church hierarchy wanted to remain above "the jungle world of politics," to seek out high-minded influential people upon whom to exert moral persuasion in order to effect social change. In 1966, the Catholic Community Relations Council (CCRC) moved into the Chancery (the main headquarters building of the diocese) and was integrated into the diocesan structure. According to Father Emile Farge, the CCRC director, it thereby gained "more of a handle on power than before."[65] Father Farge claimed he alone controlled social action activities in the diocese, that neither the bishop nor the diocesan chancellor had tried to "keep this office out of delicate or possibly explosive affairs." Still, Farge admitted that "[t]he difficulty with this alliance is that one must act in a socially acceptable way."[66] Bishop Morkovsky sought "to get people influential in the establishment to meet together and to find that they have the same high ideals." This circle of people would then be "broadened step-by-step so that the establishment would be influenced."[67] Obviously, maverick political actions by individuals like Gonzales fitted neither the philosophy nor the strategy of institutional social action in the Galveston-Houston Diocese.

Failing to Deliver?: The Huelga Schools and Oxford Place

During the Chicano boycott of Houston public schools, the Catholic Church failed its children—at least in the opinion of one community newspaper, *Papel Chicano*. The newspaper was bitterly disappointed by pastors who refused to allow religious facilities to be used as *huelga* schools. In 1971 the paper reported that one parish wanted $400 a month rent, plus cost of utilities, which prompted the editor to charge that the church put "exploitation" ahead of the education of children.[68] Another article assailed a pastor as "a racist gringo priest" who had "no right" ministering to Mexican Americans, and claimed that the majority of the Catholic schools had refused to support the school boycott.[69] Although several parishes and individual priests did help the boycott in different ways, backing for the *huelga* schools was uneven, and some Chicanas and Chicanos obviously resented the lukewarm support.[70]

Papel Chicano also considered the diocese's involvement in Oxford Place harmful to Chicano interests in Houston. About a year and a half after the opening of the housing project, the newspaper denounced it as "Another Well-Meaning Instant Slum." *Papel Chicano* argued that Oxford Place was an example of misguided thinking by churches "who were very rapidly destroying the very people [they] sought to help." The newspaper charged that the project was plagued by overwhelming problems: bad race relations within the complex and in the surrounding white neighborhood, high unemployment and student dropout rates, and lack of public transportation to outside areas with good jobs. *Papel Chicano* further argued that the church-related managing agency (and by association the Galveston-Houston Diocese) was to blame for not providing the necessary support to ensure success for Oxford Place residents.[71]

The project administration had failed to provide tutoring for students to succeed in the white schools of the area, the newspaper charged, and there had been no leadership training, no education in race relations, and no programs to organize the residents to protect themselves from the racism of the surrounding community. "To have done this kind of work would have caused the people in Oxford Place to stand up for themselves in the schools and community," the editorial asserted, "and neither of these two religious sects [Catholic and Episcopalian] want any whites to actually know these minorities are living in 'their' communities." Ultimately, the writer argued, the problem at Oxford Place was "the unwillingness of the churches to really break the poverty cycle."[72]

At least some Chicanos considered the diocese's indirect approach to social change a failure. Some of the more disaffected voices in the community charged that it was not only ineffective but also disingenuous: not only did it not work, but also it was not really *supposed* to work, they implied. However, that conclusion reflected more the times' political hyperbole and personal estrangement some felt toward the Church than it did an accurate understanding of the diocese's policies and actions toward Chicano social issues. Clearly, racial conflict between Chicanos and blacks had marred the early history of Oxford Place.[73] That is not to say, though, that the Catholic Church in Houston had conspired to thwart Chicano aspirations for equality. The Church had indeed been supporting *el movimiento*, albeit through more conservative means than appealed to more militant Chicanas and Chicanos.

Legitimation or Control?: The *Encuentros*

The activism of the late 1960s and early 1970s culminated in an institutional response by the hierarchy of the U.S. Catholic Church called an *encuentro*, a meeting to address problems. Father Edgard Beltrán, an activist-priest from Latin America, suggested the idea in the fall of 1971 while visiting the Archdiocese of New York. The idea soon gained support in the U.S. hierarchy and thus the first Encuentro Hispano de Pastoral (Pastoral Congress for the Spanish-Speaking) became a reality in June 1972. For the first time, the Catholic Church in the United States provided a national forum for leaders of Spanish-speaking communities throughout the nation to air their grievances. Two hundred and fifty delegates met in Washington, D.C. to examine the place of the Spanish-speaking in the Church. "It was a meeting," said Bishop Patricio Flores, "called by the [C]hurch not to praise, but to make a self-evaluation and correct what is wrong." What was "wrong," essentially, was that Mexican-origin and other Spanish-speaking peoples—25 percent of the U.S. Catholic population—had virtually no voice in the institutional Church and were not adequately served by it, pastorally or socially. Adequate representation was the central theme of the national *encuentro*: "[I]f we are 25 per cent of the church, we should participate in 25 per cent of . . . the committees of the national church," Bishop Flores demanded.[74] The three-day meeting produced seventy-eight conclusions and demands calling for "greater participation of the Spanish-speaking in leadership and decision-making roles at all levels within the American church."[75]

The crescendo of Chicano demands struck a responsive chord within the U.S. Catholic Church. On the national level, for instance, the Church responded by naming more Mexican American bishops.[76] Locally, Houston's Bishop Morkovsky opened the door to greater Mexican American participation and voice in the Church. In the months after the national *encuentro*, similar regional and diocesan meetings took place, and the findings of these smaller forums and the motions of the national meeting were then presented to the Bishops of the United States in November 1972 to serve as a basis for a comprehensive pastoral plan for Spanish-speaking Catholics.[77] Houston hosted the Southwest regional *encuentro* in October 1972. In July, two months prior to the meeting, Bishop Morkovsky named Father John McGrath, the Oblate pastor of St. Patrick Parish, interim coordinator of the ministry for the Spanish-speaking. In appointing an Anglo to this position, Bishop Morkovsky was not slighting Chicanos or their social activism. As Morkovsky made clear to Father McGrath, this was a temporary position meant to start discussions about developing a "pastoral" plan; "the social part" of the ministry remained in the hands of such people as the well-known activist sister, Gloria Gallardo, and Father John McCarthy, who earlier had facilitated much of the diocese's support for the striking farmworkers. In addition, Bishop Morkovsky ordained more Mexican American laymen as permanent deacons in Houston's predominately Mexican parishes. In July 1972 the local Catholic newspaper featured three such appointees, Manuel Betancourt, Benigno Pardo, and Valeriano Leija, proudly posing in surplice and cassock outside Immaculate Heart of Mary Church. Coming in the wake of the national *encuentro*, Bishop Morkovsky's actions signaled his recognition that Chicanas and Chicanos comprised at least 25 percent of the diocese and, as such, their needs were one of the hierarchy's "special areas of concern."[78]

As the year 1972 drew to a close, Mexican Catholics in Houston and throughout the nation entered a changed relationship with the institutional Church, especially as it affected their struggle for social equality. The Galveston-Houston Diocese, like the national Church leadership, had begun to respond systematically to pressures from Chicanas and Chicanos. It had put in place the *encuentro*, an institutional structure that could serve as a springboard for further changes. It now seemed possible to build a critical mass of homegrown clergy and sisters who could leverage their power in the struggle for social justice. Those who interpreted these developments optimistically saw in the *encuentros* legitimation of Chicano protest and concessions from the Catholic Church in the United States. Some even called the conclusions drawn up at the proceedings the "Magna Charta of Hispanic Catholics."[79]

But others were less optimistic. Had the Church co-opted the Chicano Movement, channeling protest into a controlled environment of its own creation? At the Houston regional *encuentro*, poet Lalo Delgado extemporaneously harangued attendees for seventy minutes about the long-standing neglect of Mexicans by the Catholic Church in the United States, and the festering discord many Chicanas and Chicanos felt toward the institution. At the same meeting, national lay leader Pablo Sedillo hinted at co-optation, reminding listeners that similar meetings had taken place before, with nearly identical conclusions, yet nothing had changed. Sedillo voiced what many Mexican Catholics had experienced historically: "To date there has been a commitment of words, lip service, but no real action." [80] Ultimately, Sedillo offered a cautiously optimistic assessment of the *encuentros* and the juncture that Mexican Catholics and the institutional Church had reached. Although he did not see the *encuentros* as a panacea, Sedillo perceived a significantly altered relationship between Mexican Americans and the institution in 1972. "The Mexican Americans are not asking for pity, for handouts, [or] for a box of groceries. We're beyond that traditional help," Sedillo explained. The Catholic Church in the United States was "beginning to respond" to the needs of Mexican Catholics, Sedillo stated, adding that he hoped the rhetoric would beget meaningful action. [81] The lay leader viewed the reactions of the Church hierarchy in the 1960s and early 1970s in historical perspective, and correctly recognized them for what they were, a response to activism by Chicanas and Chicanos.

Conclusion

During the mid-1960s and early 1970s, the Catholic Church lent uneven and circumspect—if unprecedented—support to the Chicano quest for social justice in Houston. Catholic activism during the Chicano Movement gave rise to the Encuentro Hispano de Pastoral of 1972, an airing of grievances at the highest levels of the U.S. Church. This national meeting elicited commitments from the Roman Catholic hierarchy, symbolizing the progress Mexican Catholics had made toward greater participation in society and the Church and suggesting the possibility of further progress. Ignited by the laity and taken up by priests and sisters, the Chicano Movement prodded the Catholic Church toward greater support of Chicanos' social and political goals. The intense dialogue between the Chicano Movement and the Church also resulted in an improving pastoral relationship. Mexican and Mexican American Catholics had come a long way since Archbishop Robert Lucey of San Antonio described them in 1941 as "a people apart, ostracized and held in social and economic subjection." [82] No longer pariahs and increasingly becoming participants in the Bayou City's life by the early 1970s, Mexican Americans could now count on one of their own—Chicano Bishop Patricio Flores—to voice their concerns in the halls of power. In addition, the Galveston-Houston Diocese now dedicated greater resources and attention than ever before to both the material and spiritual needs of Mexican and Mexican American parishioners. In 1972 Mexican and Mexican American Catholics in Houston faced the future with mixed feelings. Some looked forward to brighter times; for others, however, the clouds of the past darkened the vista. But one thing was clear: in raising their voices in protest, Mexican Americans brought significant changes to Catholicism in Texas and the Southwest.

Notes

1. *Papel Chicano* (Houston), September 16, 1971.

2. Harvey G. Cox, "'The New Breed' in American Churches: Sources of Social Activism in American Religion," *Daedalus* (Winter 1967): 135–50; Patrick H. McNamara, "Social Action Priests in the Mexican American Community," *Sociological Analysis* 29 (1968): 177–85.

3. Chávez quoted in Moisés Sandoval, ed. *Fronteras: A History of the Latin American Church in the USA since 1513* (San Antonio, Tex.: Mexican American Cultural Center, 1983), 384.

4. *Texas Catholic Herald* (Houston), February 11, 1965, 10. A Spanish immigrant, Crespo was well known for his civic involvement and business activities in the Mexican community since the 1930s; see Thomas H. Kreneck, *Mexican American Odyssey: Felix Tijerina, Entrepreneur and Civic Leader, 1905–1965* (College Station: Texas A&M University Press, 2001), 67, 69, 71; Arnoldo De León, *Ethnicity in the Sunbelt: A History of Mexican Americans in Houston* (Houston, Tex.: University of Houston, Mexican American Studies, 1989), 74, 83. *Texas Catholic Herald* (Houston), October 3, 1969, 1; September 18, 1970, 1, 11.

5. *Texas Catholic Herald* (Houston), October 3, 1969, 1, 6. For similar sentiments, see Alberto Carrillo, "The Sociological Failure of the Catholic Church toward the Chicano," *Journal of Mexican American Studies* 1 (Winter 1971): 75–83.

6. *Texas Catholic Herald* (Houston), October 13, 1972, 10; *Houston Chronicle*, February 19, 1970, 1, 4 (sect. 3).

7. See document #43, Marta Cotera, "La Conferencia de Mujeres por La Raza: Houston, Texas, 1971"; document #44, Francisca Flores, "Conference of Mexican Women in Houston—Un Remolino [A Whirlwind]"; and document #45, Anna Nieto Gomez and Elma Barrera, "Chicana Encounter," in *Chicana Feminist Thought: The Basic Historical Writings,* ed. Alma García, 155–64 (New York: Routledge, 1997).

8. Editorial, *Compass* (Houston), October 1967, 4, October 1968, 10–11.

9. *Papel Chicano* (Houston), February 3, 1971, 9, February 29, 1972, 11.

10. "Listen, Christian," *Compass* (Houston), October 1968, 4. Some Internet sources attribute slightly varying versions of this poem to Bob Rowland.

11. For studies and essays from the 1970s that focus on institutional racism and discrimination within the Catholic Church, see Juan Hurtado, "An Attitudinal Study of Social Distance between the Mexican American and the Church" (Ph.D. diss., United States International University, San Diego, 1975); Antonio R. Soto, "The Chicano and the Church in Northern California, 1848–1978: A Study of an Ethnic Minority within the Roman Catholic Church" (Ph.D. diss., University of California, Berkeley, 1978); Carrillo, "Sociological Failure of the Catholic Church"; José Roberto Juárez, "La Iglesia Católica y el Chicano en Sud Texas, 1836–1911" *Aztlán* 4 (Fall 1974): 217–55; Raoul E.

Isais-A., "The Chicano and the American Catholic Church," *El Grito del Sol* 4 (Winter 1979): 9–24. More recent works include Alfredo Mirandé, *The Chicano Experience: An Alternative Perspective* (Notre Dame, Ind.: University of Notre Dame University Press, 1985), chap. 6; Alberto L. Pulido, "Race Relations within the American Catholic Church: An Historical and Sociological Analysis of Mexican American Catholics" (Ph.D. diss., University of Notre Dame, 1989).

12. Eduardo N. López to Bishop John L. Morkovsky, ca. November 1970, Our Lady of Sorrows Parish File, Archives of the Diocese of Galveston-Houston (hereafter, ADGH).

13. Ibid.

14. Ibid.

15. For details of Flores's life, see Martin McMurtrey, *Mariachi Bishop: The Life Story of Patrick Flores* (San Antonio, Tex.: Corona, 1987).

16. *Texas Catholic Herald* (Houston), October 24, 1969, 1; ibid., June 30, 1972, 7.

17. McMurtrey, *Mariachi Bishop*, 55; Sandoval, *Fronteras*, 397–98; *Texas Catholic Herald* (Houston), October 24, 1969, 1. See also Juan Romero, "Charism and Power: An Essay on the History of PADRES," *U.S. Catholic Historian* 9 (Spring 1990): 147–63.

18. Rev. Ralph Ruiz to Rev. L. C. Reyes, December 8, 1970, PADRES Collection, Catholic Archives of Texas (hereafter, CAT).

19. Las Hermanas Proposal, Leonel Castillo Collection, Houston Metropolitan Research Center (hereafter, HMRC); Sandoval, *Fronteras*, 405–407.

20. *Houston Post*, April 21, 1971, clipping in Huelga Schools Collection, HMRC; "Qué Pasó Sheet," PADRES Collection, CAT. See also Sister Teresita Basso, "The Emerging 'Chicana' Sister," *Review for Religious* 30 (1971): 1019–28.

21. Las Hermanas Conference Program, Huelga School Collection, HMRC; *Texas Catholic Herald* (Houston), November 26, 1971, 12, December 10, 1971, 1; *Papel Chicano* (Houston), October 28, 1971, 11, November 9, 1971, 2. For an in-depth study of the national organization, see Lara Medina, *Las Hermanas: Chicana/Latina Religious-Political Activism in the U.S. Catholic Church* (Philadelphia: Temple University Press, 2004).

22. Clipping, *Houston Post*, April 21, 1971, Huelga Schools Collection, HMRC; "Spanish-Speaking Sisters Unite," *Texas Catholic Herald* (Houston), April 8, 1971.

23. Quotes from Lora Ann Quiñónez, C.D.P. and Mary Daniel Turner, S.N.D. de N., *The Transformation of American Catholic Sisters* (Philadelphia: Temple University Press, 1992), 72–73.

24. "Pastoral Letter from the Bishops of the United States," August 25, 1963, Provincial Records, Archives of the Oblates of Mary Immaculate (hereafter, "US Bishops' Pastoral" and AOMI); clippings, *Texas Catholic Herald* (Houston), October 14, 1966, June 23, 1967, and September 15, 1967, in Diocesan Chancery Collection, CAT.

25. "US Bishops' Pastoral," AOMI; clipping, *Texas Catholic Herald* (Houston), June 23, 1967, Diocesan Chancery Collection, CAT.

26. *Texas Catholic Herald* (Houston), June 23, 1967, clipping in Diocesan Chancery Collection, CAT; "US Bishop's Pastoral," AOMI.

27. For a fuller accounts, see Marilyn D. Rhinehart and Thomas H. Kreneck, "The Minimum Wage March of 1966: A Case Study in Mexican-American Politics, Labor, and Identity," *The Houston Review* 11 (1989): 27–44; Joan Hart Cohen, "To See Christ in Our Brothers: The Role of the Texas Roman Catholic Church in the Río Grande Valley Farm Workers' Movement, 1966–1967," (master's thesis, University of Texas at Arlington, 1974); and Charles Ray Chandler, "The Mexican-American Protest Movement in Texas," (Ph.D. diss., Tulane University, 1968).

28. *Texas Catholic Herald* (Houston), June 24, 1966, 1.

29. "La Marcha . . . Valley Farm Workers' 491-Mile March for Justice," in *Harris County PASO 5th Anniversary and Salute to Valley Farm Workers* (Houston: Harris County PASO, 1966), pamphlet in Mexican American Collection, HMRC.

30. *Texas Catholic Herald* (Houston), July 1, 1966, 1, 6.

31. "La Marcha"; *Houston Chronicle*, July 5, 1966, 6.

32. "La Marcha"; *Houston Chronicle*, September 1, 1966, 19 (sect. 1), September 4, 1966, 10 (sect. 1); Chandler, "The Mexican-American Protest Movement in Texas," 244.

33. "La Marcha"; *Houston Chronicle*, September 5, 1966, 1, 18 (sect. 1), September 6, 1966, 1 (sect. 1).

34. *Houston Chronicle*, September 7, 1966, 13 (sect. 1), September 9, 1966, 11 (sect. 1); *Texas Catholic Herald* (Houston), September 9, 1966, 1, 6.

35. Rhinehart and Kreneck, "The Minimum Wage March," 39–44; Chandler, "The Mexican-American Protest Movement in Texas," 245; for similar assessments, see De León, *Ethnicity in the Sunbelt*, 173–74; David Montejano, *Anglos and Mexicans in the Making of Texas, 1836–1986* (Austin: University of Texas Press, 1987), 284–85.

36. Quoted in Rhinehart and Kreneck, "The Minimum Wage March," 44.

37. Bishop P. F. Flores, "Mission and Vision, Mexican-American Apostolate," TMs (mimeographed), n.d. [ca. 1971], Hector García Collection, HMRC.

38. *Texas Catholic Herald* (Houston), December 5, 1969, 1; *Houston Chronicle*, April 8, 1970, 1 (sect. 4); clipping, *Texas Catholic Herald* (Houston), February, 5, 1971, PADRES Collection, CAT; McMurtrey, *Mariachi Bishop*, 57–58.

39. *Texas Catholic Herald* (Houston), October 24, 1969, 1.

40. *Texas Catholic Herald* (Houston), October 1, 1964, 2, October 24, 1969, 1, October 2, 1970, 1; Flores, "Mission and Vision."

41. Flores became auxiliary bishop of San Antonio on May 5, 1970. Later that year, in December, a PADRES "action group" was initiated in Houston. Moisés Sandoval, *On the Move: A History of the Hispanic Church in the United States* (Maryknoll, N.Y.: Orbis, 1990), 72; "Qué Pasó Sheet," PADRES Collection, CAT.

42. Father Lawrence Peguero was PADRES diocesan director in Houston during the

early 1970s, but his bootstraps philosophy contrasted dramatically with more militant priests like Flores. While Flores attacked societal barriers, Peguero described himself as "a firm believer in the American system." A contemporary recalled that Houston PADRES was insignificant in the social arena and that Peguero was simply "not interested in social issues." Father Peguero believed that the function of the Church was "strictly a moral one," that it was "not the function of a priest to be a leader in social work." Although at times he expressed support for some Chicano causes, Peguero's career and philosophy were summed up in the Franklinesque homilies he was fond of repeating: "We don't have any poor people in our neighborhood—only lazy ones"; and "The only thing that has not been tried against poverty is work." See PADRES booklet (undated, ca. 1971), PADRES Collection, CAT; *Houston Post,* March 5, 1970 (Close-up sect.), clipping in Our Lady of St. John File, ADGH; *Houston Chronicle,* October 2, 1970, 5 (sect. 2); interview with Bishop John E. McCarthy, Austin, Texas, October 18, 1991 (hereafter, McCarthy interview). For social activism of PADRES in other places, see Moisés Sandoval, "The Church and El Movimiento," in *Fronteras,* 401–402. De León, *Ethnicity in the Sunbelt,* 206, briefly mentions PADRES emergency relief activities in Houston in the 1970s.

43. *National Catholic Reporter* (Kansas City, Mo.), August 13, 1971, 1; Résumé of Gloria Graciela Gallardo, Leonel Castillo Collection, HMRC.

44. "MAEC preparing," *Texas Catholic Herald* (Houston), August 6, 1971, 1; De León, *Ethnicity in the Sunbelt,* 185–189. See also Guadalupe San Miguel, *Brown, Not White: School Integration and the Chicano Movement in Houston,* University of Houston Center for Mexican American Studies Monograph Series no. 3 (College Station: Texas A&M University Press, 2001). Leonel Castillo parlayed his high-profile activism into a successful run for the office of city controller, and later served as the first Mexican American director of the Immigration and Naturalization Service under President Jimmy Carter. Thomas H. Kreneck, *Del Pueblo: A Pictorial History of Houston's Hispanic Community* (Houston, Tex.: Houston International University, 1989), 201–202.

45. *Papel Chicano* (Houston), September 26, 1970, 3, 5, October 24, 1970, 5, January 16, 1971, 7, February 20, 1971, 5, April 1, 1971; clipping, *Houston Post,* April 21, 1971, Huelga Schools Collection, HMRC.

46. "San Jose Clinic," TMs, Mexican American Small Collection, Box 2, HMRC; *Texas Catholic Herald* (Houston), April 17, 1970, 12.

47. Much of the effort was carried out through the Bishop's Committee on the Inner City, the Council on Community Relations, and the Council of Catholic Women. See Catholic Charities of the Diocese of Galveston-Houston 1967 Annual Report, Provincial Records, AOMI; Morkovsky Memorandum to Monsignor Ganter, May 22, 1968, Blessed Sacrament Parish File, ADGH; clipping, *Texas Catholic Herald* (Houston), November 12, 1965, St. Stephen Parish File, ADGH; clipping, *Herald,* June 19, 1970, Diocesan Chan-

cery Collection, CAT; *Herald,* April 3, 1970, 6, May 3, 1970, 3; clipping, *Texas Catholic Herald* (Houston), June 17, 1966, *Texas Catholic Herald* Parish Photograph Files (St. Stephen); clippings, *Texas Catholic Herald* (Houston), March 17 and 31, 1972, *Texas Catholic Herald* Parish Photograph Files (Immaculate Heart of Mary); Bishop's Pastoral Letter, September 23, 1968, Provincial Records, AOMI; clipping, *Herald,* December 5, 1969, Diocesan Chancery Collection, CAT.

48. *Houston Post,* November 13, 1965, clipping in LAC scrapbook; TMs in LAC scrapbook; "Minister's Quarterly Report," Folder 2, Box 1; "History, Structure and Purposes of the LACK Project," Box 2, Folder 1, all in VISTA Collection, HMRC. Note: The LAC Project was also known as "LACK."

49. Flier in LAC scrapbook; LACK Project *Voice,* Box 1; LACK Project Director's Report, Box 2, Folder 2, all in VISTA Collection, HMRC. An offshoot organization of LAC that involved some East End priests was The East End Mission (TEEM). *Texas Catholic Herald* (Houston), January 23, 1970, 12.

50. Oxford Place was managed by an "interfaith and interracial staff" led by director Lupe Maciel, a Baptist, and four Spanish and non-Spanish surnamed office personnel, two Catholics and two Baptists. *Texas Catholic Herald* (Houston), April 24, 1970, 2; "Report of Self-Study Committee of Houston Metropolitan Ministries," undated, ca. August 1970, Organizations File, Leonel Castillo Collection, HMRC. The Galveston-Houston Diocese entered into two other ecumenical agreements to provide low-cost housing, Pleasantville Village in 1967 and Houston Home Ownership Corporation in 1969, though these were not exclusively aimed at Mexican Americans. Robert C. Giles, *Changing Times, The Story of the Diocese of Galveston-Houston in Commemoration of its Founding* (N.p., 1971), 63.

51. *Texas Catholic Herald* (Houston), April 3, 1970, 6.

52. LAC Project Director's Report, September 1967, Box 2, Folder 2, VISTA Collection, HMRC. On the national level, the hierarchy of the Catholic Church in the United States formed the Campaign for Human Development in 1969 to empower the poor and attack root causes of inequality. See Bernard F. Evans, "Campaign for Human Development: Church Involvement in Social Change," *Review of Religious Research* 20 (Summer 1979): 264–78.

53. Bishop John L. Morkovsky to Reverend Antonio Gonzales, July 28, 1966, Provincial Records, AOMI; Provincial John A. Hakey to Bishop John L. Morkovsky, August 6, 1966, Provincial Records, AOMI.

54. *Texas Catholic Herald* (Houston), July 15, 1966, 3.

55. Cohen, "To See Christ in Our Brothers," 24–25; McCarthy interview; Bishop John McCarthy, interview by Jan H. Cohen, March 10, 1972, Houston, Texas, OH 27, Texas Labor Archives, University of Texas at Arlington Special Collections.

56. *Texas Catholic Herald* (Houston), July 15, 1966, 3.

57. Ibid., March 24, 1967, 3.

58. *Alamo Messenger* (San Antonio), February 7, 1969, clipping in Episcopal Collection, CAT; see also *Texas Catholic Herald* (Houston), December 5, 1969, 1.

59. *Houston Chronicle*, August 20, 1967, 24 (sect. 1).

60. Bishop John L. Morkovsky to Reverend Antonio Gonzales, August 21, 1967, Provincial Records, AOMI.

61. *Houston Chronicle*, August 20, 1967, 24 (sect. 1).

62. Morkovsky to Gonzales, August 21, 1967.

63. Ibid.

64. Provincial John A. Hakey to Bishop John L. Morkovsky, February 13, 1968, Provincial Records, AOMI. In February 1968, Father Gonzales was reassigned to Houston. Back in the city, the priest renewed his political activities. His interests ranged from PASSO and the Democratic Party to La Raza Unida Party, and eventually even the Republicans. In the opinion of a contemporary, Gonzales "lost touch with reality in the heady world of the Chicano movement," and was "used" by politicians. Within six months of his return to Houston, Gonzales was again in trouble with his bishop and his association with the diocese was temporarily suspended while he explained reports of "irresponsible" behavior. This episode was apparently smoothed over, as within a week he was back at his post and communicating with the bishop regarding his latest political activity, a meeting with a representative of the incoming Nixon administration. Father Gonzales eventually left the priesthood. See Provincial John A. Hakey to Bishop John L. Morkovsky, February 13, 1968; Morkovsky to Gonzales, February 14, 1968; Morkovsky to Gonzales, November 27, 1968; Gonzales to Morkovsky, December 5, 1968, all in Provincial Records, AOMI; *El Sol* (Houston), March 22, 1968, April 26, 1968, May 3, 1968; McCarthy interview.

65. Undated memorandum from Father Emile Farge (ca. August 1968), Organizations File, Castillo Collection, HMRC.

66. Ibid. Farge described his job as social action director as one of "exposing people to people" [through the Catholic Interracial Committee], maintaining contact with grassroots organizations, and "political activities, especially pushing the good legislation, good political candidates." In the late 1960s, he led an effort to build an ecumenical social action coalition, the Joint Strategy and Action Committee, which was "motivated by the common knowledge of the problem that many in our Greater Houston area are disenfranchised from real participation in the life of the city." He described the effort as "the only realistic ecumenical group working on the race-culture crises." See Farge letters and memoranda from 1968 to 1969 in Organizations File, Castillo Collection, HMRC.

67. Memorandum from Bishop Morkovsky to Father Farge, February 14, 1969, Organizations File, Castillo Collection, HMRC.

68. *Papel Chicano* (Houston), February 20, 1971, 2.

69. *Papel Chicano* (Houston), September 16, 1971.

70. *Papel Chicano* (Houston), August 22, 1970, 4, November 21, 1970, 2, January 16, 1971, 7, February 20, 1971, 5; *Texas Catholic Herald* (Houston), September 11, 1970, 8.

71. "Oxford Place, Another Well-Meaning Instant Slum," *Papel Chicano* (Houston), September 16, 1971.

72. Ibid.

73. Houston Council on Human Relations, *The Black/Mexican-American Project Report* (Houston, Tex.: Houston Council on Human Relations, 1972), 6.

74. Moisés Sandoval, "The Organization of a Hispanic Church," in *Hispanic Catholic Culture in the U.S.: Issues and Concerns,* ed. Jay P. Dolan and Allan Figueroa Deck, 141–42 (Notre Dame, Ind.: University of Notre Dame Press, 1994); Bishop Flores quoted in *National Catholic Reporter* (Kansas City, Mo.), July 7, 1972, 1, 2.

75. *Texas Catholic Herald* (Houston), November 3, 1972. See also National Conference of Catholic Bishops, *Hispanic Ministry: Three Major Documents* (Washington, D.C.: United States Catholic Conference, 1995), 8, 29; Sandoval, *On the Move,* 79–82.

76. Sandoval, *On the Move,* 74–79.

77. Sandoval, *On the Move,* 79–82; *National Catholic Reporter* (Kansas City, Mo.), July 7, 1972, 2; *Compass* (Houston), October 1972, 4.

78. *Compass* (Houston), October 1972, 4; Bishop John L. Morkovsky to Reverend Robert J. McGrath, July 11, 1972, St. Patrick File, ADGH; Morkovsky to Reverend Edward F. Brauman, June 3, 1971, Immaculate Heart of Mary Parish File, ADGH; photo, *Texas Catholic Herald* Immaculate Heart of Mary Photo File, ADGH.

79. Sandoval, *Fronteras,* 429, quoting Archbishop Francis Furey of San Antonio, Texas.

80. *Texas Catholic Herald* (Houston), October 20, 1972, 2, October 13, 1972, 10.

81. Sandoval, *On the Move,* 81; *Catholic Herald* (Houston), October 20, 1972, 2.

82. Quoted in Jay P. Dolan, *The American Catholic Experience: A History from Colonial Times to the Present* (Garden City, N.Y.: Doubleday, 1985), 374.

Contributors

STEVEN M. AVELLA is a professor of history at Marquette University and a priest of the Archdiocese of Milwaukee. He received his Ph.D. at the University of Notre Dame and has taught at St. Francis Seminary, Milwaukee, Cardinal Stritch University, and Marquette. He has published works on Chicago Catholicism, the Archdiocese of Milwaukee, and other topics related to Catholic life in the Midwest. He recently completed a manuscript on the role of the Catholic Church in the development of Sacramento, California.

ANNE M. BUTLER graduated from the University of Maryland, College Park, completing her doctoral studies with Walter Rundell, a Texas native, widely renowned for his Walter Prescott Webb scholarship. Butler is the immediate past editor of the *Western Historical Quarterly* and a Trustee Professor, emerita, of Utah State University. She has published extensively on various aspects of western cultural history, especially concerning women. In 2003 and 2006, she received awards from the Catholic Press Association of the United States and Canada for her essays about Roman Catholic nuns in the American West.

MICHAEL E. ENGH, S.J., is professor of history and dean of the Bellarmine College of Liberal Arts, Loyola Marymount University, Los Angeles. His research and publication focuses on the history of Los Angeles and the history of religion in the American West. He cofounded the Los Angeles History Seminar at the Huntington Library in 1991 to foster the exchange of works in progress in a collegial setting.

RICHARD FRANCAVIGLIA is Professor of History at the University of Texas at Arlington, where he also serves as Director of the Center for Greater Southwestern Studies and the History of Cartography. As a historical geographer, he is especially interested in how religion helps shape perceptions of places in the American West. His numerous publications include *The Mormon Landscape: Existence, Creation, and Perception of a Unique Image in the American West* (1978), and *Believing in Place: A Spiritual Geography of the Great Basin* (2003).

WILLIAM ISSEL is Professor of History and former Director of American Studies at San Francisco State University. He is the author of *Social Change in the United States, 1945–1983* and coauthor of *American Labor and the Cold War*. His work concerning religion in the American West has appeared in *Journal of Urban History, U.S. Catholic Historian,* and the anthology *California Jews*.

MATTHEW PEHL is a graduate student in American History at Brandeis University. He is currently writing his dissertation, which examines religion, class, and culture in twentieth-century Detroit. Prior to enrolling at Brandeis, Pehl served as the S. George Ellsworth editorial fellow at the *Western Historical Quarterly*.

GINA MARIE PITTI was raised in Sacramento, California, and received her Ph.D. from Stanford University in 2003. She has taught courses in Chicano/a history, women's history, and immigration history at Stanford University and Arizona State University. A recent recipient of the Ford Postdoctoral Fellowship, she is currently working on a book project, *In Pursuit of One Parish Life? Mexican Americans, Race, and Religion in Northern California*.

ROBERTO R. TREVIÑO is Associate Professor of History and Assistant Director of the Center for Mexican American Studies at the University of Texas at Arlington. He received his Ph.D. from Stanford University and taught previously at the University of Colorado at Colorado Springs. He is the author of *The Church in the Barrio: Mexican American Ethno-Catholicism in Houston* and other publications about religion and ethnicity in U.S. history.